# 50 HIKES

## IN ORANGE COUNTY

## OTHER BOOKS IN THE 50 HIKES SERIES

*50 Hikes in Michigan*

*50 Hikes in Michigan's Upper Peninsula*

*50 Hikes in Wisconsin*

*50 Hikes in Minnesota*

*50 Hikes in Ohio*

*50 More Hikes in Ohio*

*50 Hikes in Western Pennsylvania*

*50 Hikes in West Virginia*

*50 Hikes in Kentucky*

# 50 HIKES
## IN ORANGE COUNTY

SECOND EDITION

Karin Klein

THE COUNTRYMAN PRESS
A division of W. W. Norton & Company
*Independent Publishers Since 1923*

For information about special discounts for bulk purchases, please contact W. W. Norton Special Sales at specialsales@wwnorton.com or 800-233-4830

Library of Congress Cataloging-in-Publication Data

Names: Klein, Karin, author.
Title: 50 hikes in Orange County / Karin Klein.
Other titles: Fifty hikes in Orange County
Description: Second Edition. | Woodstock, VT : The Countryman Press A division of W. W. Norton & Company, [2016] | Series: 50 hikes | Includes bibliographical references and index.
Identifiers: LCCN 2015046467 | ISBN 9781581573336 (paperback : alk. paper)
Subjects: LCSH: Hiking—California—Orange County—Guidebooks. | Orange County (Calif.)—Guidebooks.
Classification: LCC GV199.42.C22 O736 2016 | DDC 796.5109794/96—dc23
LC record available at http://lccn.loc.gov/2015046467

The Countryman Press
www.countrymanpress.com

A division of W. W. Norton & Company, Inc.
500 Fifth Avenue, New York, N.Y. 10110
www.wwnorton.com

10 9 8 7 6 5 4 3 2

*In memory of Irene and Irving Klein,*
*who lovingly set my feet on the path.*

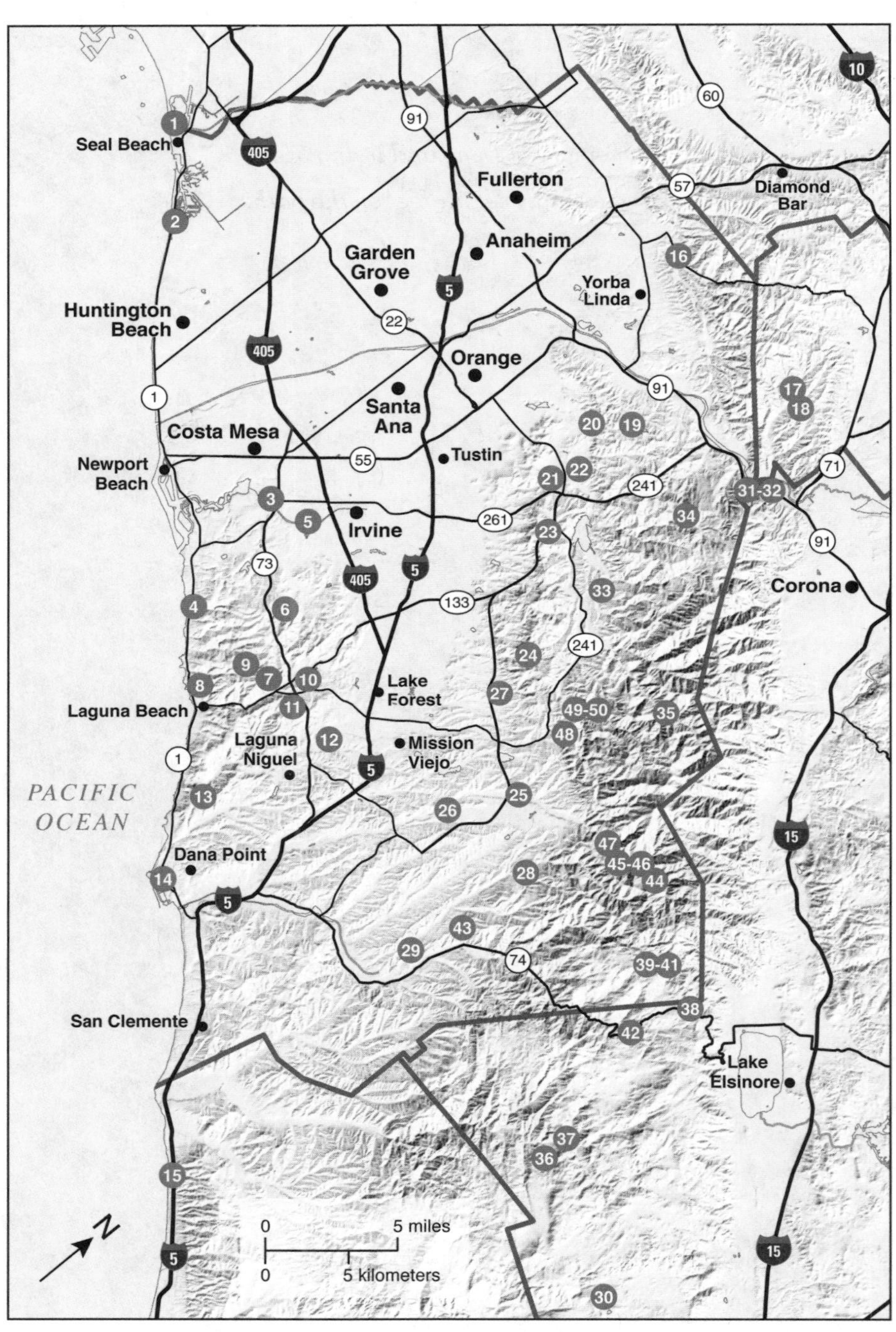

Seal Beach
Huntington Beach
Costa Mesa
Newport Beach
Fullerton
Anaheim
Garden Grove
Orange
Santa Ana
Tustin
Irvine
Yorba Linda
Diamond Bar
Corona
Lake Forest
Mission Viejo
Laguna Beach
Laguna Niguel
Dana Point
San Clemente
Lake Elsinore
PACIFIC OCEAN
N
0 5 miles
0 5 kilometers

# Contents

## III. SANTA ANA MOUNTAINS HIKES | 157

# Acknowledgments

The people involved in hiking or caring for nature—the two overlap tremendously—are a generous crowd in the habit of sharing their great stores of information.

Bob Allen is an extraordinarily knowledgeable biologist and wildflower expert. He identified from photos—with startling speed and wonderful humor—every plant that was beyond my store of information. Ron Vanderhoff has been a constant source of new information about the flora of Orange County. His forays in its most remote spots have been fascinating to follow online; even better are the hikes he leads for the Califonia Native Plant Society.

Co-naturalist Len Gardner has been my partner and teacher on many hikes and my co-conspirator in researching uses of wild plants; he provided valuable ideas and information on a regular basis throughout the process. Michael Hearst was my first, best, and funniest nature instructor.

The following experts took the extraordinary time to back-read many chapters for accuracy, also providing valuable new information and ideas: Mert Hill on geology; county historian Phil Brigandi; and Len Gardner and Joel Robinson, head of Naturalist For You, for just about everything else.

Debra Clarke, wilderness/trails manager for the Trabuco Ranger District of the Cleveland National Forest, obtained special access permits for me to enter closed areas and graciously loaned me rare books on plants and on Native Americans. Claire Schlotterbeck helped on many fronts, from information to access, on Chino Hills State Park. I also was lucky enough to meet and hike with Mike Boeck and Michael Hazzard. Between the two of them, these men know all the corners of the Santa Ana Mountains. Bob Huttar provided the lore of Silverado and Limestone canyons, Jenn Starnes at the Irvine Ranch Conservancy provided updates for the second edition on the hikes and landscape changes for the areas it manages, and John Kaiser told me how to find the Alpine Village. Orange County archivists Jean O. Pasco and Chris Jepsen went out of their way to provide historical photos. *Los Angeles Times* colleague Louis Sahagun guided me to the sea turtles.

But the biggest thanks go to my husband, Amnon Meyers, for amazing help, and we're talking about a lot more than moral support. Amnon hiked most of these trails with me, carrying the heavy backpack and sharing the wonder of nature as well as the anxious hour spent driving 8 miles down a winding dirt mountain road on two tires and two rims. He set up everything computer-driven and fixed all the technological glitches. Everyone should have a hiking computer scientist for a spouse.

Thanks also to my daughter, Aviva, for hiking several of these trails with me even after the really scary rattlesnake episode, and getting all her own lunches and dinners during the more intense times on the book; my son, Sam, for taking charge of the technical tasks on photos; and my daughter, Talya, for long-distance writing support.

The Society of Professional Journalists provided the resources and time necessary for this project by awarding me the 2006–07 Eugene C. Pulliam Fellowship for Editorial Writers.

Friends Lauren Heitner, Melodye Shore, and Laurel Jacob were amiable and helpful companions on several hikes.

This book never would have come my way had it not been for my friend Kristina Lindgren. Thanks also to my reassuring acquisitions editor Kim Grant.

Everywhere I went on the trails, I met people who helped, either by fixing my camera on the spot, telling me about their favorite trails, or even changing a tire. Even if I didn't like hiking so much, it would be worth it to go out on the trail just for the people.

# Introduction

There it is on the map, so easy to miss among the vastly bigger counties surrounding it. Orange County is a tiny place geographically, just 789 square miles. Amazing to consider that more than 3 million people fit into that space, largely in suburban tracts, making it California's second biggest county by population.

All the more surprisingly, laced throughout this crammed county you can find lovely and diverse stretches of linked wilderness, more than 600 miles of trails that invite hikers of almost every description. In fact, Orange County's expansive hiking scene was ironically created in large part by its equally expansive construction. As mitigation, developers often were required to dedicate swaths of environmentally valuable land as open space. Others did so to leave a legacy. Combined with existing parks, a national forest, and open spaces preserved by the work of dedicated community activists, Orange County encompasses a variety of hiking experiences within easy distances of its suburban sprawl.

Once-degraded wetlands previously covered with oil pumps, their restoration just completed, draw crowds of birds including the endangered least tern. The last major link of the South Coast Wilderness was completed in 2007, providing an easy walk to the county's only natural lakes, one named for a hippopotamus that escaped from an animal park and made its home there for a short time. A climb over a ridgeline with big views brings you to a little gully on the other side; a sycamore there is the infamous hanging tree where two bandits from a famous gang were lynched in the 1850s. In the Santa Ana Mountains you can find mining adits from the 1800s, waterfalls, forests of conifers, and forever views without a house in sight.

To see, touch, and understand the surroundings of Orange County is to forge a palpable link to a rich natural history. You walk on ground that, back in dinosaur days, formed the floor of a shallow sea, and stroll wetlands that were the stomping grounds of Ice Age mammals that left their bones behind tens of thousands of years ago. You scent the pungent white sage that Native Americans burned in ceremonies 1,000 years ago, see the stones they pounded their acorns on, taste the lemonadeberry they made a tart drink from, and observe the tiny doveweed they threw into creeks to stun fish for easy catching—an early example of better living through chemistry.

Tread paths through yellow fields of high mustard, an exotic plant strewn some 250 years ago by the padres who, it is apocryphally said, sought to leave a golden trail from mission to mission. With your fingers, trace the ridges in a scallop shell fossil more than 15 million years old. Hold the hard fruit of the stinking gourd that pioneer women used 150 years ago as darning eggs; its pounded roots made a strong soap. Smell the char of ash-strewn acreage left by recent wildfires at the same time that you marvel at showy flowers that blossom only after a catastrophic fire, evidence that this wilderness is no stranger to fire and actually thrives on a limited amount of it, though in recent decades, too-frequent fires have also been a major cause of habitat destruction. Colorful stories and lore lie all along the trail for those who know their signs; this book is your guide to them.

## THE ECOLOGY

Orange County, like much of California, has a Mediterranean climate—which, just as the name implies, is much like the area around the Mediterranean Sea. Hot and dry during the summer and early fall, temperate and rainy (though not all that wet) during the winter, Mediterranean climates occur on western sides of continents, between 30 and 45 degrees latitude on both sides of the equator. California and the actual Mediterranean are the only such areas in the Northern Hemisphere, and by far the largest. Much smaller zones exist in Australia, Chile, and South Africa.

The long annual dry spell—the area receives an average of 15 inches of rain per year, almost all of that from November to April—means that brush-covered hills throughout the county often turn brown by June, and most streams are seasonal, drying within weeks of the most recent rain. As a result, the prime hiking season in Orange County starts in November, after the first rains, and extends through about May. Waterfalls are flowing, hills are green.

Wildflowers begin popping up in January and reach their height in February and March. The late bloomers show themselves in April to May, and only a few hardy souls, like tiny golden tarweed and the giant white-and-purple trumpets of jimson weed, are still around in summer. Though ocean breezes keep the coast at fairly comfortable temperatures through most of the year, inland valleys and canyons can reach searing temperatures in summer. Start hikes early in hot weather; the dryness of the air means that temperatures drop significantly at night, so you can get off to a cool start.

Unlike the crisp autumns of eastern states, the fall months here bring some of the hottest temperatures and the hot, fierce Santa Ana winds from the desert, prime conditions for the wildfires that have blackened several portions of the county over the past several years. Catastrophic fires in 2007 and 2008 caused major damage in some of the county's key habitat and hiking areas, including the Cleveland National Forest, Chino Hills State Park, and Carbon Canyon and Santiago Oaks regional parks.

The Orange County wilderness contains five main types of habitat, each with its own way of surviving frequent drought and wildfire. Coastal sage scrub, made up of low shrubbery such as buckwheat, sagebrush, and grassland that's soft enough to bushwhack through, greens up in winter rains. After a long summer, the scrub is brown and tinder-dry. Chaparral—a version of which is found in every Mediterranean climate—consists of large, woody shrubs like toyon and laurel sumac, growing 8 feet and higher, with tough, thick leaves that retain water. They're impenetrable to hikers unless you crawl along the ground. Grasslands are perhaps the most fragile areas, and the ones most affected by the activities of white settlers, who introduced annual, invasive grasses that add to fire danger and choke out the graceful, perennial bunch grasses that are native to this land. It's rare now to find a meadow covered mainly with those grasses. The gnarled limbs of sycamore and coast live oak make woodlands a shady, inviting place to hike. And riparian areas offer the beauty of running waters and water-loving plants like the California wild rose—as well as the dangers of poison oak. Of course, there's also the extraordinary coastline for which Orange County is famous, and several of these hikes will take you there.

As it happens, the first overseas explorers and settlers in this area were from around the Mediterranean Sea, especially Spain. They brought with them plants that, perfectly suited to local conditions, became invasive pests. Sometimes beautiful and useful pests, such as wild radish and mustard, they nevertheless steal territory from native plants, create wildfire hazards, and at this point remain an indelible part of the local landscape.

The hiking landscape of Orange County is still changing, usually for the better. Three large tracts of open space should offer excellent hiking in years to come. At the former El Toro Marine Corps Air Station, the city of Irvine is working on opening the Great Park, hundreds of acres of combined groomed and natural open space. This would be dwarfed by the preservation of 32,000 acres of Rancho Mission Viejo, set aside as mitigation for a vast construction project in the foothills of the Santa Ana Mountains. In 2010, the Irvine Company transferred 20,000 acres of open land on its private nature preserve to the county parks system, although management of the land remains under the Irvine Ranch Conservancy and access is limited to docent-led activities and occasional days for open exploration.

## WHAT TO BRING

One of the great aspects of hiking in Orange County is that elaborate gear is seldom needed, and even hiking boots are unnecessary for many trails. Regular sneakers are not a good idea, though, as even moderate hikes require good tread. My personal favorite is trail runners, which are lightweight, low cost, and have excellent tread. Some trails do call for more specialized footwear, such as hiking sandals or shoes, and I'll point those out in the individual trail descriptions.

Clothing should fit the hike. If you're walking on an exposed ridgeline on a warm day, a brimmed hat prevents all sorts of suffering. Shorts are great on a wide truck trail, but you'll probably want long pants for narrow canyon and stream walks where poison oak prevails. Generally, the best idea is to dress with maximum flexibility. Cargo pants with zip-off lower legs, a light long-sleeved shirt layered over a short-sleeved shirt in case you get hot. Light colors keep you cooler, but avoid white-white if you want to see birds, which can be startled by the unnatural appearance of pure white.

Sunscreen and water are musts. If your hike is longer than a mile or two, bring at least a liter, and pack more for extensive hikes and those with significant climbs. This is arid country, and there is no water along the trails that can be counted as safe to drink. I like to fill a plastic bottle halfway with water, put it at a tilt in the freezer overnight, then fill it all the way in the morning. That hunk of ice at the bottom keeps it chilled for hours. Propping the bottle at a tilt keeps the bottom of the bottle from bulging out and increases the surface area of ice that touches the water.

Bring a trail map, a whistle—there should be one for every member of the hiking party—and compass. In the places where trails are not well maintained or marked, a compass can be vital. If you're technologically inclined, a GPS device is even more helpful. There are models that strap on your wrist like a watch.

A small first-aid kit is smart even on minor outings. Even trivial troubles, like the beginnings of a blister, can make a hike miserable or cut it short if left uncushioned.

An emergency medical technician who is also an outdoorsman taught me how to pack a lightweight kit that takes up almost no space. It can even be tucked into the large pocket of cargo pants. Assemble the following:

- Several plastic bandage strips and antibiotic ointment
- A couple of feet of gauze, rolled
- A couple of feet of duct tape, rolled
- A small multi-use knife that includes scissors and a corkscrew
- Several packages of individually packaged alcohol prep wipes to clean wounds and to wash off the oil from poison oak exposure
- An individual packet of uncoated aspirin
- A couple of large safety pins

Put all of the above into a disposable latex glove. Fold over the fingers of the glove and insert it, opening first, into another latex glove.

This prepares you for most of the mishaps you might encounter. Scrapes and cuts get an immediate cleaning with an alcohol prep wipe, followed by a dose of antibiotic ointment and bandaging. With some gauze and duct tape, you can bandage almost anything. If you need serious bandaging, use the knife or its scissors attachment to cut a T-shirt into a continuous 3-inch-wide strip that can be pinned with a safety pin. A quick arm sling is fashioned by pulling the bottom of a T-shirt up to the shoulder and pinning it. The aspirin is for symptoms of heart attack; EMTs recommend chewing it, not swallowing it whole.

I also recommend that you bring a small, unused, and sealed plastic bottle of water, 12 ounces or so, on hikes of more than a couple of miles. If there's a nasty wound, this serves as a debriding tool. Use the corkscrew attachment of the knife to puncture a small hole in the bottle and squeeze the bottle to squirt the water with enough pressure to clean the wound.

I used to recommend commercial poison oak wash in case you accidentally brushed into some of the highly allergenic plant, but then discovered that UC Davis' Integrated Pest Management program recommended washing the exposed skin with a mild solvent such as rubbing alcohol. It's important to rinse off afterward, using your sealed bottle of water. I've used alcohol prep wipes ever since and have never gotten a rash. They're cheap and lightweight—or you could carry a small bottle of rubbing alcohol.

Bring extra water and a hat for sunny ridgeline hikes and wear light, loose clothing. Learn the symptoms of heat exhaustion and heat stroke—which include feeling faint, dizzy, or confused, and having rapid heartbeat—and treat symptoms immediately before they can worsen. Rest in the shade, have a drink and spritz with water, loosen or remove clothing, and seek medical help or a ride from a ranger if you're on or near a trail that can be traversed by SUV. On the hikes I lead, participants tend to worry about snakes and mountain lions, but I have found that the biggest and most common dangers to hikers are dehydration and heat exhaustion. You might want to consider packing a couple of cooling scarves, the type that have beads that expand and help keep you cool when soaked in a bit of water. They weigh almost nothing and take up no real room, tucked into whatever bits of spare space your pack has.

This will sound obvious, but it's surprising how often people neglect to do it, and the results have occasionally been tragic: If you have special medical needs, bring your medication on the trail and let a companion know you have it and where it is. This includes epinephrine injectors for severe allergies, inhalers for asthma, and medications for heart ailments. The backcountry, with its insects, vegetation, and steep hills, is exactly the place most likely to test these conditions.

None of this precludes the wisdom of calling 911 on your cell phone in an emergency (although in large sections of the Cleveland National Forest, reception is poor to nonexistent), or seeking medical attention for non-emergency situations as soon as you return to civilization.

## TRAIL SAFETY—AND RESPECT

Properly equipped, you face little danger on the area's trails. Most are so well marked that getting lost is not an issue, unless you go off on your own without a well-mapped plan. Here are the main hazards you might face on the trail, and the best ways of avoiding or coping with them:

**Ticks.** They're especially abundant in spring, just waiting for a host to come along while they hang out in overgrown scrub or stream habitats. Avoid sitting on logs, check yourself every once in a while, especially at the nape of the neck and on the midriff. Once you get home, it pays to strip down and check yourself in a mirror.

Lyme disease is relatively rare in Orange County, and for a curious reason. Through much of California, nymphal ticks feed off the blood of the western fence lizard. UC Berkeley scientists have found that a substance in the lizard's blood—they believe it to be a protein—appears to kill off the Lyme bacterium.

Still, ticks are more than just repulsive. In 2007, Rocky Mountain Spotted Fever was found in some ticks of the South Coast Wilderness area. Some people use insect repellent, with varying success, and others tuck their hiking pants into their socks, and their shirts into their pants, to give ticks very little way to find an unprotected patch of skin. I find that just checking once in a while works fine.

**Poison oak.** Usually grows as a vine, intertwining with chaparral in riparian and canyon areas. Even on an open trail, before touching plants, check for the distinctive glossy leaves growing in sets of three. In summer, the leaves often turn a vivid red. Beware in winter, when the leaves fall off and bare branches give no hint of the danger.

Contrary to its name, poison oak is not poisonous, but most people are allergic to its resin, called urushiol. Lucky is the rare person who doesn't react to it. Native Americans are said to have woven the supple stems into baskets. Most exposed people will develop a weepy, extremely itchy rash a couple of days after exposure. Systemic reactions can be more serious.

In most of the county's hiking situations, you can avoid poison oak by sticking to the trail and watching where you put your hands, as well as by wearing long pants and sleeves. But there are some hikes in this book where poison oak contact is unavoidable. Wear long sleeves and long pants in these areas; in the worst thickets of it, gardening gloves can be handy. I've found a commercially sold poison ivy and oak block to be effective; it's a physical barrier, not a chemical one. But don't spread it on skin that's already been exposed.

If you come into contact, this is where your packet or bottle of rubbing alcohol comes in handy on the trail. Beyond that, you generally have a few hours after exposure during which the resin stays on the exterior of the skin and can be washed off. When you get home from a hike where there was poison oak, even if you think you didn't touch it, head straight to the laundry room and throw everything you've been wearing into the washing machine with plenty of detergent. Then go take a shower. If you're going to a hike that you know has thick poison oak and it will be a long drive home, a change of clothes in the car (bring a plastic bag for the exposed clothing) can literally save your skin.

Naturalist lore holds that mugwort, which often grows near poison oak, will remove the resins if rubbed on the skin shortly after exposure and will alleviate the related rashes and itching. If you're stuck without better remedies, and you can identify mugwort with certainty, it can't hurt.

**Rattlesnakes.** Generally, they're even more eager to avoid you than the other way around. Who gets bitten by rattlesnakes? Most commonly young men, especially inebriated ones, because instead of leaving the snakes alone, they sometimes try to pick them up. Stay on the trail, not because rattlers won't stretch themselves across it, but because you can see them more easily that way. That said, I have had a couple of scary interactions with Southern Pacific rattlesnakes, the most aggressive ones in Orange County. There always seems to be a rash of rattlesnake encounters on the trail during the first warm weekend in April, when the rattlers usually emerge from winter hibernation.

A hiking staff can act as a block between you and a snake. Bites are very rare, but if you are bitten, use that part of your body as little as possible. Call 911 for help getting off the trail and to a hospital quickly. Bites can be life-threatening.

**Mountain lions.** Encounters between mountain lions and people are quite rare in Orange County, but they have occurred. In 2004, a bicyclist was killed, and another seriously injured, by a cougar attack in Limestone Canyon & Whiting Ranch Wilderness Park, where cougars are occasionally spotted.

Though mountain lions have been known to stray occasionally into the South Coast Wilderness, they are an extreme rarity there and do not stay long. Cougars are more common in the Santa Ana Mountains and surroundings. Still, I talk to naturalists all the time who lead hikes in the mountains, and only a couple of them have ever seen a mountain lion.

If you see one, do not run. Stand as big as you can, facing the lion. If you're wearing a jacket, lift up your arms with the jacket hanging from them to create a bigger profile. Shout in a big, deep voice. If it comes toward you, throw stones or use your hiking staff to hit it. In other words, don't act like prey.

**Hiking alone.** One of the reasons people love to hike is to get a moment away from other people. It would be unrealistic to say never hike alone. But save solo hikes for easier trails that aren't terribly remote. If the trail requires bushwhacking, rock scrambling, or other activities where injury is more likely, or if it involves a distance where a sprain or heat exhaustion could impair your ability to return safely, go with a companion, especially in areas without cell phone reception.

Though these tips should prepare you for much of what you'll find on hiking trips, it's important to use caution and common sense in the wilderness and to realize that you're in an unpredictable environment—the very thing we love about the wild. Get used to observing your levels of energy and hydration. Don't hesitate to turn around if it feels like the full hike might be a little too much for you today. It's not as important to get to the "goal" as it is to enjoy your time in a natural setting. One skilled naturalist I know has such a keen eye for interesting detail that occasionally his hikes don't quite make it out of the parking lot. That's part of why I don't give estimated times for these hikes. They take as much time as you feel like spending at your chosen pace.

Keep the wilderness safe as well as yourself. Staying on the trail is more than a safety tip for humans. It's also vital to keeping coastal sage scrub healthy and wild. Off-trail exploration and hiking is allowed in most of the national forest, but not the cutting of new trails. Neither is allowed in county or state parks. Keep your dogs out of parks where they are prohibited; even when dogs are kept on leash, the scent of this unfamiliar predator or its droppings can disrupt the patterns of wild animals, forcing them to use energy that they need to survive.

Horses have the right of way over hikers, and hikers over bicyclists. But don't make an issue of it when a biker is hurtling down your trail. Whether the biker hits the hiker, or the hiker hits the biker, nobody comes out happy. Bikes are allowed on most trails in the county.

## HOW TO USE THIS BOOK

The hikes are divided into three sections: coastal (including the South Coast Wilderness of the San Joaquin Hills), foothills, and Santa Ana Mountains. Each trail description will include the length, type, elevation gain, degree of difficulty, and any special instructions like the need for certain equipment or extra water. Bring the book with you on the trail, both for the directions and maps, and for the phone numbers to contact for each hike. On one of my hikes in the Cleveland National Forest, the rangers locked a gate, not realizing my car was still in the campground. Because I happened to be right next to a cell phone reception area and had the number of the nearest ranger station, help came within minutes.

In the ensuing chapters, there will be descriptions of the history and ecology of the area to be hiked, including an overview of what you will find there and the best seasons and times of day for hiking. Directions to the trailhead will usually be from the nearest freeway. Sometimes toll roads can shave time off the drive, but directions from these roads are not included.

Take your time reading the trail descriptions, which will take you step by step through the features of each hike. They will lead you to visible fossils, point out local plants, and tell you what Native Americans and later settlers used them for. They will tell you which birds to look and listen for and about the colorful characters who lived—or died—along these trails. You'll come out with a richer experience than a pretty walk. It's worthwhile to look through the descriptions of other hikes, where you'll learn about plants and history that might be relevant to your hike as well.

## THE 50 HIKES

Orange County has far more than 50 hikes in it. If the only criterion for being in the book was a nice stroll through sage scrub, chaparral, or oak woodland, you'd be taking something the size of *War and Peace* onto the trail with you. I have tried to select hikes for their variety and their unique features—fossils, animals, extraordinary histories, exceptional beauty and remoteness, amazing views, signs of ancient settlement by Native Americans, or unusual geological features. I'll also confess to being a sucker for water in this often dry landscape: lakes, ponds, creeks, and especially waterfalls. A few new hikes have been included in this second edition.

This book is mostly for the beginning to intermediate hiker, though a few more strenuous outings also are included. Within these categories, I also looked for hikes scattered throughout the county so that people could enjoy the outdoors without a long drive.

Though the title says these hikes are in Orange County, "in" is loosely defined as being within the Orange County area. Several hikes are just outside the county's borders.

## MORE INFORMATION

Chances are that once you have walked some of these trails, you will have a thirst to learn more and to become an expert yourself. Appendix I provides a directory of the groups that offer guided hikes and other nature activities. Appendix II lists some of the best books and resources for educating yourself about the wild and doing your own identifications of plants and animals along the trail.

Appendix III lists annual parking and access passes so you can visit often. Passes are no longer required to park in the Cleveland National Forest, but be aware that the situation is complicated. You can park for free, but using any "developed" amenities such as a picnic table or bathroom could mean you're required to have a Forest Adventure Pass, in the unlikely event that a ranger comes upon you at such moments.

One of the greatest experiences is to introduce children to nature. At the beginning of one hike I was leading, a preschool-age girl cried and clung to her mother because she was afraid of going out on the trail into what was actually a tame environment. After a half-hour of learning about the plants, birds, and bugs around her, she began skipping along the trail and asked, "Can we have my birthday party here?" That remains one of my favorite all-time hikes. Appendix IV is all about children. It lists the hikes in this book that they are most likely to enjoy and refers you to spots that don't offer anything that could be called a hike, instead providing an inspiring introduction to the outdoors. One of the best places to see fossils is in a city recreation building in south Orange County. Free parking, easy access, beautiful building, great exhibition.

## THE PACT

This book will guide you to many sites with extraordinary finds: fossils, Native American artifacts, rare flowers, awe-inspiring wildlife. This implies a trust between the writer and reader that you will tread lightly and leave these marvels untouched and untaken, both for the next hiker and for the sake of preserving the wilderness intact. Many a writer of hiking guides has been dismayed to see damage to beloved wilderness areas because they had made people more aware of those trails. Leave nothing behind you on the trail; take no items, all of which have their place and purpose in the wild; and resist any urge to catch or otherwise bother the animals.

Though the book frequently refers to the historic uses of plants, the flora in the wilderness also should be left undisturbed, both for the health of the

plant and for yours. The people who used these plants knew them intimately, but a little bit of knowledge can be dangerous. Edible wild fennel looks almost exactly like poison hemlock when it turns brown.

## THINGS CHANGE

Each of these chapters is written with the most recent information about conditions, access, and fees. But hiking conditions change fast in Orange County. Wildfires can put trails out of commission for years. Landslides change the contour of a hike. Financially strapped agencies raise their fees, sometimes substantially, or limit their hours, or both. As I mentioned earlier, access to 20,000 acres of Irvine Land Reserve property could change once this land is transferred to the county. It's wise to call before heading out on a hike; I have provided the phone numbers and websites for all hikes where those are available.

I look forward to traveling these paths as your companion.

THE "WIDOWMAKER" CONE OF COULTER PINE

# I.

# COASTAL HIKES

# San Gabriel River to Turtle Overlook

**LOCATION**: Seal Beach/South Long Beach

**TOTAL DISTANCE**: 3 to 4.5 miles

**TYPE**: Out and back

**TOTAL ELEVATION CHANGE**: Level

**DIFFICULTY**: Easy

**SEASON**: Year-round

**FEES ETC.**: None. Leashed dogs allowed.

**MAPS**: USGS Seal Beach, Los Alamitos

**TRAILHEAD COORDINATES**: N 33°44.816′ W 118°06.754′

**CONTACT**: Aquarium of the Pacific (www.aquariumofpacific.org)

This first hike is also the oddball of the book; in places, it's certainly the winner for ugliest. But the lower San Gabriel River also is a candidate for most fascinating. Along its dreariest little stretch, in the midst of industrial power plants and oil tanks, swims a wonder story of nature: A resident colony of endangered green sea turtles, which can grow up to 5 feet long and 500 pounds. This is the northernmost group ever found, hundreds of miles from its more usual haunts.

This hike is like whale watching; you aren't guaranteed a sight of the turtles, which sometimes move closer to the mouth of the river, but they are year-round residents, and in several visits to this spot, I have always been treated to at least a glimpse of them.

This hike starts about a mile south of the turtles, at the marina. You can catch views of the river as it meets the ocean and walk the hiking-biking path that offers occasional glimpses of nature that thrives even when its natural habitat has been channelized and replaced with steep banks of rocks.

## GETTING THERE

From the Seal Beach Boulevard exit off the San Diego Freeway (I-405), turn southwest on Seal Beach Boulevard, heading toward the ocean. Drive 2.8 miles and make a right on Pacific Coast Highway. Travel 0.9 mile and make a left onto First Street. After 0.4 mile, turn right onto Marina Drive. Go 0.2 mile on Marina Drive, crossing over the San Gabriel River, to where it makes a sharp right turn, becoming North Marina Drive. Do not make the turn; rather, continue straight into the marina and park.

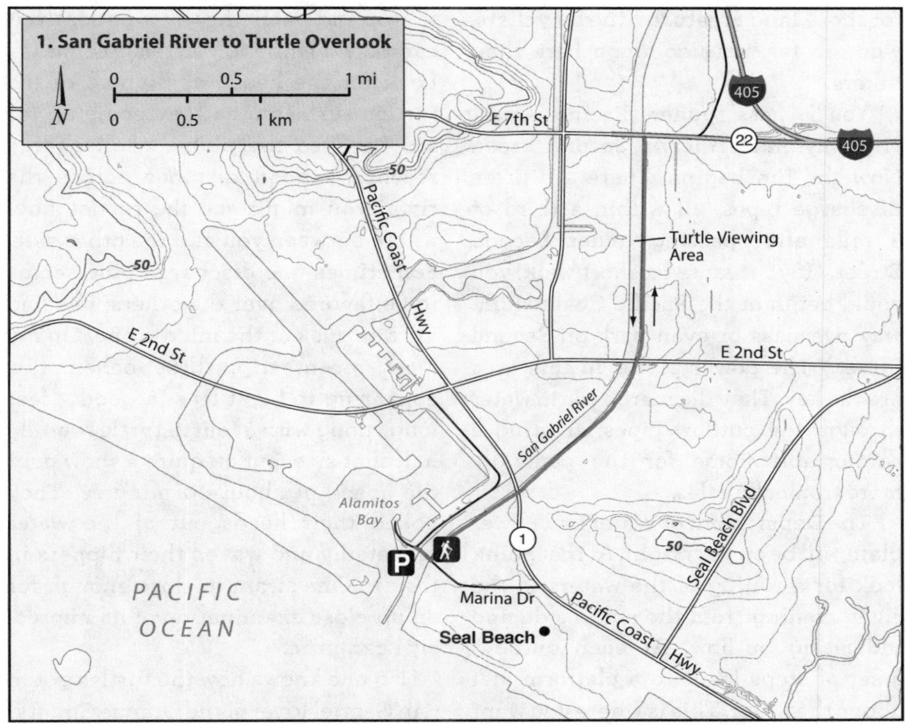


## THE TRAIL

It's pleasant to start this hike with a stroll around the picturesque marina, but whether or not you choose this option, cross back on Marina Drive over the river to its southeast side and enter the paved bike path that runs along its southern flank, walking away from the ocean.

Though the river looks more like a small canal at this point, it is teeming with living residents that can be seen by those with a sharp eye and the patience to observe carefully. Snowy egrets are the easiest to spot, hunched over by the banks of the river. If you see them walk around, notice that at the bottoms of their stiff black legs, they have bright-yellow feet. Brown pelicans are common, and occasionally a red-tailed hawk will sail overhead. This is the hawk with the piercing, almost electronic-sounding cry that's used in movies to signal the presence of any hawk. On a recent walk I heard a mockingbird sing an impressive medley of tunes, as well as the *witchity, witchity* song of the common yellowthroat, and a wrentit, with a call that sounds like a dropped ping-pong ball. Belted kingfishers and blue herons are often seen around here, and ospreys are occasionally spotted.

A close look at the water below frequently might reveal stingrays gliding along the bottom and even occasional sharks. Silvery fish called mullet make frequent leaps from the water. While watching the river life, keep an eye out for those land creatures, the bicyclists, who are far more common here than hikers.

You'll pass under Pacific Coast Highway, and farther on, Second Street. Now the fun begins. There are three discharge pipes, all within a third of a mile after passing under Second Street. (If you wanted a short walk, you could begin at the Pacific Coast Highway overpass or even park on Second Street.) The power plants in this area are the key. They discharge warm water through the outflow pipes, creating a comfortable home for the generally more tropical turtles.

The Department of Water and Power plant will be on your right. At that point, look for a roiling of the waters in the river, coming from the south side and indicating outflow. At each outflow, a set of steps leads to a platform just above the water. This is where you want to stop and watch the water patiently; it can take a while for turtles to emerge. Look for the heads or flippers of the turtles surfacing as they come up for air. Because the plume of discharge reaches a good distance across the river, you might see the turtles anywhere between you and the other side. Sometimes one discharge pipe seems to be favored over the others; I've had my best luck at the middle one. On my most recent trip, three behemoths, appearing to be at least a good 3 feet long, along with a fourth turtle roughly half that size, put on quite a show over the space of about 20 minutes. They poked their heads out of the water repeatedly and waved their flippers in the air. One swam in close enough for an up-close examination of its impressive carapace.

No one knows how the turtles got to San Gabriel River at the Orange County-

Courtesy of Aquarium of the Pacific

WORKERS FROM AQUARIUM OF THE PACIFIC RETURN A GREEN SEA TURTLE TO ITS HOME IN THE SAN GABRIEL RIVER

Hugh Ryono

A SEA TURTLE SWIMS IN THE SAN GABRIEL RIVER

A SNOWY EGRET ON THE BANK OF THE RIVER

Long Beach border, or when they arrived. Sightings have been reported since the late 1980s and were mostly scoffed at until scientists confirmed the local turtle population in 2008. It's believed they might be a breakoff group from a colony that lived in San Diego Bay, also near a power plant, and that very recently was considered the northernmost group of the turtles.

As of this writing, scientists at Long Beach's Aquarium of the Pacific had only begun to study the San Gabriel River turtles and were unsure whether they numbered as few as eight or in the dozens. In addition, the animals that lived in the warm effluent appeared to mature faster than in their historic environment, another nature puzzle. While observing the turtles, the scientists also have seen seal lions swim up to this same spot to forage for food.

After you've had your fill of turtle watching, retrace your steps, with the ocean always within your sight. A return to Marina Drive makes this a 3-mile walk; continuing on to the mouth of the river adds a mile round-trip and provides some pretty scenery, including a fairly decent chance of seeing dolphins, which sometimes swim partway into the river.

# Bolsa Chica Ecological Reserve

**LOCATION**: Huntington Beach

**TOTAL DISTANCE**: 4.8 miles (easily shortened by skipping one or two spur loops)

**TYPE**: Triple loop

**TOTAL ELEVATION GAIN**: 20 feet

**DIFFICULTY**: Very easy

**SEASON**: Year-round

**FEES ETC.**: Free. No dogs allowed.

**MAPS**: USGS Seal Beach

**TRAILHEAD COORDINATES**: N 33°42.677′ W 118°03.669′

**CONTACT**: Bolsa Chica Conservancy (714-846-1114, www.bolsachica.org)

It's hard to believe that just a few years ago, Bolsa Chica Ecological Reserve was the site of a decrepit Huntington Beach oil field, its wetlands degraded by duck hunters who built a dam that cut it off from the ocean to encourage migratory ducks to stop off there. Decades of community activism and lawsuits fought off dense development in the area and gained support for a restoration project. Many of the oil wells were pulled out, and in 2006 the wetlands were reopened to the ocean. Within two years the birds came back in force, following the return of scallops, top smelt, halibut, small sharks, and a host of other sea life, to the point where one of the problems naturalists now face is such an abundance of birds that they occasionally crush each others' nests. This is an extraordinary success in a state that has lost 90 percent of its coastal wetlands.

Bolsa Chica is a wonder still in progress. Expanded trails might open; one trail listed here, along Pacific Coast Highway, might eventually close to make way for restoration of the dunes. Here I outline a 4.8-mile hike but you have opportunities to cut it shorter by skipping the flood channel and/or the loop around Bolsa Pocket—or just stroll as long as you please. On clear days, the Port of Los Angeles and the Palos Verdes Peninsula beyond seem like they're just a few blocks away. A guide to southern California's birds makes this a richer experience, and don't forget binoculars.

## GETTING THERE

From the San Diego Freeway (I-405), take the Warner Avenue exit 5.5 miles south, nearly to Pacific Coast Highway. Just before the highway, turn left into

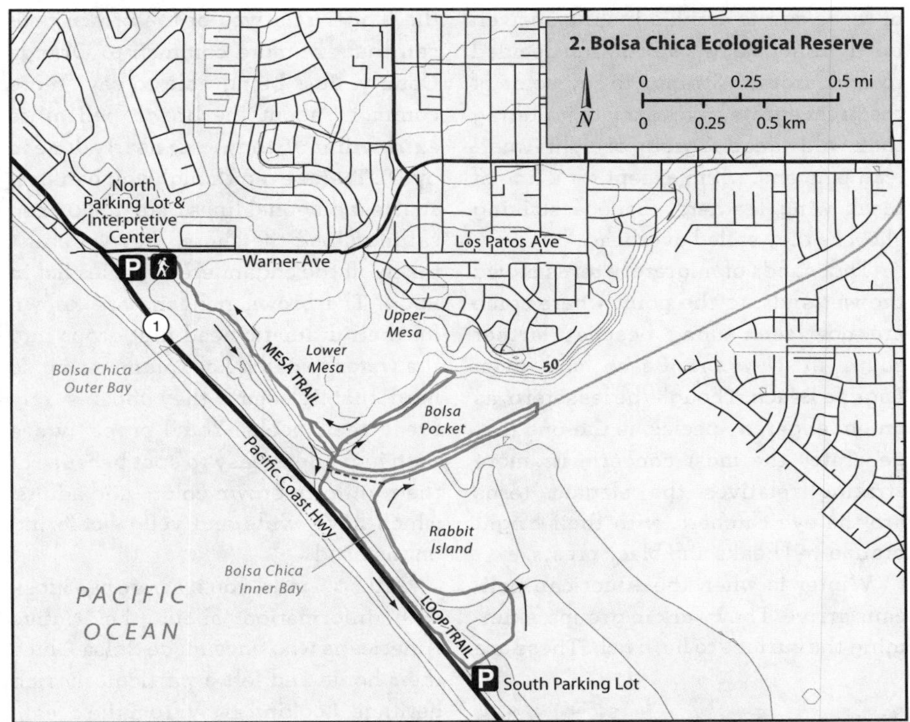


the parking lot where you see the blue-gray mobile home that serves as a small interpretive center.

## THE TRAIL

If the interpretive center is open, it's worthwhile to drop by and find out more about the wetlands. From the parking lot, walk east along the shoulder of Warner Avenue across the bridge over the Bolsa Chica Outer Bay channel. On my most recent visit, it appeared that a footbridge was being constructed across the channel so that people won't have to walk on the busy street. After crossing, turn right onto Mesa Trail, marked with a visitors' kiosk. Follow the trail along the lower mesa, which has some interesting plants seldom seen elsewhere in Orange County. A particularly pretty plant here is St. Catherine's Lace; a form of wild buckwheat from the Channel Islands with bluish leaves. In spring it blossoms with big clusters of tiny, fragrant, white to pink flowers.

But the main attraction is the extraordinary variety and number of birds. In the Outer Bolsa Bay, you'll almost always see both snowy egrets and their larger, more elegant cousin, the great egret, feathered an even purer white. It's a rare visit when you don't see at least a couple of great blue herons.

You don't have to be a bird watcher to be awed by the amount and variety of feathered life here. During recent visits, I've seen green and great blue herons, an osprey, a kestrel and a particularly rare species for this area, the reddish egret, which performs a crazy fishing dance to herd its prey. A couple of these egrets arrived in 2005, driven north from Baja by a storm, and decided to stick around. Strange to say, some of the great egrets have taken to imitating their wild dance. A group of eight American pelicans, white except for a line of black wing feathers, made a striking show as they sailed overhead.

Thousands of migratory terns crowd the wetlands, to the point where some are now seen along beaches farther south in Newport Beach and even Laguna Beach. Though the least tern, as an endangered species, is the one that generates the most concern, its more striking relatives the elegant terns are the eye catchers, with their bright orange-red beaks and black crests.

Winter is when the American pelicans arrive. They work in groups, skimming the surface to herd fish. These are the bigger relatives of the brown pelican that are more common to Orange County. Just being able to say "more common" about the brown pelican is extraordinary; they were nearly done in by DDT, and even though you can now see neat diagonal lines of up to 20 or so sailing along the shore, they were just taken off the endangered species list in 2009. The brown pelicans are known for their dramatic head-first drops into the water to catch fish, plummeting so hard that it seems they must surely break their necks. You'll probably see both juveniles—easy to spot because of their uniform brown color—and adults, which have white and yellow coloring on the head.

A PELICAN AT THE FLAP GATE OF BOLSA CHICA

After 0.8 mile, you'll arrive at a kiosk with information about the Native Americans who once made Bolsa Chica their home and left a particularly rich heritage. Looking away from the ocean, you can see a development of large, shoulder-to-shoulder houses built on the upper mesa of Bolsa Chica; a wealth of finds was discovered here during construction, including cog stones, stones shaped into something like a gear wheel. No one knows the purpose of the cog stones, a rare find dating back as much as 8,000 years; archaeologists speculate that they had religious significance. Cog stones can be seen at the Bowers Museum in Santa Ana.

At the kiosk, you're also standing right next to much more recent history. During World War II, fears of a Japanese submarine attack along the coast prompted the creation of 16 defense sites from Santa Monica to Newport Beach. One of those was here on the mesa of Bolsa Chica, where a large bunker and series of tunnels were constructed, along with two gun turrets. Next to the

GREEN HERON

kiosk, both north and south, you can see the round metal-and-concrete remains of those turrets. The palm trees up on the mesa were on the grounds of the old duck hunting club, which was responsible for the damming of the wetlands from the ocean in 1900.

Continuing on Mesa Trail, you soon come to an overlook area with various pictures of birds and other wildlife that can be found in the wetlands. This is a good place from which to observe the wetlands plants, particularly pickleweed, which actually looks like a plant made up of thousands of miniature pickles, though it turns pink or reddish in fall. (For more on pickleweed, see the Bayview Trail chapter.)

From the overlook, turn right to take the steps down to the flap gate and tide gate, used to regulate water flow. You can often see fish on both sides of the gate as you cross the water here so it's no surprise that this is a particularly popular hangout for fish-eating birds. You can often find a pelican or two sitting by the gate and clumps of snowy egrets huddling on shore.

Once on the other side of the bridge (1 mile from the start), turn left on the paved but sometimes crumbly Loop Trail that runs just east of Pacific Coast Highway. There are remnants of old sand dunes here, and plans for restoring them; this trail would eventually be eliminated. The clumps of sharp leaves growing about 2 feet high are called spiny rush; you can also find bright-yellow beach primrose along this trail, along with brilliant purple clusters of sand verbena.

After 0.6 mile on the Loop Trail, you'll reach the south parking lot of the wetlands. Turn left, walking through the parking lot and over a wooden bridge. Then go up the steps and turn left to walk on the eastern side of the Loop Trail. To your right behind the fence is an area where birds can nest undisturbed.

At 1.8 miles from the start of the hike, you'll see an outlook area to your right, with benches for viewing. Another viewing area is located on a knoll at 2.4 miles. Just past this knoll, turn right onto the flat trail that goes along the flood control channel, the favored home of a variety of ducks. (If you want to shorten your hike by a mile, turn left to return to the tide gate and climb the stairs back up to the overlook on Mesa Trail.)

After a half mile of walking along the channel, cross the bridge to your left and return on the other side. You'll find yourself between the channel and Bolsa Pocket, a pond where hawks and other raptors can often be found brooding on the snags of trees. This is also a good place to look for great blue herons; don't forget to look up in the trees as well as in the water.

This path will take you back to the tide gate; at this point, you will be 3.5 miles into the hike. Go up the steps to the Mesa Trail overlook and immediately turn right onto an unmarked loop trail that will take you to the other side of Bolsa Pocket, another particularly rich place to look for raptors and other large birds. Again, this trail can be skipped to shorten the hike by a half-mile.

After returning to the overlook once more, turn right onto the Mesa Trail where you started.

# Bayview Trail

**LOCATION**: Upper Newport Bay Ecological Reserve

**TOTAL DISTANCE**: 3 miles

**TYPE**: Out and back, plus a short loop

**TOTAL ELEVATION GAIN**: 100 feet

**DIFFICULTY**: Easy

**SEASON**: Year-round

**FEES ETC.**: Free. Leashed dogs allowed. Good for children.

**MAPS**: USGS Tustin, Newport Beach

**TRAILHEAD COORDINATES**: N 33°39.168′ W 117°52.147′

**CONTACT**: Peter and Mary Muth Interpretive Center (949-923-2290, www.ocparks.com /unbic)

Carved out during the glacier period of the Pleistocene, Newport Bay is the most distinctive feature along the Orange County coastline, a spot that has been a favored neighborhood from the Ice Age to the current Affluent Newport Beach Epoch. Fossils of mammoths, bison, and giant sloths have been found in the upper bay, which was also the site of several Native American settlements. This easy and popular trail takes you along one edge of the bay to its fine interpretive center, nestled into a bluff with full-on views. You'll see all manner of shorebirds, and almost certainly egrets, great blue herons, and quite possibly an osprey searching for its prey from overhead. Strange to say, given its suburban character, this hike could present your best chance of spotting a bobcat.

## GETTING THERE

Take the Jamboree Road exit from Highway 73, heading south. On Jamboree, travel 0.1 mile to Bayview Drive, and turn right. Pass the first stop sign and look for parking along the street.

## THE TRAIL

On the bay side of Bayview Drive, several small trails lead to the wide blacktopped riding, hiking, and equestrian path known as Bayview Trail. Turn right, away from Jamboree Road. Newport Bay has more than 10 miles of trails around its perimeter. Though there is no getting away from the development that surrounds the bay, Bayview Trail is quieter and has less housing within near view. This part of the trail has numerous non-native plants including thistle, black mustard, and pepper trees.

Some 500 feet along the trail, you might want to take the posted small nature loop that brings you closer to the marsh and more native vegetation such as pickleweed and cordgrass. Pickleweed is an edible, salt-loving plant with tiny leaves that look like miniature pickles. The plant got its name from that quality and the salty taste. You might find the plant in both green and red; the leaves turn redder as they take up more salt. Native Americans used it both for its flavor and as a remedy for constipation.

It's likely that you'll see mullet taking athletic leaps of several feet out of the water, and a variety of shorebirds. The bay provides habitat for the endangered clapper rail.

With its abundance of plant and animal life, and the nearby sources of fresh water, it's no wonder that the bay has a long history of inhabitation by Native Americans, who first settled here nearly 9,000 years ago. Tongva Indians lived here starting 2,000 years ago. Various archaeological digs have been conducted in the area, finding occasional bone beads and bits of obsidian—a sign that the Native Americans traded, because the volcanic glass is not indigenous to this area.

White settlers grazed sheep and cattle on the hills around the bay; the Spanish settlers called it Bolsa de Gengara, or bay with high banks. It got its present-day name from a steamer that in the 1870s would carry loads of lumber into the bay during high tide, making the bay a "new port."

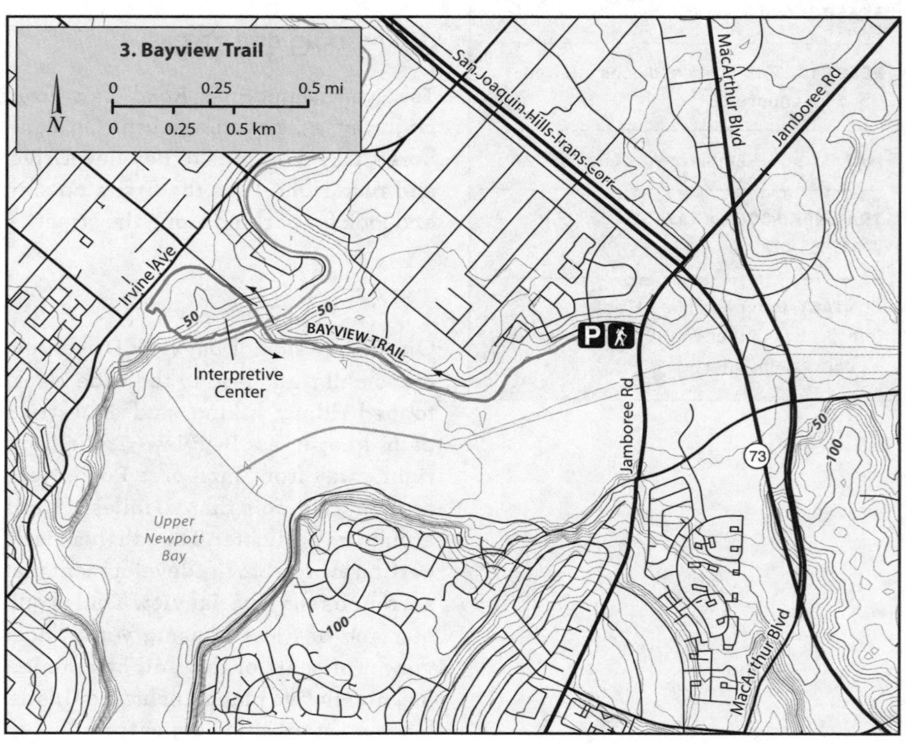

BLUE HERON IN THE DELHI CHANNEL

During the early to mid-1900s, a salt works operated in the bay until floods destroyed it. On Shellmaker Island, companies dredged shells from the bay for use as a supplement for chicken feed. After looping back to the paved trail, continue along the main path.

But what's that smell? You might notice a definite rotten-egg stink along the way, as though there's been a sewage spill. This is a natural phenomenon of the marsh. Bacteria necessary for the decomposition of dead plant and animal matter generates a foul-smelling gas. You might get the pleasant surprise of seeing a bobcat; the bobcats around the bay have become somewhat accustomed to humans. One, informally dubbed Babe, will stroll along paths as though it's one of the hikers.

At nearly a mile, you'll come to the timber-floored bridge over Delhi Channel. On the bluff above here is a thicket of coastal cholla cactus, the favored nesting spot for the cactus wren, whose numbers have been falling in recent years.

At 1.1 miles, just after crossing the

bridge, find an opening in the chain-link fence. Go through it and right on the dirt trail that runs parallel to the paved trail. Then turn left into the delivery drive for the Peter and Mary Muth Interpretive Center to reach the front entrance.

Open every day but Mondays, the interpretive center is definitely worth a visit. It was built into the bluffs with a roof that could be covered with soil and grasses, both to minimize its impact on the native vegetation and as an insulating mechanism. Much of the wood, and the tile in the bathrooms, is recycled from other buildings.

The center regularly screens a short film about the bay and has created engaging interactive exhibitions about its natural history. You can pick up fliers for a variety of programs, most of them targeted for children, but there also are kayaking trips, birding walks, and interpretive hikes.

Outside the center, turn right and go up to the parking lot for the entrance to a network of trails set amid an impressive plant-restoration project. The interpretive trails include signs to inform you both about coastal sage scrub and the plants particular to this area.

You can explore the meandering trails for a couple of miles, or take the first trail that curves down to the cattail-lined channel at the bottom of the gentle slope, a prime place for spotting egrets and great blue herons, as well as ducks, coots, and other birds. Turn left on the trail, walking along the channel until it brings you back to the paved Bayview Trail. Return as you came.

# Crystal Cove Tide Pools

**LOCATION**: Crystal Cove State Park

**TOTAL DISTANCE**: 4.2 miles

**TYPE**: Loop

**TOTAL ELEVATION GAIN**: 100 feet

**DIFFICULTY**: Moderately easy

**FEES ETC.**: $15 day parking fee. No dogs allowed on the beach. Collecting of tide-pool animals, shells, or rocks prohibited.

**MAPS**: USGS Laguna Beach

**TRAILHEAD COORDINATES**: N 33°34.719′ W 117°50.479′

**CONTACT**: Crystal Cove State Park (949-494-3539, www.crystalcovestatepark.com)

With 3 miles of probably the most pristine coastline in Orange County, plus canyon backcountry, Crystal Cove provides a choice of very different hiking environments. This hike will take you along the ocean bluffs of the park and down to the tide pools, near unusual geological formations. Crabs, anemones, and other animals show off their amazing adaptations to spending part of each day underwater, part of it in the open air. The last section of the hike goes through a historic neighborhood of cottages that have been refurbished for rental to visitors. The outing is scenic throughout and cooled enough by sea breezes for any time of day and any season of the year. You'll want to do this walk at low tide, both to see the tide pools and to walk easily from cove to cove.

This hike also calls for different footwear, since you're almost certain to get your feet wet in the tide pools; at the same time, they'll need protection from sharp rocks and shells. Waterproof hiking sandals provide traction and protection enough for both the paved trail and for tide pooling; think of any shoe that you wouldn't mind walking in after it's gotten soaking wet.

## GETTING THERE

Take the Laguna Canyon Road (CA 133) exit south from the San Diego Freeway (I-405) 8.8 miles until it ends at Broadway and North Coast Highway in Laguna Beach. Turn right and drive 4.2 miles to the traffic light for Los Trancos parking lot. Turn right into the parking lot.

Or, from the corner of MacArthur Boulevard and East Coast Highway in Newport Beach, drive 2.6 miles to the Los Trancos light and turn left into the parking lot.

## THE TRAIL

To time your hike, it's a good idea to pick up a tides and times booklet, which will give you the correct times for high and low tides throughout the year. They're often free at surf shops or chambers of commerce in coastal towns. Look for a so-called "negative tide" (indicated by a number with a minus sign), which means the water is below the average low-tide line. Tides of -1.0 or more are best.

From the Los Trancos parking lot, walk out to the traffic light and cross Pacific Coast Highway, entering the access road to the historic district. About 100 feet in, take the paved trail heading to the right. Do not veer onto the dirt paths to the left; those will take you to other beach-access points.

Along the trail, the healthiest plants you'll generally see will be silvery in color, with almost a blue tint. In late summer, some of the branches end in clusters of what look like messy rosettes of the same color, or in a reddish-pink. These plants are saltbush, which, as its name indicates, has an extraordinary tolerance for the high content of salt in the soil; it can excrete salt through its leaves. Sometimes you can even see salt crystals on the plants. Saltbush was among the plants eaten by the Native Americans who lived in Crystal Cove for more than 9,000 years, mainly in El Moro Canyon.

The Mexican government granted land in El Moro Canyon for a cattle ranch during the 1830s, but the rancher went into debt and sold it to new investors, including James Irvine. Crystal Cove would eventually become part of

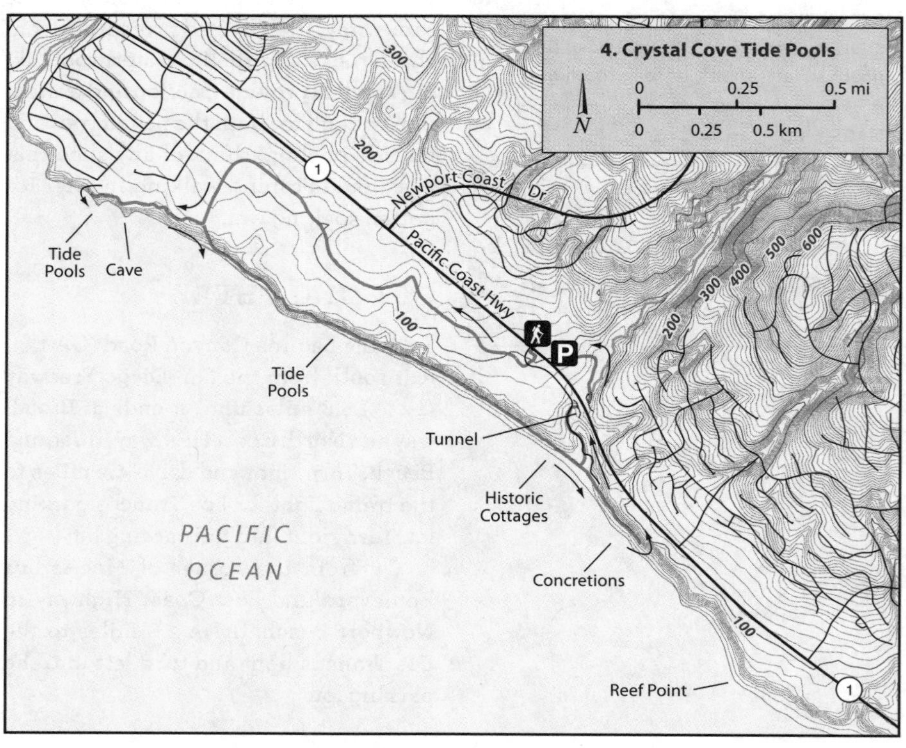

CONCRETION AT THE ROCKY BIGHT TIDE POOLS AT THE HISTORIC COTTAGES

the mammoth Irvine Ranch that spread throughout much of central Orange County. In the 1920s, the Irvine Company leased land to Japanese farmers who built homes, barns, and a community school (which can still be found in the park's historic district) and sold their produce at roadside stands. But the residents were sent to an Arizona internment camp during World War II, losing their homes and farms. They never returned.

The Irvine Company leased out additional land for a private beach vacation resort, allowing the construction of 46 cottages. At the same time, a tenting encampment sprang up in the park's southern area, at the mouth of El Moro Canyon, and eventually became a mobile home park. After the state bought the land for its park, longtime residents of both communities fought for years to keep their homes, but both lost their battles. The funky cottages were refurbished into vacation rentals, and the 300-unit mobile home park, whose residents were evicted in 2006, was razed; as of this writing, campground construction was under way.

The ocean is so clean relative to much of the region that an experimental replanting of kelp forests began here; the thinking was that the lack of pollution would give the kelp the best chance of survival, and so far it seems to be working. Dolphins have long been a fairly common sight along the shore here; I've seen them as well as sea lions on several recent visits.

After you've walked for 1.3 miles, the path turns left, adjacent to a golf course. Then, as you near the northern edge of the park, the walkway goes under a chain-link archway, so it looks like you're walking through the belly of a caterpillar. This protects you against stray golf balls. Shortly after entering the "caterpillar," you'll see stairs leading to Treasure Cove.

At its northern end are a sea cave and shale cliffs that look as if the rock has been twisted and folded to make their own series of waves. This occurred when the rock, part of the Monterey Formation, was some 5,000 feet undersea, and more gelatinous in consistency. A catastrophic event—an earthquake, perhaps—caused the gelatinous rock to slide. Think of the folding that would occur if you pushed a floor rug against a wall.

Here's where the wet part of the hike comes. You'll walk around the cave, treading carefully over the rocks, into pristine Little Treasure Cove. As you go along, examine the rocks for tide-pool life. One ubiquitous sight is groups of small barnacles dotting the rocks. The barnacle, related to the shrimp, is an invertebrate that begins life as larvae that swim freely. Eventually, though, they attach their heads to a rock, using the "cement glands" between their antennae, which secrete a strong adhesive. They will remain upside down for the rest of their lives and build a limestone shell around themselves with a trap door at the top. While the tide is low and they are exposed to air, the trap door is tightly closed. Once covered with water, though, they open the trap door and stick their legs out to sweep for plankton.

Flowerlike sea anemones are also easy to spot. In the little pools where they are covered with water, they look like green sunflowers. But at low tide, they close up and cover themselves with bits of broken shell and rock, as a sort of sunscreen to keep themselves moist. That's one of the reasons that taking shells and rocks from marine reserves like this is not allowed. Visitors also like to poke open anemones in the center; there's a slight sucking feeling as the anemone closes in on what it thinks is prey. But what's also happening is that the anemone is stinging with a neurotoxin that it uses to kill its prey, such as small fish. Because the anemone's sting cannot penetrate the skin on our fingers, it has now wasted some of its poison without getting a lunch in return.

The small fish with a white dot on each side, up near the fin, are opal-eye fingerlings; the tide pools are their nursery. But the small sculpin you see often on the bottom of the pools remain that size and will live out their lives in the tide pools.

Depending on how low the tide is, you can try going north to visit additional coves. But make sure you turn around before the tide starts coming in. Once you get back to Treasure Cove, it's easy to walk south along the beach past Pelican Point until you come to the historic cottage district. Just south of the cottages is a particularly large and interesting tide-pool area called Rocky Bight. Here you'll see rounded rock formations looking like spaceships several feet in diameter. These are concretions that also date back to when the area was underwater; they were formed by pieces of wood that fell to the ocean floor and were surrounded by sediment and then by cementing material filling the spaces in the sedimentary rock, with the wood acting as a sort of nucleus.

If the tide is particularly low, walk out between the little "canyons" between the tide-pool rocks, especially where you see mussel beds. This is a great place to find ochre sea stars and bat stars. Also in among the mussel beds you can almost always find plenty of light-colored gooseneck barnacles. One look at the shape of its "head" and the long flexible "neck" will make the reason behind its name clear. Avoid stepping on mussels to the extent possible; studies have found that this weakens their hold on the rocks and diminishes the mussel beds.

When you're done examining the pools, walk back to the picturesque historic cottages. To return to your car, walk uphill from the cottages on the paved road until you come to a small traffic circle on the right. To the far right, you'll find a tunnel going under Pacific Coast Highway, its walls covered with children's colorful paintings. After emerging from the tunnel, take the paved trail heading uphill to the left, which will bring you back to the Los Trancos parking lot.

CONTORTED-ROCK CAVE AT TREASURE COVE

# San Joaquin Wildlife Sanctuary

**LOCATION**: Irvine

**TOTAL LENGTH**: 2.5 miles

**TYPE**: Loop

**TOTAL ELEVATION GAIN**: Flat

**DIFFICULTY**: Very easy. Stroller and wheelchair accessible.

**SEASON**: Year-round

**FEES ETC.**: None. Check out docent-led hike offerings. No dogs allowed.

**MAP**: USGS Tustin

**TRAILHEAD COORDINATES**: N 33°39.649′ W 117°50.463′

**CONTACT**: Sea and Sage Audubon Society. (949-261-7963, www.seaandsage audubon.org/SJWS/sjws.htm)

It's been a pleasure to watch the San Joaquin Wildlife Sanctuary evolve over the past 15 years. This used to be an uninviting, geometrically arranged checkerboard of rectangular recessed ponds separated by nearly bare levees and surrounded by development. Now it's a model of restoration thoughtfully planned and carefully executed. The ponds look more natural in shape and setting; they're nestled within native plants selected to provide habitat for birds and butterflies. Development still surrounds the marsh, but the greenery softens—and in many spots hides—the view.

What you *can* see here are birds—lots of them, especially shorebirds. The large, dramatic-looking American pelican, pure white with a line of black wing feathers, visits here in winter. In summer, watch for Caspian terns, which look rather like flashy gulls, with a black cap contrasting with a white head and vivid orange-red beak. Giant egrets and great blue herons are practically commonplace. Nesting boxes have been planted throughout the 300-acre sanctuary to draw a variety of other birds. There are monthly bird-watching hikes and don't miss an opportunity to sign up at Audubon House for one of the semi-regular bat hikes, which fill up fast.

This pleasant oasis is convenient enough to drop by on your way to or from work for a little decompression. Children, the elderly, and people with physical disabilities find it easy to take in a little nature on the flat, well-combed paths, which are liberally dotted with benches for resting or just taking a little quiet time. The heavily interconnected trails allow you to walk as little or as much as you want without getting lost. This particular hike, complicated though its twists and turns are, will take

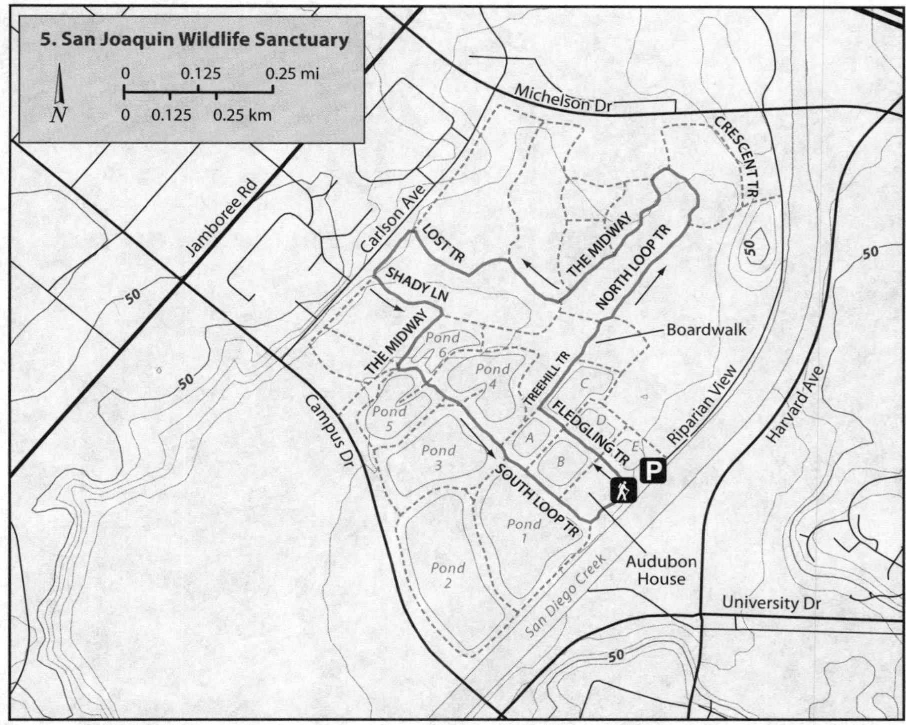


you to the sanctuary's more charming corners and avoid most of its noisier stretches along busy streets.

## GETTING THERE

Take the Jeffrey Road exit from the San Diego (I-405) Freeway and turn east onto University Drive. Travel 3.1 miles to Campus Drive, a light, and turn right. Cross San Diego Creek and almost immediately find Riparian View, a narrow access drive, on your right. Drive a half-mile and turn left at the marked entrance to the sanctuary.

## THE TRAIL

Pick up a map at Audubon House and walk back toward where you came in, up the little drive, but instead of going to the exit, take Fledgling Loop to the left. You almost immediately reach Pond E to your right. This and its neighbor Pond D are two of the more mundane-looking ponds, but they also always seem to be the ones teeming with shorebirds—avocets, grebes, and black-necked stilts.

The marsh got its start as a birding location of sorts in the late 1800s, when the natural marsh that was once here was also the home of the 20-Ranch Club, a private duck-hunting club, which constructed duck ponds amid the marsh. Now, the area is part of the Irvine Ranch Water District's high-tech settling-pond system that cleanses the waters of adjacent San Diego Creek of contaminants from urban runoff. In the 1990s, the water district began the task of turning those ponds into a true habitat for wildlife.

A MARSHY ENCLAVE

At 0.25 mile, the trail ends at a T. Make a right onto Treehill Trail. After about 500 feet on Treehill, which is planted with sycamore and matilija poppies, you reach a point next to Pond C where Treehill turns to the right. Stay straight into the boardwalk that crosses through a marshy area thickly planted with mulefat. Twice along this section, I've seen bobcats—one time a mother with her kitten—suddenly slipping out of the thickets of mulefat and back in. You'll pass mature willow trees before the boardwalk ends at a T. Turn right onto North Loop Trail (it's unmarked at this point) and then, just about 100 feet later, make the first left turn, next to a large butterfly bush with

purple flowers in season, looking similar to a lilac bush.

As you make the left, North Loop continues as a gravel path that runs parallel to a water channel that becomes a narrow, unmarked pond on the left. At 0.6 mile, continue on North Loop as it makes a left turn, ignoring Crescent Trail on the right, and walking through a densely planted area of cottonwood and willow trees with a woodsy feeling. At 0.8 mile, Crescent Trail intersects again with North Loop Trail. Here, make another left, again staying on North Loop, but then after 100 feet, turn left onto The Midway. On this trail, creek-like channels will parallel your path on both sides. One mile from where you started, pass Willow Path, which goes off to the right.

At 1.2 miles, turn right onto North Loop Trail again and 600 feet later, left onto Lost Trail. This is one of the most scenic and intimate trails in the sanctuary with willows making an archway above your head and cattails growing along the creek and marsh areas alongside the trail.

This lovely little trail will take you to one of the ugliest areas, a bare patch right behind an apartment complex. But you won't be here long. Turn left and after a tenth of a mile, turn left again onto Shady Lane, which ends at 1.8 miles at The Midway. Turn right here and then, after another tenth of a mile, turn left onto South Loop Trail. The ponds along here have more natural, irregular shapes surrounded by lush growth. Ducks, Canada geese, and many other birds inhabit these ponds and the plants around them. Little spur trails head off in either direction as you walk along, most of them with benches. One of these, on the right at 2 miles, leads to the tip of a mini-peninsula that pokes into the middle of horseshoe-shaped Pond 5.

In late spring, California wild rose gives off its delicious scent. Continue 0.4 mile, passing the intersection with Fledgling Loop, and look for the opening to a little cultivated garden on your left, after you have passed Ponds A and B. Take the pathway through the garden, back to Audubon House.

# Bommer Canyon

**LOCATION**: City of Irvine Open Space Preserve

**TOTAL DISTANCE**: 2 to 12 miles

**TYPE**: Loop or out and back

**TOTAL ELEVATION GAIN**: Level, or up to 1,200 feet

**DIFFICULTY**: Varies

**SEASON**: Year-round

**FEES ETC.**: Free, docent-led tours plus one open-access day per month.

**MAPS**: USGS Tustin

**CONTACT**: Irvine Ranch Conservancy (714-508-4757, www.irlandmarks.org)

You can pick your outing in one of the most conveniently located undeveloped canyons in Orange County. Within its gently rising walls are broad grasslands and riparian areas with flat, easy trails, a pond and coastal sage scrub, and reminders of its cattle-ranching history. The Irvine Ranch Conservancy offers a wide variety of outings in the limited-access canyon, from birdwatching to weekly yoga classes. A bonus is that the canyon is open once a month for the people to choose their own hikes. The mouth of the canyon is always accessible to the public for shorter walks or bird watching at the pond.

## GETTING THERE

Take the Culver Drive exit southbound from the San Diego Freeway (I-405). Drive 2.7 miles to Shady Canyon Drive and turn left. It's 1.2 miles to the Bommer Canyon entrance on the right. Parking is inside the locked gate during scheduled events and open-access days. To use the public areas of the canyon during non-event days, park at the Turtle Rock Nature Center by driving another quarter of a mile along Shady Canyon and turning left on Sunnyhill. Then make another left onto the park road. The center also offers a short interpretive nature trail and a labyrinth.

## THE TRAIL

There's a perceptible difference between coastal parks that are always open to the public and those with restricted access. Quiet, carefully maintained and more gently used, Bommer Canyon is a tranquil spot located an easy couple of miles off the freeway. The only downside is the audible rush of cars on the San Joaquin (73) Toll Road just over the ridgeline.

Infrequent use of the canyon makes it a haven for wildlife. In addition to the usual tracks of coyotes, rabbits, deer, and bobcats, you're likely to find scat of the Western toad (who ever imagines an amphibian leaving behind trail scat?) and elusive gray fox. The birdwatching here is prime; on a recent docent-led birding trip, more than 30 species were logged within a couple of hours, including the tiny but flashily colored Allen's hummingbird, belted kingfisher, and migratory Western bluebirds, with their bright blue backs and red breasts.

The monthly open-access days give you the chance to explore Bommer at your own pace and level. The trail through the canyon floor is easy; the canyon's classic 3-mile loop involves a moderate climb to the ridgeline, with views that extent to the ocean and far inland. On the other side of Bommer Canyon, you'll look into Shady Canyon, an equally pretty spot. More challenging hikes offered weekly are 7 to 10 miles long. The trails generally involve well-groomed terrain. Particularly popular are the 3-mile moonlit hikes, when you might come across such night animals as owls and bats (in summer).

Both canyons are part of the City of Irvine's ambitious Open Space Pre-

BIRDWATCHING IN BOMMER CANYON

OLD CATTLE CHUTE

serve program and managed by the Irvine Ranch Conservancy, which hosts the docent-led hikes there. Go to the conservancy's website for both a listing of events by month and online registration.

Once included within the vast Rancho San Joaquin of the early 1800s, Bommer Canyon was part of the land purchased in the 1860s by a partnership that included James Irvine, who a few years later became the sole owner. It became the center of the Irvine Ranch's cattle operations during most of the 20th century.

An out-of-use corral and historic ranching equipment are located along the main road, and the conservancy is planning a new hike describing the ranching days, when the Irvine Company was more about cattle than buildings. The ranch house burned down; a loose reconstruction of the cattle camp including a chuck wagon, barbeque pit, and stage has been built and is available to rent for private parties and campouts.

# Laurel Loop

**LOCATION**: Laguna Coast Wilderness Park

**TOTAL DISTANCE**: 3.5 miles (with optional 3.5-mile extension)

**TYPE**: Loop

**ELEVATION GAIN**: 600 feet

**DIFFICULTY**: Moderate

**FEES ETC.**: $3 day parking. No dogs allowed.

**MAPS**: USGS Laguna Beach

**TRAILHEAD COORDINATES**: N 33°34.797′ W 117°45.791′

**CONTACT**: Laguna Coast Wilderness Park (949-923-2235, www.ocparks.com /parks/ lagunac)
Laguna Canyon Foundation (949-497-8324, www.lagunacanyon.org)

Laurel Loop is by far the most popular hike in the 6,400-acre Laguna Coast Wilderness Park and one of the most gratifying in the county, packing a bouquet of sights into a moderate trek that includes ocean vistas, peaceful oak woodland, earthquake faults, and marine fossils from when much of Orange County lay undersea. On the lucky days after rain, there's even a waterfall.

## GETTING THERE

From the San Diego Freeway (I-405), take the Laguna Canyon Road (CA 133) exit south toward Laguna Beach. Travel 5 miles, under a toll-road overpass to the light at El Toro Road. Two hundred feet after the light, see the sign on the right indicating the entrance to the Willow Canyon staging area of Laguna Coast Wilderness Park. Park in the gravel lot.

## THE TRAIL

After paying at the iron ranger near the entrance to the parking lot, sign in at the table and from that point head straight up the main double-truck trail, Willow Canyon Road, not the more narrow Laurel Canyon Trail, which will be your return route. Soon, the trail begins to climb. The first quarter-mile is steepest, passing large rock formations; watch out for fast bikers swooping downhill. Just after the boulders, the incline grows noticeably easier.

Coastal sage scrub plants such as California buckwheat give way to chaparral, especially laurel sumac, sometimes called the "taco plant" because of the way its leaves fold along the middle. The dried-flower clusters of this plant are shaped like miniature Christmas trees and in fact used to be sprayed and

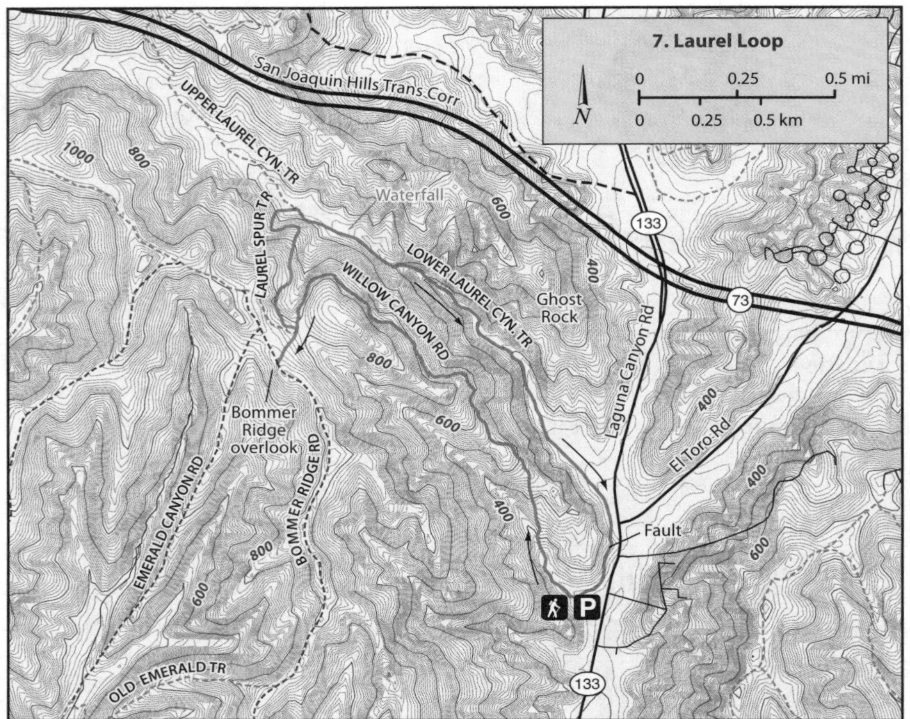


set on stands to be the trees in children's train sets and toy villages. Across the canyon, notice that the ridgeline forms several sharp points in a line; these are volcanic rises, caused by interconnected lava chimneys.

The oldest human fossil in the county came from the Laguna Coast area. The partial skull called Laguna Woman was found in 1933 by a 17-year-old amateur archeologist. First carbon-dating put Laguna Woman at 17,000 years old, but subsequent evidence has cast doubt on that age. Still, it is known that Native Americans inhabited the canyon and coastal areas thousands of years ago, and their uses of local plants are well documented.

The park used to serve as grazing grounds for the vast Irvine Ranch—a major reason why you'll see invasive cheatgrass and oat grass on both sides of the trail. After decades of work by Laguna Greenbelt, a group dedicated to the idea of a swath of wilderness surrounding Laguna Beach, the public park came about through a combination of developer's agreements, donation by the Irvine Company, and direct purchase by the city of Laguna Beach.

A wildflower guide is a helpful companion here; something is always blooming for at least the first six months of the year. In the earlier months, you're sure to see buttercups, with their glossy deep-yellow petals, as well as fringed pinks—which are fiery red, not pink, with ragged-edge petals. Blue dicks, or wild hyacinth, forms a bunch of tiny lavender flowers at the end of a stalk about 18 inches tall, and so slender it's hard to believe it can hold up the flowers.

At 1.4 miles up Willow, you'll reach two trails heading to the right. Continue past them, 500 feet to the T where Willow meets Bommer Ridge (Post 3) and enjoy the vista across the canyons into Crystal Cove State Park and, on a clear day, to the ocean.

Option: At this point you can double your jaunt into the 7-mile "Eight is Enough" hike to aptly named Emerald Canyon. Turn left on Bommer Ridge, walking 1 mile before turning right at Old Emerald Trail (Post 13), a narrow and steep trek down to Emerald Canyon Road. You're at one of the prettiest, greenest spots in the park, thick with oak and Mexican elderberry. Turn right, climbing out of the canyon (make sure to turn around once in a while to enjoy the heart-stopping vista) to Post 4. Here, turn right and in 500 feet, you'll be back at Post 3, the juncture of Bommer Ridge and Willow Road.

Head back downhill on Willow, turning left on the lower trail, Laguna Spur, at Post 2. After a half mile, you'll reach a T to Lower Laurel Canyon Trail. Turn right into a pretty oak woodland.

Travel this scenic little path for 600 feet until you come off the dirt path onto a rocky ledge that affords a vista of steep-walled Laurel Canyon. If you're here shortly after good rains, water will be flowing from the creek path behind you, over the rocks, and down the 50-foot Laurel Falls. You can walk closer to the falls to see and hear it, being careful of the sheer drop. The flat, stepped rocks here, many of which will stay dry even when the creek is flowing, are a popular spot for a rest and a bite to eat.

Follow the trail downhill from here until you reach another creek crossing, and if there's water in the creek in late winter or spring, you have a good chance of spotting tadpoles in the water or tiny frogs on the rocks.

The next creek crossing is a few hundred feet off. Right after you've made it, look directly across the creek at a roughly tube-shape rock on the ground. Jutting from the end are several particularly well-defined pectens, or scallop fossils, from when this area lay undersea; they are at least 5 million years old. You might want to explore the other large rocks in the streambed; several show imprints and pieces of marine fossils.

As you descend a slight incline to the fourth creek crossing, you'll probably notice the savory aroma of black sage. It grows along the path to the left, with slightly rubbery, veined long leaves. This is one of the most common plants of sage scrub, and the sage that Native Americans used for flavoring meat.

Soon the pleasant shade of the woods ends. As you pass the steep wall to your left, across the meadow you can see a favorite landmark, known as "Ghost Rock" or "Casper Rock," a large rounded outcrop pocked with caves that are placed so that they look like eyes and a grinning mouth with one tooth. As you continue, you'll notice a sud-

CAN YOU SEE THE FACE OF GHOST ROCK?

den change in the cliff to your right. A wall of mostly greenery gives way to a wall of mostly rock. Look in the fold of the cliff side where this change begins; there's a slight depression in the ridgeline between two rises. This is an earthquake fault; long ago, there was an uplift on the right side, exposing the older Vaqueros Formation with the shell fossils you saw; to the left is the younger, sandstone Topanga Formation, with its many caves.

About 200 feet farther, as you approach a wooden stile, look to your right to find a rounded boulder about 100 feet off the trail with a much shorter, oblique rock face appended to the right. Use binoculars to search amid the dark-green moss on this shorter section for brighter green leaves growing close to the rock. In May and June, fragile yellow flowers rise from these leaves. This is the Laguna dudleya, a plant so rare that this rock is one of a handful of spots in the world where it grows—all of them around the Laguna Beach area. The plant, unlike its showier cousin the chalk dudleya, cannot be transplanted or propagated; the best we can do for it is leave it alone. Gathering this plant is illegal and punishable by a whopping fine—and the plant would die, anyway.

You'll begin a short ascent, but two-thirds of the way up, check out the big step in the rock that goes across your path. This is another earthquake fault. Note the striations from the two sections scraping against each other.

EARTHQUAKE FAULT

As you descend from this mini-hill, you'll see a small sandstone cave on the trail to your right. This is a favorite with children. Enjoy your photo op here and finish the last hundred feet or so back to the table where you started.

# Guna Peak and Emerald Canyon

**LOCATION**: Laguna Coast Wilderness Park

**TOTAL DISTANCE**: 10 miles

**TYPE**: Out and back

**TOTAL ELEVATION GAIN**: 1,300 feet

**DIFFICULTY**: Strenuous

**SEASON**: December to May

**FEES ETC.**: Free. Dogs prohibited.

**MAPS**: USGS Laguna Beach

**TRAILHEAD COORDINATES**: N 33°33.039′ W 117°47.788′

**CONTACT**: Laguna Coast Wilderness Park (949-923-2235, www.ocparks.com /parks/ lagunac)

Landlocked Emerald Canyon is one of the most inaccessible hiking trails in the South Coast Wilderness, but quite likely its most beautiful, sheltered by trees, fed by a creek, and with a bonus waterfall near its end point. There are slightly shorter ways to get there than this 10-mile hike, but this route is worth the extra mile for several reasons. It takes you to Guna Peak, with knockout coastal views. At 740 feet, Guna is sort of the Everest of the coastline. Or maybe the Annapurna. After you get your fill of ocean and island vistas, a ridgeline trail offers views into two green canyons on either side, and a close-up of an interesting experiment in saving a troubled toad. The hike is at its best in February and March, after good rains bring water to the falls and the hills have had a chance to green up, though Emerald Canyon tends to stay green well into spring and even early summer.

## GETTING THERE

Take the Laguna Canyon Road (CA 133) exit south from the San Diego Freeway (I-405) until it ends at Coast Highway. Turn right on North Coast Highway one mile to Viejo Street. Turn right on Viejo and after 0.1 mile, make a left onto Hillcrest Drive, then an immediate right onto Dartmoor Street. Follow Dartmoor Street to the end and park on the residential street before the park gate.

## THE TRAIL

Begin the ascent to Guna Peak on Boat Spur Trail, a paved road that quickly turns to gravel and dirt. Postcard views of the picturesque artist's colony of Laguna Beach begin almost immediately to the south. You'll quickly come across a gravel road that forks left; you stay straight on the more gently curving spur road. A habitat restoration project along this trail has brought the area close to the scenery you might have encountered a couple hundred years ago. Except for a scattering of exotic grasses, all the plants are native members of the coastal sage scrub community.

Especially common here is white sage, with its strong aroma and leaves with a white, powdery look. This is the sage that the area's Native Americans traditionally used and still use today in ceremonies, by binding several leafy branches together, drying them, setting the tip on fire, and then extinguishing the flame. The smoking bundle is then waved around each person's body. These smudge sticks are commonly sold in stores with a spiritual orientation.

At 0.7 mile, having climbed 500 feet, you reach the intersection of the Boat Spur and Boat Canyon Road. Your path to Emerald Canyon is to the right, but for now, make a hairpin turn left to go to the lookout point on Guna Peak, 0.3 mile away and on top of a buried water tank. On clear days, you'll catch sight of Crystal Cove and Newport Beach to the north, and even more captivating views than before across Laguna Beach and a series of coves south to Dana Point, where the land juts farthest into the ocean. Santa Catalina and San Clemente islands are visible to the southwest.

After enjoying the view, return to the juncture of the two trails and, at 1.4 miles from the start, head northeast on Boat Canyon Road, with views into the two lush canyons on either side—Emerald Canyon to the north and Boat Canyon to the south. A utility road forks right;

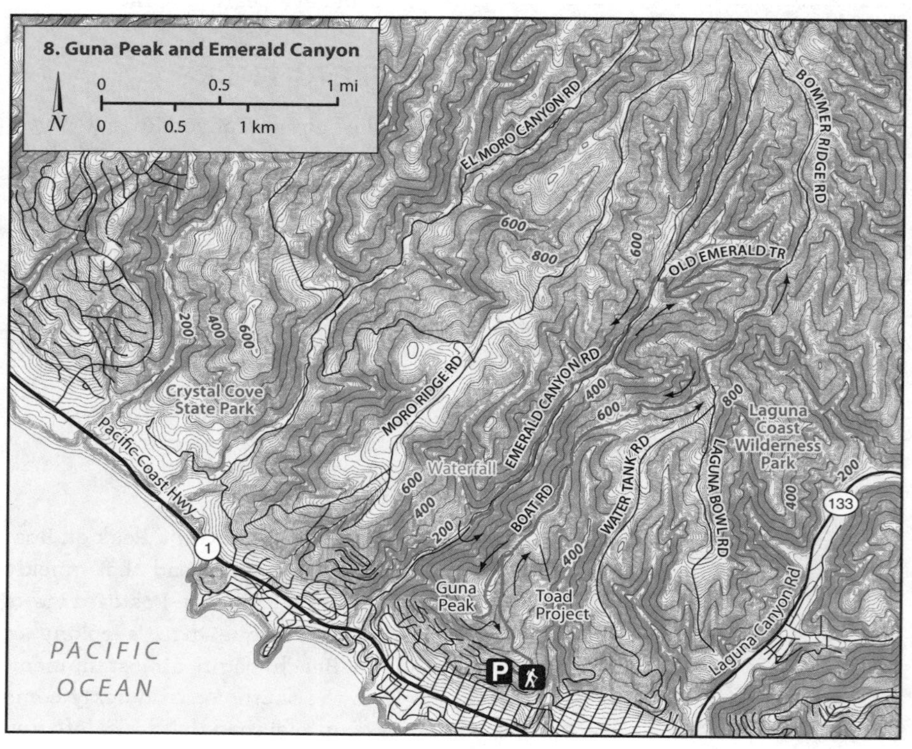

THE VIEW FROM GUNA PEAK ACROSS LAGUNA BEACH

continue straight ahead. Though the trail has level spots, there's also a fair amount of up-and-down rolling, with elevation gains or losses of as much as 200 feet each.

At 1.5 miles, note the shallow rectangular trenches dug on both sides of the trail, with a couple of them very close to you on your right. After rains, the trenches fill with water. These humble little depressions in the ground are part of a joint project in several Orange County open spaces to restore populations of the Western spadefoot toad, listed as a federal and state species of concern.

The toads get their name from a wedge-shaped structure on their hind feet that they use like a spade to dig burrows during the hotter, drier seasons. It only takes a little rainfall, collecting in vernal pools or even ruts in a dirt road, to start their breeding season, which lasts from January through May. But development has erased many of those ponds, and pools that form in park roads are often run over by bicyclists or trucks. As a result, the toad's population is declining.

The trenches are an experiment in seeing whether creating small pools

WALKING THE BOAT CANYON RIDGELINE

will encourage the toads' reproduction. Judging from the number of black tadpoles swimming there on a recent February morning, the experiment seems to be working.

When you reach the intersection with Bommer Ridge Road, turn left and continue on the up-and-down ridgeline trail.

At 3.3 miles, you'll find the marker on the right for the Old Emerald Trail, a single-track, ridgeline trail that descends on your left through sage scrub for 0.7 mile to the bottom of Emerald Canyon. There, you find an utterly different world.

Turn left onto Emerald Canyon Road and wander this classically scenic creek-side trail under a canopy of old oaks and amid willows and sycamores. Look for sandstone caves along the way, as well as patches of California wild rose and towering elderberry with blossoms that smell like cloves. Emerald Canyon is as good as its name, the greenery here is nothing short of lush. The trail narrows, with dense growth on both sides, providing a sense of solitude and escape from the outside world. Watch out for stems of poison oak that occasionally stray into the trail. Uphill to your left are Bommer Ridge and Boat Canyon Road, the trails you hiked in on; to your right is Moro Ridge, the borderline between Laguna Coast Wilderness Park and Crystal Cove State Park.

This lush section of trail was closed for four years, after intense rains washed out two gullies in 2010. The area of damage was too large to reroute the trail, so a 60-foot bridge was installed and the trail reopened in 2014, roughly 0.6 miles from Old Emerald. The trail descends so gradually that the elevation change is hardly noticeable, until a short section becomes noticeably steeper. At this point, 1.3 miles after beginning on Emerald Canyon Road, look to your right to see the seasonal waterfall, only 20 feet high but more than twice as wide. This is your turnaround point. Emerald Canyon Road is landlocked and a half-mile more of walking would bring you to the back fence of the Emerald Bay gated community.

# Little Sycamore–El Moro Canyon Traverse

**LOCATION**: Laguna Coast Wilderness Park and Crystal Cove State Park

**TOTAL DISTANCE**: 8.7 miles one way or 5-mile loop (Alternate start from Willow Canyon staging area reduces length of the hike to 6.3 miles)

**TYPE**: Shuttle

**TOTAL ELEVATION GAIN**: 800 feet

**DIFFICULTY**: Moderately strenuous

**SEASON**: October to July

**FEES ETC.**: $3 parking via iron ranger at Laguna Coast; $15 at Crystal Cove

**MAPS**: USGS Laguna Beach, Laguna Coast and Crystal Cove park maps

**TRAILHEAD COORDINATES**: N 33°36.520′ W 117°45.834′

**CONTACT**: Laguna Coast Wilderness Park (949-923-2235, www.ocparks.com /parks/lagunac)
Crystal Cove State Park (949-494-3539, www.crystalcovestatepark.com)
Laguna Canyon Foundation (949-497-8324, www.lagunacanyon.org)

I'm a fan of shuttle hikes—the ones where one car is left at the trailhead and the other at the destination. They allow you to max out on scenery, packing in a load of different sights . . . all without having to climb up that horrendous hill you just got down.

This shuttle hike, from a section of Laguna Coast Wilderness Park 7 miles inland all the way to the waves lapping on the beach at Crystal Cove State Park, sends you up a quiet, remote-feeling canyon—only recently opened to the public—to a scenery-encompassing ridgeline, along creeks and through oak forests. In springtime, you'll see a bounty of wildflowers, especially lush patches of California wild rose and steep hills covered with purple fiesta flowers. Along the trail, you'll find caves and *morteros*, ancient bedrock mortars of the Native Americans. There's even a solitary valley oak about two-thirds of the way down El Moro Canyon—a more sinuous and majestic relative of the coast live oaks that dot most trails. It was badly burned in the Great Laguna Beach Fire of 1993, but is making a comeback. Leave a car at the ending point, at the state park, and drive from there to the start in the wilderness park. If you're less of a shuttle-hike fan, there's also a nice five-mile loop you can do within this section of the county park.

## GETTING THERE

Take both cars to the end point at Crystal Cove State Park. From the San Diego Freeway (I-405), take the exit for Laguna Canyon Road (CA 133) south, toward Laguna Beach, traveling 8.8 miles until the road ends at Broadway and N. Coast Highway. Turn right and drive 2.5 miles to the light at El Morro Elementary

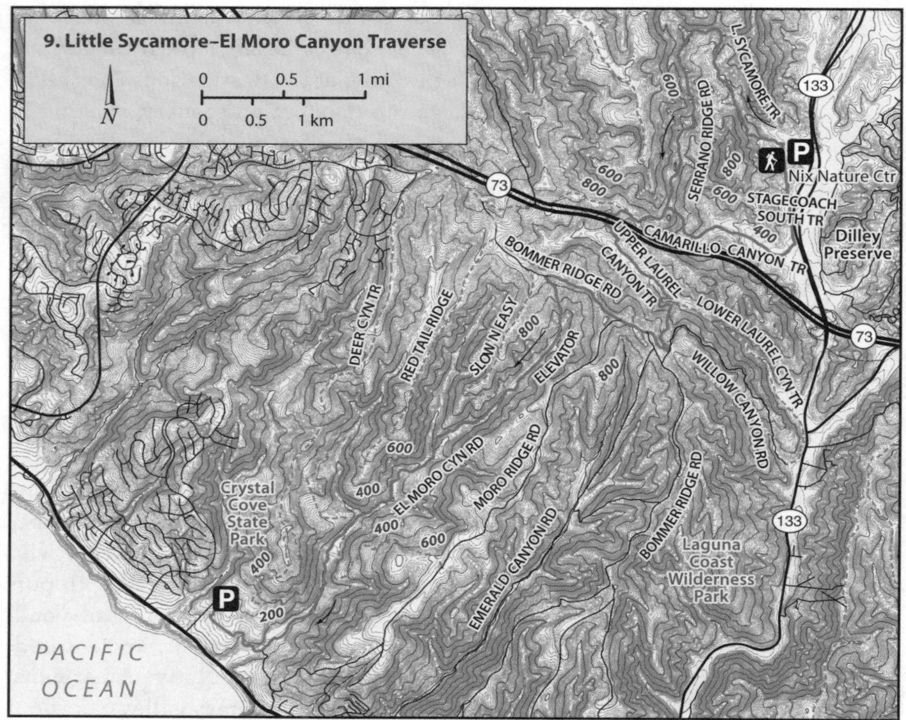


School. Turn right onto the narrow park access road and at 0.2 mile, turn right again on the road leading past the new campground and downhill to the large parking lot. Park toward the back of the lot, away from the beach.

Take one car to Little Sycamore Canyon by returning on Coast Highway to Broadway. Turn left on Broadway and travel 6.3 miles to the entrance to Nix Nature Center. There will be a left-turn lane before the turn. Turn left, going across the southbound lanes of Laguna Canyon Road into the dirt parking lot.

## THE TRAIL

You'll start in the Little Sycamore area of Laguna Coast Wilderness Park, the newest section of the park to open. A 3,200-home housing development was planned for this land until 8,000 people, mostly Laguna Beach residents, marched down the canyon in protest in 1989. The Walk, as it's still known among Lagunans, prompted Irvine Company chairman Donald Bren to rethink his plans and offer to sell the land; nearly 80 percent of Laguna voters chose to tax themselves to buy the parcel for a park.

Now the only development on the land is the Nix Nature Center. With its floor-to-ceiling windows facing the hills, the center was designed to meld education with the environment in which it sits.

The sights often begin in the parking lot, especially if you're hiking early on a springtime morning. California quail are a common sight; entire broods of the birds can be seen running across the parking area and nearby scrub.

EL MORO CANYON WOODLAND

Families of rabbits hop around, the young play-boxing each other. The center of the parking area is a golden oval of fiddleneck in early spring, and an extensive habitat restoration has filled the nearby area with deep-purple Parry's phacelia and the yellow pansy-resembling flower, Johnny jump-ups.

Head up Little Sycamore Trail, passing two intersections with Mary's Trail. After a quarter-mile of climbing through brush, the trail levels out somewhat and enters an area of chaparral. Look back for views over the canyon. Close as you are to Laguna Canyon Road, the trail at this point takes on an otherworldly feeling as you cross small bridges over even smaller streams. In later spring, the trail is lined with such flowers as fringed pink and splendid mariposa lily. Earlier in the season, lavender-pink clusters of canyon pea flowers hang from sumac and lemonadeberry. The dramatic rock bluffs along the opposite wall of the canyon are pocked with multiple caves.

The last thousand feet of the trail turn steep again, and rocky. Exactly 1 mile from the start, the trail ends at Serrano Ridge Trail. Turn left here and walk along the ridgeline that offers views in every direction. Below you to the right is Shady Canyon, a particularly verdant

CAVE IN EL MORO CANYON

canyon that's part of the City of Irvine Open Space Preserve and managed by the Irvine Ranch Conservancy. Though you will see trails into the canyon, public entry is not allowed without prior permission.

To the distance in the north, you can see the high-rises of the Newport Center and to the west and south, you catch glimpses of the ocean. During later spring, much of the trail is lined with bush mallow, a large shrub with flowers all along its branches that look like pale lavender cups. On my most recent hike here, I found numerous velvet ants. They look like large, fuzzy ants in vivid black and red, or sometimes black and white, but are actually wingless, stinging wasps.

After walking nearly a mile on Serrano Ridge, you get your first sight of the San Joaquin Hills Toll Road, a behemoth of a freeway that, despite years of protest and lawsuits attempting to stop its construction, cuts through the heart of the wilderness park and mars what would otherwise be an impressive view. A half-mile later, you'll reach Camarillo Canyon Road on your left.

(If you'd prefer to do the five-mile loop, turn here and descend a steep section to reach a small oak woodland below dotted with a nice variety of wildflowers. Unfortunately, the noise from the toll road above is a regular presence through this otherwise pleasurable stretch. After 1.1 miles on Camarillo, turn left on Stagecoach South Trail, climbing into low rolling hills that lead to switchbacks that guide back down to the parking lot in 1.6 miles.)

After slightly less than 2 miles along Serrano Ridge, the trail will take you under the toll road into the Laurel Canyon section of the park. (The trail just before the underpass crossing that continues parallel to the toll road would cut the length of the hike significantly, but is also on land managed by the Irvine Ranch Conservancy and, like Shady Canyon, off limits to the public at this time.) On the other side of the toll road, turn left on Upper Laurel Trail and descend into a pretty scene of oak trees, a creek, and lots of lavender verbena.

A half-mile farther—3.5 miles from the start—you reach a juncture with Lower Laurel Trail and the Laguna Spur Trail. Turn right on the spur trail. Climb for a half-mile until you reach Willow Canyon Road. This is the point where, if you have chosen to begin the hike at the Willow staging area, the two hikes converge.

Turn right on Willow Canyon and then another immediate right onto a diagonal spur through a sage scrub area. Along the way on this trail, you'll see a wooden cross planted in the ground. A ranger says the cross was supposedly erected by a hiker as a memorial to his cat. A tenth of a mile on this trail will take you to Bommer Ridge, where you'll turn right. The views from here are a pleasure . . . the hills of Crystal Cove State Park ahead of you and clear views to the ocean. The trail can be a little confusing in its markings. You'll reach Gate 12 at 4.4 miles from the start of the hike, but continue toward the right on Bommer Ridge Road. You'll be able to look through the entire length of El Moro Canyon to the ocean. At 5 miles, turn left into El Moro Canyon, marked with a kiosk.

At this point, the trail into the canyon is called The Elevator, and you'll soon find out why. It makes a sharp descent into the canyon and the last 75 feet or so of the descent are so steep and eroded, some people are more comfortable going down on their rumps. The elevation loss is more than 300 feet in less than a tenth of a mile.

After successfully negotiating the descent by whatever part of your body seems useful for the task, you are on El Moro Trail. Ignore the trail going off to the right and continue straight into an area full of bush mallow, sticky monkey flower, and cobweb thistle, a native thistle that looks as though it's laden with lacy webs.

Just before you have traveled one mile on the El Moro Trail, you'll enter a dense oak-woodland area with the feel of a primitive forest. Five hundred feet later, a short spur trail on the left takes you to a large cave.

A quarter of a mile farther, 6.4 miles from the start of the hike, the trail begins a moderate descent. Look here for where the power poles shift from the left side of the trail to the right. At the first pole on the right, you'll see a small clearing leading off from the main trail. Here, less than 10 feet from the trail, is a large rock that offers a lovely vista down the canyon. Ground into this rock are several very even holes, no more than a couple of inches deep. These are the *morteros* that Native American women would use with a small hand-held rock to crush acorn meat from the abundance of local oaks into meal.

The acorn meal had to be rinsed repeatedly to rid it of tannins before it was edible, a tedious job. Some women tied the meal into bags and then weighted the bags down with a rock in a creek, to let the running water do the leaching job for them. The meal then was made into small cakes high in calories and protein, making them a staple of the Native American diet.

In springtime, as you continue down the trail, there are areas to the left where purple fiesta flowers vividly decorate entire vertical walls. Closer to the mouth of the canyon, you will see several large patches of California wild rose. With their single tier of pink petals, they're not as visually dramatic as the cultivated roses sold in florist shops, but their scent is heavenly. In the days of the ancients, as now, the rose hips were used to brew a tea rich in vitamin C.

The canyon ends at a recently built bridge, bulky and imposing looking in a setting this rural, that will take you over the degraded creek crossing. At 3.3 miles after you entered El Moro Canyon, or 8.3 miles from the start, you reach the mouth of the canyon and the parking lot where you left the second car. If you'd like to end with a beach visit, there's a passageway across Pacific Coast Highway to the ocean.

# Mariposa Trail Loop

**LOCATION**: Laguna Coast Wilderness Park

**TOTAL DISTANCE**: 3.5 miles

**TYPE**: Double loop

**TOTAL ELEVATION GAIN**: 600 feet

**DIFFICULTY**: Moderately easy

**SEASON**: Mid-May to late June.

**FEES ETC.**: $3 day parking. No dogs allowed. Hiking-only trails.

**MAPS**: USGS Laguna Beach

**TRAILHEAD COORDINATES**: N 33°35.712′ W 117°45.589′

**CONTACT**: Laguna Canyon Wilderness Park (949-923-2235, www.ocparks.com /parks/ lagunac)
Laguna Canyon Foundation (949-497-8324, www.lagunacanyon.org)

Call me a flower dork, but every spring I set aside a couple of mornings in late May and early June to hike this figure-eight loop that includes a walk on the aptly named Mariposa Trail. Hardly anyone seems to bother with the trail, and maybe for good reason. For close to 11 months of the year, it's just a decent ridgeline jaunt among the common coastal sage scrub. But for four to six weeks in late spring, it is lined with a gorgeous flower, the weedii (pronounced weedy-eye) mariposa lily. Different from the more common, pale lavender-pink splendid mariposas, the weedii is a visual stunner, with its multicolored blossoms of cream, yellow, and reddish tones, decorated with purple rims and specks, feathered inside with yellow "hairs."

As a bonus, the coastal cholla cactus are blossoming at the same time of year with flowers that are best described as hot pink on steroids, while the chalk dudleya are sprouting showy stalks of purplish red.

The hike is in the James Dilley Preserve, named for the late Laguna Beach bookseller who in the 1960s galvanized the community around the idea of creating a greenbelt around its borders. This is the least-visited of the three major sections of Laguna Coast Wilderness Park, in large part because no bicycles are allowed on most trails. Dilley is also the location of the only two natural lakes in Orange County. The second, smaller loop will take you past the prettier and more historic of these, Barbara's Lake, a place with a particularly interesting natural history as well as a more recent story involving an escaped hippopotamus.

Though the hike is not difficult, sunny days call for a hat and, as always,

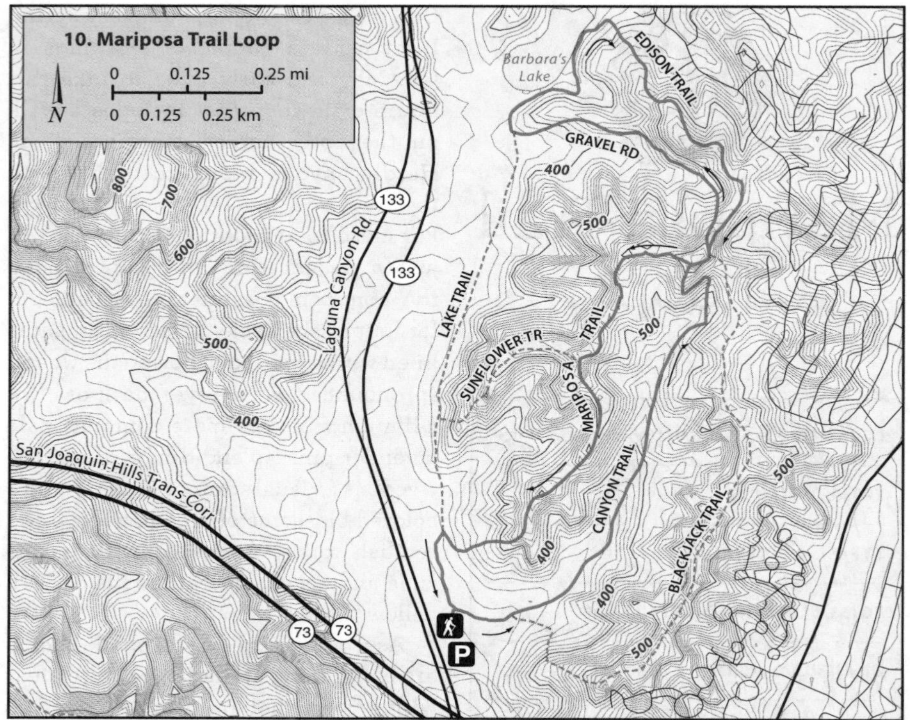


adequate water. I had a run-in with heat exhaustion on the Mariposa Trail during a particularly sweltering midday hike; the trail runs along an exposed ridgeline with no hope of shade. My mistake: Going unprepared because I figured nothing could happen to me on such a modest outing.

## GETTING THERE

From the El Toro Road exit off the San Diego Freeway (I-5), head west on El Toro Road for 3.1 miles. Turn right onto the ramp for the San Joaquin (73) toll road. (You won't have to pay a toll; this is a great little shortcut.) Follow the signs to Laguna Canyon Road (CA 133) for 0.4 mile. Turn right (north) on Laguna Canyon Road, and almost immediately make a right into the James Dilley Preserve parking lot.

## THE TRAIL

After paying the iron ranger, sign in at the table under the wooden shelter and head away from Laguna Canyon Road on the Canyon Trail. You'll pass a shady grove of sycamore trees on your right, a nice spot for picnicking or hanging out with a book or sketchpad. Ignore the marked intersection with the Blackjack Trail to your right.

At a quarter of a mile, the Canyon Trail veers left, northeast, into a quiet area with a small oak woodland, sage scrub, and a coffeeberry bush with large berries that start out red but mature to nearly black—hence the "coffee." The plant was used by Native Americans as a laxative, though it can be dangerous to ingest in significant quantities.

The trail narrows at 0.6 mile and soon begins to climb; this is a good place to start watching out for poison oak. The climb grows steeper at 0.9 mile as you work your way up the western side of the canyon, past the first coastal cholla, which is the less common of the two cacti found in Orange County. It's easy to tell them apart; unlike the more ubiquitous prickly pear, with its "beavertail" pads, the cholla is made up of slender, jointed arms.

At 1.0 mile, you reach a flat, open circle atop a water tank. Take in the view across Laguna Canyon and then look for a chain-link fence enclosure. You'll go down the small incline at the fencing. There are small concrete drainages to both sides that you can use, or you can go around the side of the fence and down the small stairs to the Ridgetop Trail. Make a left at Post 58. You quickly come to a fork at Post 61, beginning the Gravel Road to the left (not the Edison Trail to the right). After walking 0.6 mile on Gravel Road, go past the marked Lake Trail to the left, continuing 20 feet

BARBARA'S LAKE

to the Barbara's Lake Trail on the right. Turn right here at Post 35.

The lake is named for a benefactress of the park; another lake, with the drab moniker of Lake 1, lies about a half-mile north on a rather noisy trail parallel to Laguna Canyon Road.

But the trail along Barbara's Lake holds many little delights if you take the time to tread slowly and quietly. It's a place where you can often hear the *witchity, witchity* call of the common yellowthroat, and both hear and spy frogs of several different kinds. Water birds, strange to say, are not a frequent sight in spring, though you might see some mallards (broods of ducklings are common at this time of year).

It's a curious matter how, of all the places in Orange County, its only natural lakes are here, in a spot with no particular rivers or streams. Blame, or credit, faults under the land surface that shifted in such a way that they blocked the flow of groundwater, forming a natural dam that forced the water to rise to the surface. It's the same principle as the historic (man-made) dam in Santiago Oaks Regional Park.

Until recently, people thought there were three Laguna Lakes. On the other side of the lake from where you stand was a small, ephemeral pool of water that came to be known as Bubbles Pond, after the misadventures of a hippopotamus from a nearby wild animal park called Lion Country Safari, long since closed. Bubbles the hippo escaped from the park in 1978 and took up residence in the pond for 19 days. Eventually, as she wandered out, she was shot with tranquilizer darts and fell in such a way that she suffocated. A necropsy showed that poor Bubbles was five months pregnant.

Much as it made a good temporary hippo hideout, Bubbles Pond was not really a separate body of water. It was part of Barbara's Lake, cut off by the old Laguna Canyon Road, which was paved through that section of the lake. In recent years, the road was moved to the west and widened, and the two bodies of water rejoined.

After a short 0.3 mile saunter along the lake, you reach its end and find yourself practically in the backyards of some homes in the retirement community of Laguna Woods Village. The trail veers right and heads uphill, now named the Edison Trail, under a series of electrical towers. After 0.2 mile—or 2.1 miles from the start of the hike—that trail ends, with three trails forking off. Take the middle one, making a shallow left and continuing uphill, past little side paths that mainly exist to give crews access to the electrical towers. At 2.3 miles, you'll reach a T. Turn right here. At 2.5 miles you reach the juncture with Gravel Road again, and turn left onto Ridgetop. Almost immediately, you'll make a right, going back up the little incline past the little chain-link enclosure to the flat, open circle.

There, with the chain-link fence to your back, you'll find the inconspicuously signed Mariposa Trail across the clearing at 2 o'clock.

At 2.9 miles, the Sunflower Trail hooks off to the right, but you'll stay straight on the Mariposa Trail. And if you have come in the right season, it shouldn't be long before you start seeing the distinctive weedii mariposas, tulip-shaped flowers growing on top of long, slender stalks that rise 2–3 feet high. The blossoms, 2 inches or so in diameter, show remarkable variety of shape and color, some in deep gold, others more cream colored, some with more purple than yellow.

WEEDII MARIPOSA LILY WITH CALIFORNIA BUCKWHEAT ALONG THE MARIPOSA TRAIL

The coastal cholla cactus also should be in bloom; the flowers are only about an inch and a half in diameter, but an intense fuchsia color. Cholla is the preferred habitat of the cactus wren, a species that has alarmed biologists with its declining population. Take a close look at cholla "arms" that are going brown, with the skin peeling off. Underneath are the woody ribs of the plant, often called cholla skeletons. The hollow rib, with its network of holes, is a striking sight. Refrain from touching them, though. Cholla thorns are deeply irritating and seem to transfer to skin or clothes almost magically.

The last section of the trail descends somewhat steeply and ends 3.4 miles from the start, at the Lake Trail. A sign at Post 50 will indicate that the parking lot is to your left. It's only a tenth of a mile back to the Canyon Trailhead.

# Wood Canyon to Dripping Cave

**LOCATION**: Aliso and Wood Canyons Wilderness Park

**TOTAL DISTANCE**: 2.4 to 7.2 miles

**TYPE**: Triple loop

**TOTAL ELEVATION GAIN**: 300 feet

**DIFFICULTY**: Moderately strenuous

**SEASON**: Year-round

**FEES ETC.**: Free. Dogs prohibited.

**MAPS**: USGS San Juan Capistrano, Laguna Beach

**TRAILHEAD COORDINATES**: N 33°35.115′ W 117°44.702′

**CONTACT**: Aliso and Wood Canyons Wilderness Park (949-923-2200, www.ocparks.com/alisoandwoodcanyons)

The trick to discovering the many pleasures of Aliso and Wood canyons is to avoid entering via its main entrance. The trail leading from that entrance into the backcountry involves a 1.5-mile slog along the edge of a paved road in an uninspiring area that provides little sense of escaping into the wilderness.

Yet the park is loaded with natural and historical treasures, which you can best reach via lesser-known access points. This hike will take you through my favorite entrance into the park's poetic wooded area of oak and sycamore with one of the county's few year-round streams, to the hideout cave of an infamous gang. Along the way and back, you'll find a century-old corral, a private hideaway of oak woodland, and a particularly rich stand of a substance that was once as expensive per ounce as gold—and is still used today for some food colorings. With its shaded areas and relative flatness, Wood Canyon makes a good year-round outing. Shortening the hike is easy by omitting one or two of the three loops or the spur to the oak grove.

## GETTING THERE

From the San Diego Freeway (I-405), take the El Toro Road exit. Turn west on El Toro Road, toward Aliso Viejo. Travel 1 mile, make a left onto Moulton Parkway. After 1.4 miles, turn right on Glenwood Drive. After 1.4 miles, Glenwood turns into Pacific Park Drive. Continue 0.4 mile to Canyon Vistas, where you'll turn right and continue to the end of the street, 0.5 mile. Canyon View Park is on your left. Park on the street; there is no charge, but respect no-parking signs along some stretches.

## THE TRAIL

As you enter Canyon View Park, stay on the large paved walkway that runs straight through the park, near Silkwood Drive. At the end of the groomed park, the walkway heads downhill. Hop over the narrow concrete drainage channel to continue on a wide dirt pathway to the park gate and onto Wood Canyon Trail.

Just a couple hundred feet of walking will take you to an inviting spot with graceful, old oak trees and a year-round stream. Watch for poison oak all through this area. The right side of the trail is also a good place to look for mugwort, an erect plant 2 feet or so high with long, slender leaves that are green on top and fuzzy white underneath. By reputation, this plant has the ability to alleviate a poison-oak rash if rubbed over the exposed skin. At creek crossings look for wild watercress growing in the water, a mass of tiny deep-green leaves.

Aliso and Wood Canyons Wilderness Park was home to Orange County's two major Native American groups, the Acjachemen and Tongva. The confluence of creeks in the area, and its relative nearness to the ocean for the gathering of seafood, made it an ideal place to set up winter encampments.

Several years ago I volunteered at an Acjachemen archaeological site along Aliso Creek. This spot was so rich in survival resources, it resembled a Tel (mound) in Israel, with successive groups of people settling on top of the ruins of long-gone groups. The oldest of them was some 5,000 years old. Sea-

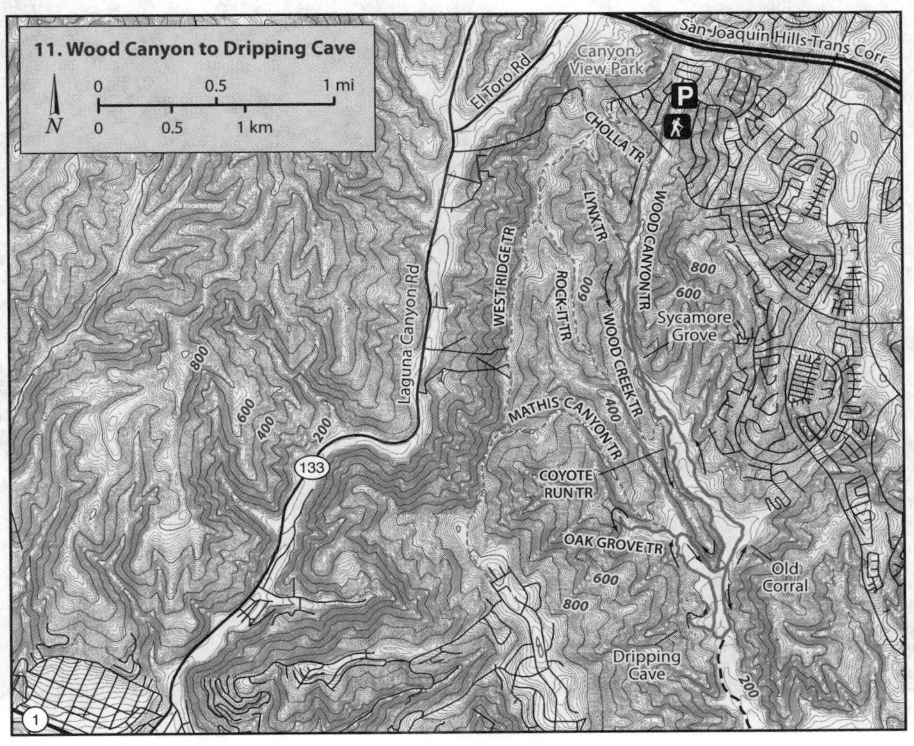

shells found in the creek bed had been there for hundreds of years at least, brought by these earlier settlers, since no such shells occur here naturally.

After walking a half-mile from your start in Canyon View Park, look on the right for the trailhead of Wood Creek Trail, which will rise to a vista point among the sage scrub, looking down the length of the canyon. The hiker-only trail then descends sharply via steep railroad-tie steps into a dense oak woodland following the creek below. Look for the many nests of wood rats nestled on the ground among the trunks of the trees, especially to the left. They look like messy wickiups, with their domed tops. Each nest contains several rooms with specialized uses: storing food, raising a family, even a bathroom.

The 1-mile trail crosses a wooden bridge to end back at the main Wood Canyon Trail. If you want to stick to a 2.4-mile hike, you can return via this trail by turning left; otherwise, turn right and begin looking for the posted Coyote Run Trail to the right.

Cross the wooden bridge back over the creek to travel along this trail where a gnarled, ancient oak provides an umbrella of shady protection (you'll know it by the bench that's been set there), abundant willows that were used by Native Americans to build their wick-

DRIPPING CAVE

iup shelters (willow bark was chewed for its salicylic acid, the active ingredient in aspirin), and a series of sandstone outcroppings on the cliffside above you. At the point where Coyote Run meets the Rock-It Trail, the signs and paths can be a bit confusing. Do not head uphill on Rock-It; instead, you'll hook to the left and then continue straight ahead (not crossing the stream again) to stay on Coyote Run. Similarly, do not turn right onto the Nature Loop.

You'll come across a good-sized patch of prickly pear cactus to your left that's especially interesting, not for the plant but for what's found on it. See what look like white and grayish growths over many of the pads? That's the sign of cochineal, a substance that in its heyday was one of the most valuable exports from the Americas and was used to color the royal purple robes of Europe. Though it looks white on the plant, even a small amount leaves an intense purple-red color when, for example, smeared across paper. The color actually comes from a tiny parasitic insect that preys solely on prickly pear. The female insect feeds on the juices of the pads and gives birth to nymphs, which secrete a whitish protective coating—the grayish white you see on the plants. The insect also produces carminic acid, the source of the red color.

Hernan Cortes brought the first cochineal dye back to Europe in the early 1500s, after he heard about the Mayans and Aztecs using it, and cochineal became the rage for coloring fabrics orange, red, or purple for the next 300 years, at which point the first synthetic red dyes were invented. The British military red coats were dyed with cochineal, which has become popular again in recent decades with concerns over the safety of artificial food coloring. If you see the words carmine or "Natural Red Dye #4" on an ingredient list, you'll know they're talking about cochineal.

Past the prickly pear, continue to where Coyote Run meets Mathis Canyon Trail. Turn left onto Mathis Trail, which quickly ends back at Wood Canyon Trail. Again, you have the option of returning via this trail by turning left, a 4.4-mile double loop. But if you want to continue to the cave, turn right.

After a quarter-mile on Wood Canyon Trail, the turnoff to Dripping Cave is on the right. Because of unclear signage, the turnoff is easy to miss; the post indicates only that the ranger station is straight ahead.

Option: At this point, if you want to add a mile to your hike, continue on Wood Canyon to Cave Rock. Turn right into Cave Rock, walking around the large sandstone outcropping where water seepage and wind have carved unusual cave formations. When you return to Wood Canyon Trail, turn left and go back up to Dripping Cave Trail.

Turn up Dripping Cave Trail and turn left when it forks to get to the good-sized overhang. The park has labeled it Dripping Cave for the water that frequently falls from its lip, but others know it better as Robber's Cave, legendarily a hiding place for the infamous Juan Flores gang. Flores gained notoriety in the mid-1800s for his lawlessness and daring escapes. Two of his men were lynched at the Hanging Tree. (For more lore on Juan Flores, see the chapter on the Hanging Tree.)

Near the cave's entrance, you'll find neat holes drilled into the walls; these were used to hang supplies. You can also see that portions of the cave roof were blackened by campfires.

Retrace your steps and turn left

THE OLD CORRAL

at the fork to continue on Dripping Springs Trail. You'll do some modest climbing and descent. Take note of the old oak, obviously hundreds of years old, its gnarled roots intertwining with the rock from which it grows until it's difficult to see where one ends and the other begins. You'll pass under an archway of willow and mulefat before the trail ends at Mathis Canyon. Here, make a left and, after 400 feet, make another left onto Oak Grove Trail. On this quarter-mile trail, you'll cross a bridge and make a gentle climb into a particularly pretty grove of oaks facing a rock wall; in winter and spring, the gurgling of the stream and the general absence of other visitors make this a serene spot to enjoy a snack, a book, or quiet time.

Retrace your steps back to Mathis and, turning right on Mathis, continue back to Wood Canyon Trail. Here, you'll make a left to begin the 2.5-mile return. This time stay on Wood Canyon all the way. On the right you'll pass a century-old corral once used for the ranch's sheep and cattle; farther along, on the left, is a gracious grove of large sycamore trees, with large stumps set among them as a resting place. You'll reach the welcome shade of the oak woodland along the creek and then climb out of the shade back through Canyon View Park.

# Pecten Reef Loop

**LOCATION**: Aliso and Wood Canyons Wilderness Park

**TOTAL DISTANCE**: 1.4 miles

**TYPE**: Loop

**TOTAL ELEVATION GAIN**: 60 feet

**DIFFICULTY**: Easy

**SEASON**: Year-round

**FEES ETC.**: Free. Dogs allowed on leash. Good hike for children. Collecting of fossils prohibited.

**MAPS**: USGS San Juan Capistrano

**TRAILHEAD COORDINATES**: N 33°35.566′ W 117°42.668′

**CONTACT**: Aliso and Wood Canyons Wilderness Park (949-923-2200, www.ocparks.com/alisoandwoodcanyons)

So far from the main section of Aliso and Wood Canyons that most people don't realize it's part of the park, and surrounded on three sides by busy streets, Pecten Reef Loop nonetheless has its own peculiar charm. If you have even a whiff of paleontologist-wannabe about you, this tiny trail is a fun spot that lets you explore for marine fossils that are 15 to 20 million years old.

You'll loop around, and then over the top of, one outcrop of the reef, which is a 10-mile-long deposit containing white limestone and mudstone that were once at the bottom of a shallow bay. Imprints and remains of pectens (scallops), clams, and oysters are easy to find, and you can be fairly certain that buried deeper within the reef are parts of ancient whales, fish, and birds, which have been found nearby during excavations for development.

There's an unusual flower here, the Pomona milkvetch, found along this trail and in only one other spot in the county. It's notable for its stalk of cream-colored, tubular flowers. But the trail's main attraction is the fossils, not the flowers or water features (though Aliso Creek flows most of the year), making this a fine little hike for any season.

In fact, the fossils are easier to spot when the growth has died back. This is also a perfect outing for children who are old enough to be excited about fossils. (It is important not to remove any fossils or disturb the rocks that contain them.) There are two nearby side trips, to Fossil Reef Park and, believe it or not, the Laguna Hills Community Center, that enhance the experience.

## GETTING THERE

Take the Alicia Parkway exit from the San Diego Freeway (I-5) and head south for 1.6 miles. Turn right on Moulton Parkway and drive for 0.6 mile to the light at Laguna Hills Drive. Turn right here and park along the street.

## THE TRAIL

Though Pecten Reef Loop is just to the south side of Moulton Parkway, there is no parking along Moulton. The best way to access the loop is via Aliso Creek Trail through a small neighborhood play area called Sheep Hills Park.

On either side of Laguna Hills Drive, where it crosses Aliso Creek, you'll find entryways to Aliso Creek Trail/Bikeway. Walk toward Moulton Parkway. To your right will be the creek; to your left, if you're here on a Saturday, will be dozens of short native and non-native creatures running around the green field. These are known to scientists as AYSO soccer players.

The path crosses under Moulton Parkway next to the rock-lined creek. On the other side of the parkway, the creek area will become more natural looking, with sage scrub and riparian growth.

You'll pass a large sign that says you're entering the wilderness park, and just beyond that, on your right, is the trailhead to Pecten Reef Loop. Turn in here on the single-track dirt trail. The creek will be to your right. You're walking through a disturbed area with mostly non-native vegetation—black mustard, horehound, and, in the stream, giant reed, which chokes large areas of the creek for miles—although there's also native willow, mulefat, coyote bush, and, in late spring, large spreading patches of stinking gourd. (If you

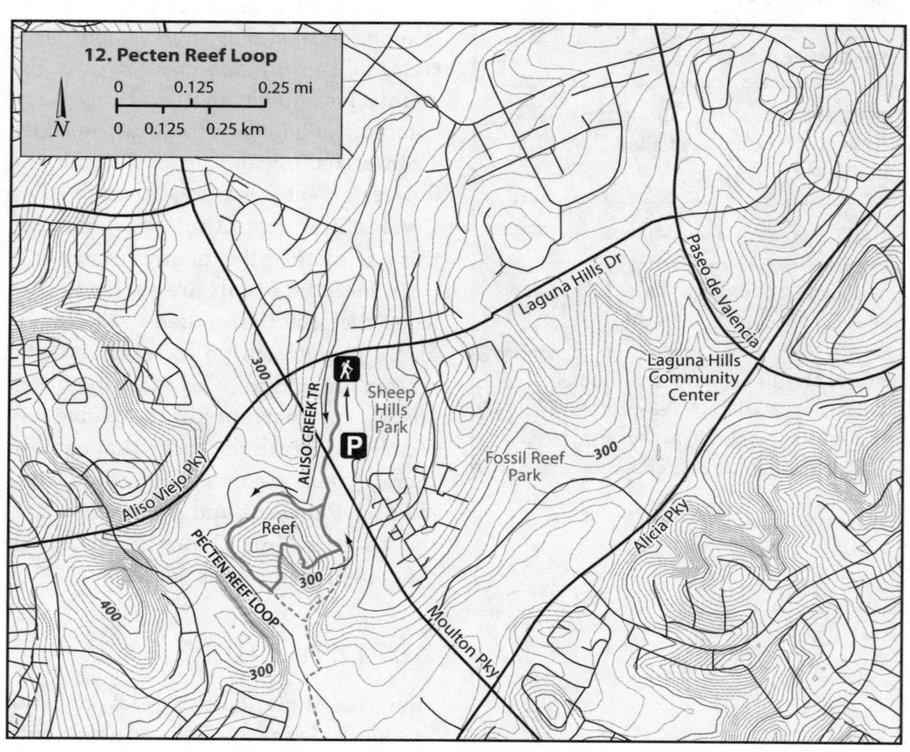

SCALLOP IMPRINT IN ROCK ALONG PECTEN REEF LOOP

press its leaves and then smell your fingers, you'll see where the name comes from.) The roots of this plant were once pounded into a strong soap. The gourds, green in spring, later turning yellow, and about the size of a tennis ball, could be made into rattles but the only animal interested in tasting this fruit is the coyote—hence its other popular name, coyote squash. Pioneer women used these hard gourds as darning eggs, back in the days when people mended socks that got holes in them.

From the start of the trail, examine the loose rocks you see along the path for the imprints of mollusks. The pectens are the easiest to identify with their radiating lines, but oyster and other mollusks are also fairly common. The large size of the pectens here indicates that this was a tropical area in its day.

The reef is part of the ancient sea floor, exposed by tectonic uplift during the last million years—the same uplift that formed the Santa Ana Mountains. Though found within the Monterey Formation, these fossils are from an older era. They formed in a shallow marine environment and then, because of earth movement, broke free of the formation in which they formed and fell into the deeper Monterey Formation. The limestone broke along faults during uplift, revealing its buried contents. Marine mud from the same era that covered the limestone contained their own fossil riches—shark teeth, plankton fossils, gigantic shark teeth, and the bones of marine mammals. The skeleton of a large baleen whale was unearthed in 1981 about a mile from here.

At 0.7 mile, turn left onto an unmarked but obvious trail that heads uphill and smells like anise from the wild fennel that grows abundantly on the slope. In the embedded rock here, the fossil finds grow much richer, with larger specimens and ones showing the remains of their shell as well as imprints. In a few spots, you can even see 15-million-year-old nacre, the iridescent mother-of-pearl that appears on the insides of some mollusk shells.

At 0.9 mile, you reach the top of the little hill, where the trail forms a small loop. Here, the size and frequency of fossil finds improves, especially in the first large embedded rock to your right. Continue exploring the rocks as the trail begins to descend on the other side of the hill. You reach Aliso Creek Trail, just a short distance from the Pecten Loop Trailhead, at 1 mile. Turn left along the bikeway to return.

If you haven't gotten your fill of fossils by this time, a 1.4-mile round-trip walk from the corner of Moulton and Laguna Hills will take you to Fossil Reef Park. Head downhill on Moulton, on the Sheep Hills Park side of the street, for 0.4 mile, then turn left on Via Lomas. At 0.3 mile, in the midst of a quiet little neighborhood, you'll find the grassy one-acre park with two large outcroppings of white limestone. Many of the fossil finds here are large and clearly formed.

The perfect end to this outing is a visit to the Laguna Hills Community Center on your way back to the freeway. After turning left on Alicia from Moulton, travel for 0.6 mile to the modern stone building at the corner of Alicia and Paseo de Valencia. The city curated many of the finds of Pecten Reef and displays an impressive collection of fossils, many of them found under your feet during the excavation for the building. Along with pectens some 7 inches across or more, there are oysters, 5-inch shark teeth, and the bones of an American mastodon and camel that also were uncovered during construction.

FOSSILS ON DISPLAY AT LAGUNA HILLS COMMUNITY CENTER

# Aliso Peak

**LOCATION**: Aliso and Wood Canyons Wilderness Park

**TOTAL DISTANCE**: 2 to 4 miles

**TYPE**: Out and back or shuttle

**TOTAL ELEVATION GAIN**: 500 feet

**DIFFICULTY**: Moderately easy

**SEASON**: Year-round

**FEES ETC.**: Free. Leashed dogs allowed.

**MAPS**: USGS San Juan Capistrano, Aliso and Wood Canyons park map

**TRAILHEAD COORDINATES**: N 33°30.766′ W 117°43.925′

**CONTACT**: Aliso and Wood Canyons Wilderness Park (949-923-2200, www.ocparks.com/aliso andwoodcanyons)

On a macro level, this h
view, view, view. Views
prettiest coastal canyon
Santa Ana Mountains.
structured, bird's-eye view
and ocean. Expansive views just about every foot of the trail (and some close-up views of a gated housing development).

But take the time to look around carefully. This is also a rare microenvironment, a place where the usual plants of coastal sage scrub and chaparral in Orange County mingle with plants seldom seen outside San Diego County and Baja California, such as summer holly and spice bush.

Because its high, coastal location brings cooling breezes and the chaparral remains green throughout the seasons, this is a pleasurable walk for almost any time of year and almost any time of day, though it's a special delight to start a couple of hours before sundown.

## GETTING THERE

From the San Diego Freeway (I-5), take the Crown Valley Parkway exit. South on Crown Valley 5 miles to the light at Pacific Island Drive. Turn right on Pacific Island, a steep uphill, traveling 1.7 miles to Talavera Drive. Make a left on Talavera, drive 0.1 mile to the start of a groomed pocket park, and park on the street.

## THE TRAIL

Walk along the wood-rail fence of the little park along the rim of Aliso Canyon to catch the vista, emerald green through much of the year. From here, you can easily see the golf course and Aliso Creek flowing into the ocean. Fed in large part by runoff that makes it a

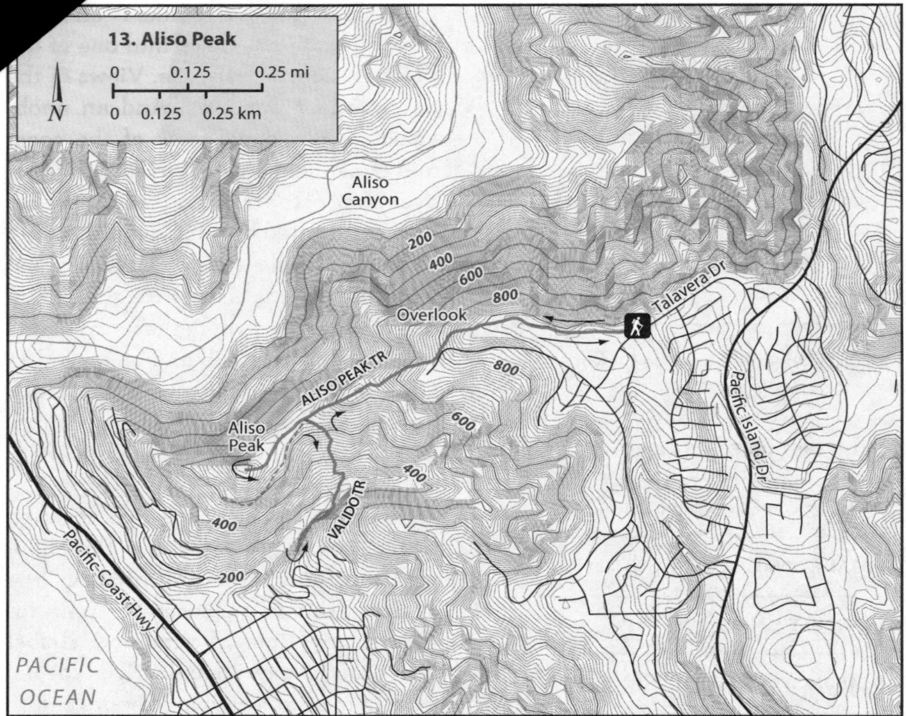


year-round stream, the creek is tainted by E. coli and other pollutants; immediately after rainstorms, the waters of Aliso Beach are regularly too foul for swimmers.

It's easy to see, looking down at the canyon from this vantage point, what a lifeline this was to the Native Americans who lived here hundreds, and even thousands, of years ago. From their settlement at the confluence of two creeks upstream, they had only a few miles to walk through this dramatic, steep-walled canyon where plants like toyon provided food along a freshwater stream to reach the ocean and its bounty of seafood. Nearby tide pools would have provided mussels, and, back in their day, abundant abalone.

Unfortunately, the public cannot walk through most of the canyon at this time. The road that goes most of the way to the coast is owned by a water management agency, which operates a treatment plant you can see as you look down into the canyon. The section closer to the coast is owned by a private resort and includes one of the county's oldest golf courses.

But you can enjoy the canyon from this aerie along with the unique mix of plants as you enter the dirt trail of Seaview Park at the ocean end of the small grassy strip. Summer holly has long, evergeen, toothed leaves and bark that can look somewhat shredded, like its close relative the manzanita. In spring it puts out similar flowers as well, small, white, bell-shape blossoms that look like lily-of-the-valley, hanging in groups along the ends of stems. In fall and early winter, these produce orange-red berries that were eaten by Native Americans. It can be easy to mistake the plant for toyon (also known as California holly) during fruiting season, but toyon berries grow in large, roughly symmetrical clusters; summer holly's fruit grows in smaller, linear groups hanging from the stem.

Another plant rare to Orange County is coast spice bush, or bush rue, a short, twiggy shrub with very narrow leaves. Its small, four-petaled white flowers smell sweet, but the berries and leaves have a spicy scent that gives the plant its name. The flowers give way to edible greenish fruit with a red blush—Orange County's only native citrus.

Picnic benches also line the pathway until, after a quarter-mile, you reach the overlook platform that gives commanding views of both the canyon and Aliso Beach and the ocean.

Continuing from here, the path grows narrow and heads steeply downhill. It levels out along the rim of a suburban cul-de-sac where you'll see lemonadeberry that is clearly being trimmed and cultivated in a tiered garden. As you continue downhill, the more wild, natural look returns. In springtime, it will be

ALISO PEAK AND THE OCEAN BEYOND

easy to spot ceanothus, or wild lilac, all along the trail, with its clusters of white flowers.

You'll reach a saddle between the overlook point and Aliso Peak ahead. To the left, the first, unmarked trail, secured with railroad ties, is Valido Trail; 30 feet ahead is Toovet Trail, a quarter-mile path that goes around Aliso Peak. But you'll continue straight and up the steep but short path—railroad-tie steps make this easier—to the top of Aliso Peak in South Laguna. A bench offers a spot to sit and take in the view. Immediately below is Aliso Beach, where the shallow waters along the coast take on an eye-pleasing aqua hue. A little farther north, waves splash against tide-pool rocks.

You've hiked 1 mile to reach Aliso Peak. At this point you can turn around and hike back up to the overlook summit, or, when you reach the saddle, turn right onto Valido Trail, which will take you into cozy, scenic Valido Canyon. It's a steep descent, made easier by log steps in places. For a while, you'll walk along a stream until the trail drops you near West Street in South Laguna, a charming, offbeat neighborhood of Laguna Beach with charmingly quirky houses along narrow streets. You can treat yourself to a coffee or lunch before heading back up the trail. (If you prefer the lazy-hikers route, you can park a second car here and not face the uphill trek.) Return up Valido, turning right when you reach the saddle to make the climb back to the overlook and picnic table.

You've reached a serene and scenic spot for watching the sun as it nestles down into the ocean for the night.

If you haven't gotten enough Aliso Canyon view by now, it's only a quarter-mile walk along Pacific Island Drive north of Talavera to reach the trailhead at La Brise for a 4-mile out-and-back (or 2-mile shuttle) hike along Aliso Summit Trail, which has arresting vistas of both Aliso and Wood canyons, the ocean seen through the canyon, and inland mountains. On one side, though, you are virtually in the backyards of the imposing homes along the ridgeline. The trail, with unvarying cultivated plants on both sides, offers little sense of nature. Still, it's clear why these houses, with their premium view, would be prized.

# Dana Point Headlands

**LOCATION**: City of Dana Point

**TOTAL DISTANCE**: 2.5 to 4 miles

**TYPE**: Loop, with optional, additional out and back

**TOTAL ELEVATION GAIN**: 150 feet

**DIFFICULTY**: Very easy

**FEES ETC.**: Free parking and entry. No dogs.

**MAPS**: USGS Dana Point

**CONTACT**: Dana Point Nature Interpretive Center (949-542-4755, www.danapoint.org/index.aspx?page=577)

Thank the Pacific pocket mouse. The presence of the tiny, endangered rodent at the Dana Point Headlands (the only other place it's found is Camp Pendleton, and there are fewer than 500 mice altogether) was what kept this prime little piece of coastal real estate from being developed into a large hotel. On a steep cliff jutting into the ocean, it's the best spot for whale watching in all of Orange County.

At first sight, this small nature preserve is pretty but unimpressive. With its groomed, fenced trails and landscape of purposefully chosen native plants, it looks like what it is: more restored than wild. Good thing the wildlife doesn't care. On my first hike there, I saw two rare birds: the cactus wren and the California gnatcatcher, an endangered songbird that mews like a kitten. Also a roadrunner and a pod of common dolphins so close to shore, I was afraid they would beach themselves. On subsequent visits, bobcats and blue whales.

In exchange for keeping the tip of the headlands open, the city agreed to the construction of more than 100 McMansions and a small hotel on adjacent property. There's no way to avoid them on this walk.

And yet the unique delights of this easy loop make it a standout—the spectacular ocean and coastal views, the wildlife drawn to this little plot of land, and even a free funicular ride. And if you extend the trip with a stroll along Dana Point Harbor, immediately below and to the south of the headlands, you can include a trip to the Ocean Institute.

## GETTING THERE

From southbound Pacific Coast Highway (CA-1), turn right on Street of the Green Lantern. It turns into Scenic

Drive and dead-ends at the Dana Headlands Interpretive Center. Parking is free in the small parking lot; if that's full, there's plentiful parking on the street.

## THE TRAIL

Start with a quick trip to the small interpretive center (open every day but Mondays) where you can borrow a pair of binoculars for free to do some whale watching. During the winter and early spring months, gray whales are either heading south from Alaska to Baja California, or heading back north with their young. March is peak viewing, with whales in both directions. During summer and fall, blue whales, the largest mammals on Earth, have become a not-uncommon sight off the Orange County coast, and there are rarer glimpses of orcas and humpbacks. Of course, sighting whales is a matter of luck, not an every-moment occurrence. But with its position jutting out from the rest of the coastline, and up on a cliff, the viewing here is as good as it gets.

The well-marked trail of decomposed granite starts right next to the interpretive center; cables on either side are meant to reinforce the idea that you should stay on the trail, avoiding the dens of the pocket mouse. In spring and early summer, the gently descending hillside is a spread of yellow from the bush sunflowers that were liberally planted to help restore the area to native habitat. But there are stands of cholla cactus, worth checking out in case

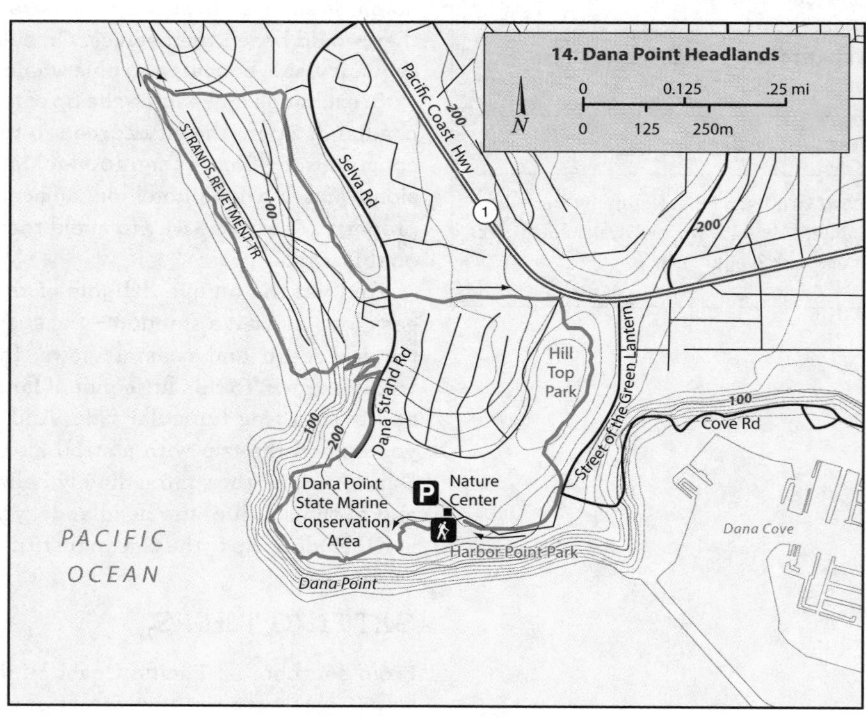

Melodye Shore

FOREVER VIEWS OF THE OCEAN AND COASTLINE FROM THE HEADLANDS

Melodye Shore

THE HEADLANDS VIEWED FROM THE BEACH

you're lucky enough to spot a cactus wren, which favors cholla as its habitat.

As the path draws nearer to the ocean it veers north, providing views of the coves and hills miles up the coast. To your left, there are a couple of viewing stops for pulling out those binoculars and seeing if you can spot whales in the distance. The path then curves back uphill on the other side of the point, and ends at a half-mile from the start.

At that point, walk on the street a couple hundred feet until you find the entrance to the winding ramp that takes you down to Strand Beach. At the bottom, there's a spectacular little cove to your left, formed by the headlands that now rise high above you.

You can explore the cove and walk north along the beach, or just turn north on the paved walkway between the beach and the mansions sprouting to your right. After a third of a mile, the walkway changes from pavement to wood decking and then ends.

Make a sharp right, going uphill for 100 feet, where you have a choice of climbing a whole lot of stairs to the cliff top or taking the little funicular that you can summon with an elevator button. The funicular isn't always running; try this walk on summer weekends if you want to be sure of finding it in operation.

At the top, turn south, or right, heading back from where you came along Strand Park. There are benches and tables for viewing the ocean (and, less inspiring, the roofs of a lot of massive houses) or having a snack. The walkway is strewn with colored marine designs.

When the walkway ends, cross the street and enter the fancifully named Passage des Palmiers—basically just an alley between housing developments on each side. There are a variety of plants along here, none of them natives and only a few of them palm trees, despite the sign.

At the end of the alley, though, you'll reach another entrance to the restored native plantings of the Headlands Preserve, and it's worth taking this little trail because this is the area where you're most likely to find the California gnatcatcher, an endangered songbird that lives in the limited range of coastal sage scrub in southern and Baja California and, as mentioned, is known for mewing like a kitten. Its habitat has been shrunk by development, and its nests are often invaded by cowbirds that lay their own eggs there. Sometimes this leads the gnatcatchers to abandon their nests; other times, they'll hatch and raise the young cowbirds.

During nesting season—from February to July—look for a small blue-gray bird flitting about. The breeding males are easiest to spot and identify because of their distinctive black caps.

The short trail ends at the sidewalk in less than a quarter of a mile. Here you have three choices: You can turn right along the sidewalk on Scenic Drive to return to the parking lot for a 2.5-mile hike; you can cross the street and explore a small but pretty section of the restored sage scrub overlooking Dana Point Harbor; or you can descend the short but steep Cove Road to the harbor itself. To your right is the Ocean Institute, which has some small but interesting exhibitions of local marine life, especially tide-pool animals, as well as a replica of the *Pilgrim*, the brig that sailed to and from Dana Point to transport hides to New England.

It's a pleasant walk along the length of the marina, with various restaurants as well as kayak and stand-up paddle rentals, and adds an easy mile-and-a-half stroll to the overall hike.

# San Onofre State Beach

**LOCATION**: San Onofre State Beach

**TOTAL DISTANCE**: Panhe-Peaceful Valley Trails, 5.5 miles; San Onofre Becaha Trails, 2.5 to 7.5 miles round trip

**TYPE**: Out and back or loop

**TOTAL ELEVATION GAIN**: 150 to 200 feet

**DIFFICULTY**: Easy to moderate

**SEASON**: Year-round

**FEES ETC.**: $15 day parking. Camping facilities available (Free parking if you park on Cristianitos Road for the Panhe-Peaceful Valley hike)

**MAPS**: USGS San Onofre Bluffs

**CONTACT**: San Onofre State Beach (949-492-4872, www.parks.ca.gov/?page_id=647)

There's a reason it's called San Onofre State Beach instead of State Park. Most visitors come for the ocean, including Trestles, the renowned surfing spot, and the fantastically shaped and colored bluffs along the ravishing beach south of the now-closed San Onofre Nuclear Generation Station. Truly, it's barely a stone's throw from the freeway, but you'd never know that as you stroll a beach that—as long as you're facing south, away from the nuclear plant—feels primordial, as though you might just come across a pterodactyl soaring off the spectacular bluffs that also block all freeway noise.

But you have another option here, the trail less followed: The backcountry of San Onofre is also worth visiting—it's the site of a 9,000-year-old Native American village; a little knoll that provides habitat for an endangered mouse; the training grounds of Marines; and the site of the first baptism in California. The last spot is on Camp Pendleton grounds, but from across Cristianitos Canyon, you can easily spot the large, white cross that commemorates the event.

## GETTING THERE

**For the beach hike:** Take the Basilone Road exit off the San Diego Freeway (I-5) just south of San Clemente and head west, then curve south on Old Highway 101. You'll pass the nuclear plant on your right and arrive at the gate to the southern section of San Onofre State Beach after 2.9 miles. During weekdays off-season, the gate is often unstaffed, so bring the right amount of money (and a pen) for the iron ranger. Continue to the parking lot where you see the sign for Trail 1 to your right, 0.2 mile south of the gate.

**For the backcountry hike:** Take the Cristianitos Road exit from the San Diego Freeway (I-5), heading east. At the quarter mile mark, start looking for legal parking along the northern (westbound) side of the street.

## THE TRAIL

**For the beach hike:** You'll set off through typical coastal sage scrub on a wide dirt trail that will curve around to a steep ramp leading down to the beach.

From the freeway, you would have no idea that to the west there were bluffs that would fall away to the sand; from the beach, you would have no idea that there's a major arterial practically overhead.

The one problem with hiking San Onofre State Beach is that northbound, the nuclear plant is perpetually in your line of sight. You could overcome this to some extent by, after heading south to whatever trail you want to climb back up, making a loop hike by taking the trail that runs along the bluffs. But the beach is prettier and quieter. I prefer to do this as an out and back.

Head north from Trail 1, toward the nuclear plant. You'll see a dramatic break in the brown shale bluffs to your right, creating a sort of private gorge. The beach is loaded with stones worn to smooth ovals by the continued wave action; as you walk, you can hear not just the breakers but the cobbles rolling against each other.

At 0.4 mile up the beach, a little more than a half-mile from the power plant, notice that the uniformly brown bluffs change to striking-looking, two-colored

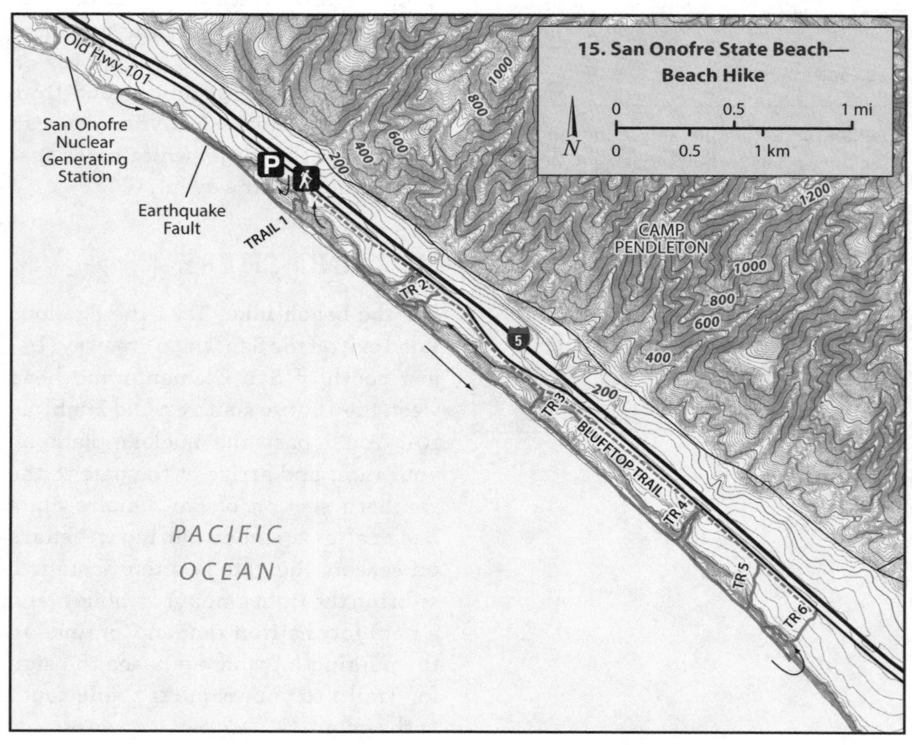

cliffs, with a white sandstone layer below and brown alluvium (basically, mud deposited by streams) above, carved by wind and water into dramatically shaped badlands. The crack between the two runs diagonally.

This is the Cristianitos Fault. The white shale is part of the San Mateo Formation, up to 5 million years old. The brown shale is part of the much older Monterey Formation, some 15 million to 20 million years old.

The Cristianitos Fault is considered inactive—which is defined as no movement for at least 11,000 years—and one of the reasons for that determination is right before your eyes. Look at the layer of cobbles just above both of these two different rocks, at the bottom of the towering alluvial deposits. The cobbles form an even line across the two; they were laid down on top of the rock when the cliffs were still under the ocean. If there had been an earthquake along the fault after these cobbles were deposited, the line wouldn't be even. Geologists have dated the cobble layer at some 120,000 years old. Therefore, the fault has been inactive for at least 120,000 years.

Despite the less-than-inspiring views of the twin-domed nuclear plant, it's worth continuing north for some of the most fantastically shaped cliffs. Then turn and head south along more beautiful scenery as far as you like. If you walk 2.5 miles, past Trail 6, the southernmost of the beach-access paths, you reach the area of the traditionally nude beach.

If you want to do the loop hike, you might want to return to the top of the

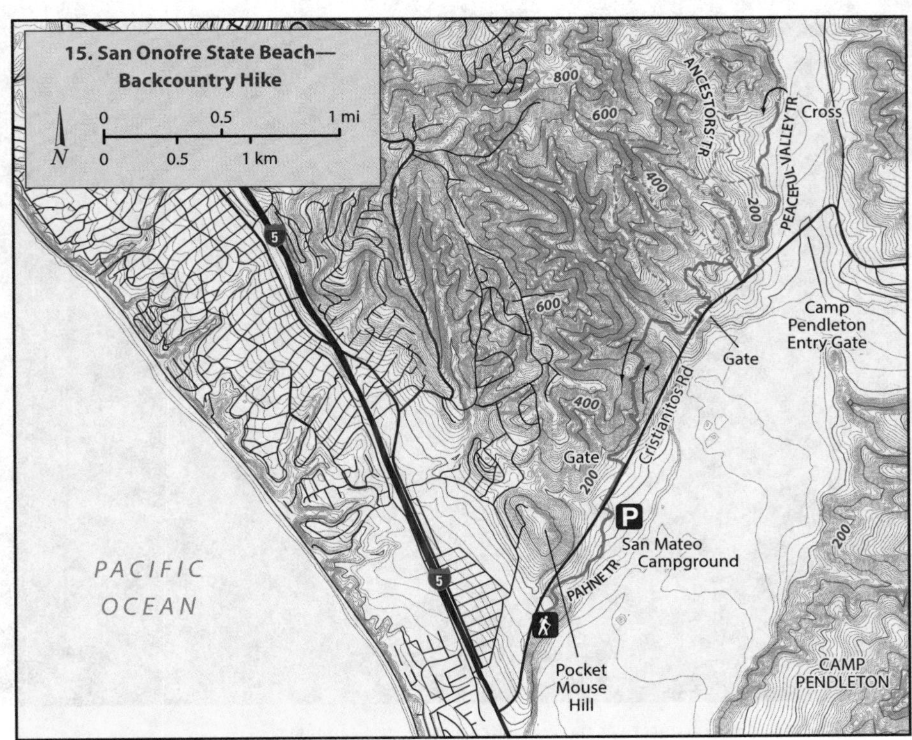

ON WEEKDAYS, YOU CAN HAVE THESE SPECTACULAR BI-COLORED CLIFFS TO YOURSELF

Courtesy of First American Corp. Historical Library

AN EARLY DRAWING OF THE FIRST BAPTISM IN CALIFORNIA

bluffs via Trail 5, which ascends through a steep-walled gorge.

**For the backcountry hike:** Along this section, the Panhe Trail, the path that for thousands of years was used by Native Americans to get from the main village to the ocean, runs alongside Cristianitos Road. Slip over the guardrail on the eastbound side of the street and join the paved trail, heading east. The trail curves around a knoll and gently descends within a half-mile to San Mateo Campground. Before you get there, though, at 0.4 mile, look up at the left to the little hill on the other side of Cristianitos Road; there might be an orange flag on top. This is known as Pocket Mouse Hill, one of only four known sites where the endangered pocket mouse lives.

It might not look like it, but you are at the site of Panhe, an Acjachemen village that was continuously inhabited for close to 9,000 years. This is considered a sacred site by the Acjachemen, where the remains of their ancestors and countless artifacts of their daily lives lie under your feet. Many artifacts, including arrowheads, already have been found in the larger area around the park. After heavy rains, it is not uncommon for bones of the ancient village's residents to be found by the creek. Camp Pendleton provided fenced land for the reburial of these remains, and for those of other Native Americans found during construction projects in Orange County.

In winter and early spring, the greenness of lower San Mateo Canyon is restful to the eyes as the creek water rushes to the ocean. It's easy to imagine the canyon looking much the same way during the wetter period when Native Americans lived here. In later spring, the non-native vegetation that those early people never saw quickly turns brown and thistles grow thick along the trails. February and March are the best months for visiting Panhe.

Walk through the campground and leave through the regular exit. Then turn right on Cristianitos Road. After 0.2 mile along the road, you'll see one of the three gates that lead to the park's backcounty fire roads on the left. Turn left up this trail and then right, running roughly parallel to Cristianitos Road as you follow it through the scrub and overlook the canyon. Camp Pendleton's land begins on the other side of Cristianitos Road. Look for what appears to be a motley collection of flat-topped huts strung together. As of this writing, the inside of the building had been set up to resemble an Iraqi village, used as part of the Marines' training.

THE CROSS ON CAMP PENDLETON LAND MARKING THE SITE OF THE FIRST BAPTISM IN CALIFORNIA

THE SPRING WHERE THE FIRST BAPTISM TOOK PLACE

After a half-mile, the fire break will turn into a single-track trail that descends and within a quarter-mile will bring you to the second gate along Cristianitos Road. Continue on the lower single-track trail rather than the fire break that goes steeply uphill. After 0.6 mile, this trail will take you to the third gate along Cristianitos Road, near the security gate to Camp Pendleton, and the beginning of the Peaceful Valley Trail. Take the lower path of this trail, which heads up into Cristianitos Canyon. The trail continues for 1.6 miles and hooks up with the Ancestors' Trail for a steep loop favored by mountain bikers, but you need walk for only about a half-mile on Peaceful Valley to get a good view of the canyon, and on the bluff top on the other side of the creek, a large, white cross on Camp Pendleton land.

This is the site of the first baptism in California, conducted in 1769. As the Portola Expedition came up from Mexico with the intent of setting up bases in Alta California before the Russians could do the same, it came across the 350 or so residents of Panhe. Two young sisters of the village were dying, and one of the priests with the expedition baptized them at a spring near the river, directly below the cross, after telling their mother that this would allow their souls to ascend to heaven.

The event gave this canyon its name: Cristianitos, or the little Christians.

The Native Americans eventually lost Panhe when it became part of the vast O'Neill Ranch, though some stayed on to work at the ranch. As the Native Americans came under the authority of the missions, they were called the Juaneños, for Mission San Juan Capistrano. In recent years, many of them have begun calling themselves by the older name Acjachemen.

Because of the careful genealogical records kept by the early missionaries in California, many modern Acjachemen know from which villages their ancestors came. In the case of the descendants of Panhe, they can say with certainly that they are standing where their forebears stood 9,000 years ago. Not many of us could match that.

After returning back to the gate that marked the beginning of Peaceful Valley Trail, return to your car along Cristianitos Road, following San Mateo Creek.

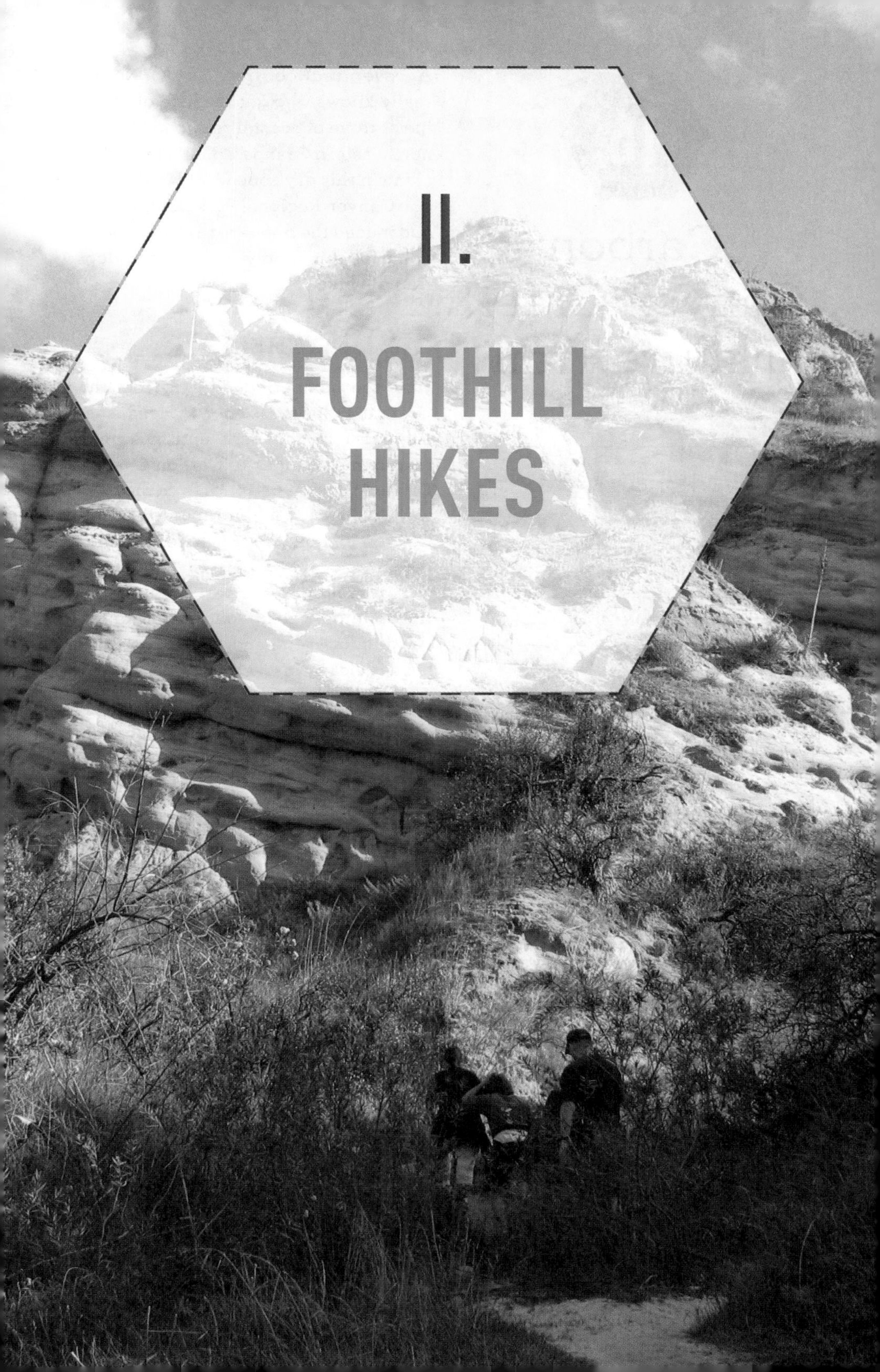

# II. FOOTHILL HIKES

# 16

# Carbon Canyon Creek Nature Trail

**OCATION**: Carbon Canyon Regional Park

**TOTAL DISTANCE**: 2.4 miles

**TYPE**: Partial loop

**TOTAL ELEVATION GAIN**: 20 feet

**DIFFICULTY**: Very easy

**SEASON**: Year-round

**FEES ETC.**: $3 on weekdays, $5 weekends. Good for children. Dogs allowed on leash.

**MAPS**: USGS Yorba Linda, Carbon Canyon Regional Park county map

**TRAILHEAD COORDINATES**: N 33°55.262′ W 117°49.768′

**CONTACT**: Carbon Canyon Regional Park (714-973-3160 www.ocparks.com/carboncanyon)

A grove of redwood trees? In OC? No one really knows who got the idea of planting a grove of coastal redwood trees in northeastern Orange County. Its oddity alone in this dry zone would make Carbon Canyon Regional Park worth a visit, and indeed the trees are the turnaround point for this family-friendly and dog-friendly hike.

## GETTING THERE

Take the Lambert Road exit from the Orange Freeway (CA 57). Head east 2.5 miles to the park entrance. The road name changes to Carbon Canyon Drive. At a point 2.5 miles from the freeway, you'll reach the entrance to Carbon Canyon Regional Park. There is a parking fee.

After entering the park, turn left on the main park road, following it to the parking lot at the end, where the trailhead is clearly marked.

## THE TRAIL

The Carbon Canyon Creek Nature Trail—the name is practically longer than the trail—is the only real hiking trail within the park, adjacent to Chino Hills State Park. And like its vastly bigger neighbor, the area surrounding the nature trail shows the scars of the 2008 Triangle Complex Fire, especially in a scattering of blackened trees and ruined benches. The first part of the trail is at its most pleasant during winter and spring when the creek is flowing, but this is an easy walk any time of year.

The way of land in Orange County tends to be from open to developed, or developed to redeveloped. Carbon Canyon Regional Park is one of the exceptions. In fact, it's the site of one of the older villages in the county, Olinda, an

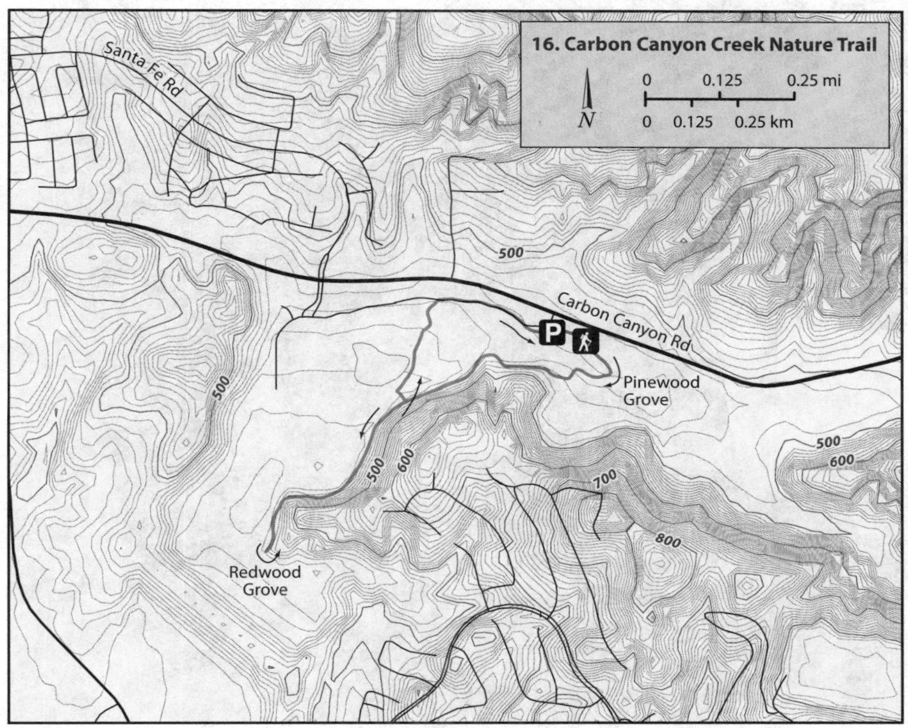


oil-boom town in the late 1800s. The boom faded out in the 1940s, and some 20 years later, the park was laid out on the site. In fact, there is no town of Olinda anymore and nothing in the park to indicate the land's past; the old buildings were replaced by an artificial lake stocked with fish, playing fields, and picnic grounds. On the drive along Carbon Canyon Road to the park entrance, though, you can still see several working oil rigs.

Just past the trailhead, you'll pass through a small grove of another non-native evergreen tree—Monterey pines, leftovers from a now-defunct Christmas-tree farm. Then, as you descend closer to the creek, you'll probably notice a handful of giant reeds, *Arundo donax*, an attractive bamboo lookalike that has become a pest throughout the region in riparian areas. The creek used to be choked with them but much of the giant reed burned in the fire as well; in fact, the dry plants fed the blaze in a chimney effect headed up-creek, giving the flames an added push into the state park.

Following the trail is easy. There are no trail intersections except for a marked set of stairs that lead to the artificial lake. That's the route suggested for the return walk.

There is one creek crossing, wet at some times of the year, muddy at others, and dry in late summer and early fall, leading you to an area beneath a dam that was built to prevent flooding of the area. You'll pass native walnut trees and non-native pepper trees, with their distinctive long, slender leaflets and pea-size reddish-pink berries. You'll also

THE REDWOOD GROVE

pass plenty of another invasive plant, poison hemlock, with its foliage resembling carrot tops (they're in the same family) and off-white blossoms. It's a graceful plant in bloom, but as deadly as its name indicates—the poison that Socrates drank.

At the 1-mile mark, you'll see the first of some 250 redwood trees in a dense, linear, 10-acre grove. These were planted in 1975—by whom exactly is unclear, but probably by the county—and are doing fairly well considering that these trees prefer moist, misty environments and that there are no naturally occurring redwood groves south of Monterey. Most of the trees have reached 60 to 70 feet high, with a few as tall as 100 feet. Underfoot, you'll feel the reason for their success: the ground is continuously damp from an in-ground watering system. If you visit on a dry, hot day, you'll immediately see the contrast between this grassy, nearly muddy ground and the parched slopes—or the dry, sandy ground on which you were recently treading. Though non-natives, these trees are hardly about to take over Orange County's open spaces. They're barely holding on where they are.

This isn't Muir Woods, the Marin County park thick with redwoods towering more than 200 feet tall, but it's worth wandering to the far end of the grove and back, enjoying the sensation of cool, damp shade before heading back. When you have walked 0.7 mile on the return, take note of the marker on the left that introduces you to the history of the extinct town; at one time, this would have been a vantage point for seeing downtown Olinda. You can take the steps down to the groomed part of the park, using the paved trail along the pleasant little lake and across the adjacent playing fields. The trail returns you to the main road; turn right and return to your car.

Post-hike, you might enjoy a scenic drive east on Carbon Canyon Drive through the steep-walled, winding canyon; there aren't many roads like this around the county. You'll also pass through the hamlet of Sleepy Hollow, which has managed to remain bucolic and isolated all these years. Also along the road, near the regional park, are privately owned hot springs that once drew tourists, but the resort has long been closed.

For more of the experience of the old oil town, check out the Olinda Oil Museum and Trail at 4025 Santa Fe Road in Brea. Visiting days are limited to Wednesday, Saturday, and Sunday at this time. The park includes the original Olinda Oil Well #1, first drilled in 1897 and still pumping.

Courtesy of the Orange County Archives

EARLY PHOTO OF THE OLINDA OIL-BOOM TOWN

# Hills for Everyone–Telegraph Canyon Loop

**LOCATION**: Chino Hills State Park

**TOTAL DISTANCE**: 5 miles

**TYPE**: Loop

**TOTAL ELEVATION GAIN**: 700 feet

**DIFFICULTY**: Moderate

**SEASON**: November to May

**FEES ETC.**: $8 day parking. Camping and equestrian facilities available.

**MAPS**: USGS Prado Dam, Chino Hills State Park map

**TRAILHEAD COORDINATES**: N 33°55.302′ W 117°42.305′

**CONTACT**: Chino Hills State Park (951-940-5600, www.parks.ca.gov/?page_iD=648)

Named for the advocacy group that fought successfully for the establishment of Chino Hills State Park, the Hills for Everyone Trail is especially popular among hikers for its picturesque climb through the bottom of a cool, green ravine by a little stream. It's also one of the few trails in the park limited to hikers only. This outing follows a loop that includes the length of Hills for Everyone, a short side trip to one of the park's springs and a return trip through a more exposed trail with views into nearby canyons and across the park's hills.

## GETTING THERE

Take the Soquel Canyon Road exit from CA 71 in Chino Hills north of the Riverside Freeway (91). Head west from the exit for 1 mile and turn left on Elinvar Drive. At 0.2 mile, Elinvar ends; forcing a left turn onto Sapphire Road. Make an immediate right turn onto Bane Canyon Road, the dirt road into the park, and drive 3 miles to the parking area near the old Rolling M Ranch and its historic ranch buildings. From the parking area, walk back in the direction you came for 500 feet to the stop sign and turn right for the Telegraph Canyon Trailhead.

## THE TRAIL

You'll ascend on Telegraph Canyon Trail, a gently rising dirt road, alongside a riparian area where you might be serenaded by a chorus of frogs. Many of the trees along here were badly burned, but it's also easy to see that the willows, at least, are shooting up quickly.

The best time to visit this area is in the winter and early spring, when the hills are green and the thin ribbon of creek is still flowing. By April many of the hills are blooming in a yellow-

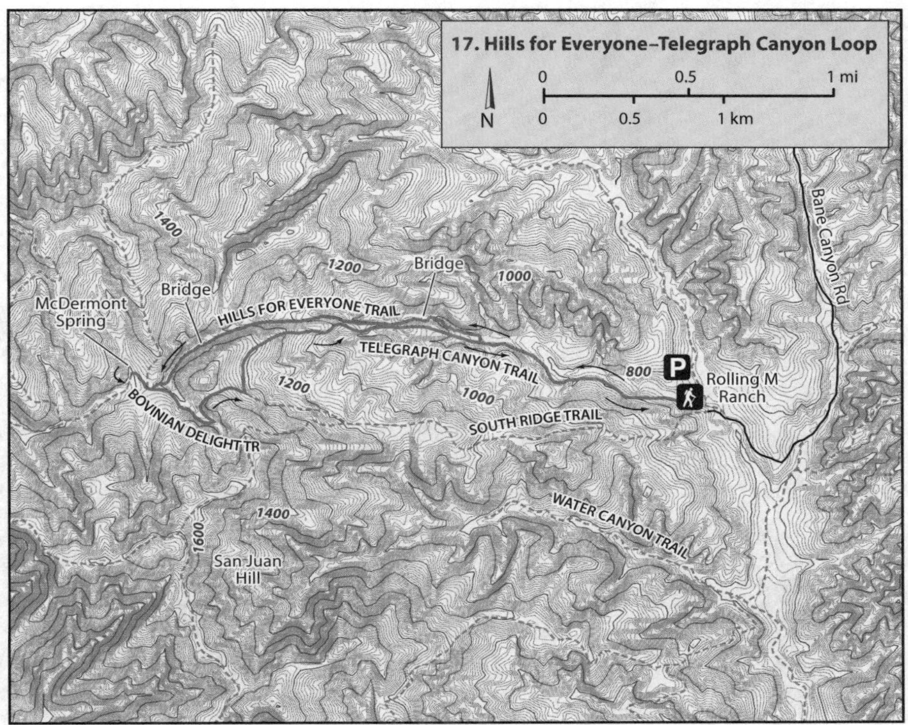


flowered sea of black mustard, a pretty sight until the plants dry into many-armed skeletons.

Access to the Chino Hills backcountry has grown more difficult in the past couple of years. The park has suffered under a triple whammy—fire, flood, and finances. The 2008 Triangle Complex Fire burned some 90 percent of the park. Because of the state budget crisis, the main part of the park is open only Fridays through Sundays (Coal Canyon is the exception). After rains (again, excepting the trails in Coal Canyon), the park closes 48 hours for each quarter-inch of precipitation; if there's a 4-inch drenching, the park is closed for 16 days. And if any more rain falls during that time, more days of closure get piled on. In a particularly wet season, it can be nearly impossible to get into the park during its prime hiking period. Call to make certain that the park is open before making the drive.

At 0.9 mile, Telegraph Canyon Trail continues straight ahead, but you'll turn right on a broad grassy path. The wide path continues uphill, but you will fork to the left almost immediately, onto the faint Hills for Everyone Trail through the ravine. This single-track trail is an immediate change from broad, exposed Telegraph Canyon Trail, which runs parallel to this path and above it most of the way to McDermont Spring. Even with the many burned trees in the ravine, this trail has a sheltered feeling. At first you walk on the right side of the little stream, past some burned interpretive signs. At 0.3 mile, a wooden bridge will take you to the other side; this bridge was built by

THE HILLS OF CHINO HILLS STATE PARK

volunteers to replace the old bridge burned in the fire. Turn right, continuing upstream. At this point, though you stay near the bottom of the ravine, the climb upward will grow steeper. Watch your footing; between fire, rains, and long periods of closure, parts of the trail were narrow and eroded on my most recent visit.

You'll find miner's lettuce along the trail, and common bedstraw, so called because it was once used to stuff mattresses. As you continue, notice that more of the trees either escaped the fire relatively unscathed or are sprouting new greenery; a canopy of oak and some walnut shelters you as you continue climbing, The 1.3-mile path veers away from Telegraph Canyon Trail and crosses another bridge shortly before climbing out of the ravine to meet up with Telegraph Canyon again at the Four Corners area. Turn right on Telegraph Canyon toward an information kiosk and sheltered picnic table. Several trails meet at this juncture, including one that wins my Best Trail Name award: Bovinian Delight, a nod to the park's ranching past.

Continue on Telegraph 500 feet past Four Corners to McDermont Spring, a cattail-dotted livestock pond that also dates back to the park's ranching days. These days, in addition providing a home for tadpoles and occasional turtles, it's a watering hole for the park's wild animals. The deep tracks around its muddy perimeter give you the perfect opportunity to check out which ones have been by lately.

You'll loop back to the trailhead via Telegraph Canyon Trail. At 0.7 mile on the return trip, you'll reach a fork; turn left here. The trail that seems to go straight ahead leads to South Ridge Trail (an alternate path back that would bring you to roughly the same area).

The plants along the sides of the trail are largely non-native—black mustard as far as the eye can see, along with thistle and invasive grasses—the result of overgrazing from when this was a ranch, and too-frequent fires. On a February day, though the hills were green, they also were covered with the dried, gray mustard from last year growing some 5 feet high; at the same time, robust, green leaves of mustard grew along the ground, promising another year's bumper crop of the plant.

At 1 mile, note the walnut trees along the path to the left, natives that aren't often seen in the Orange County area. Many of these seem to be recovering after the fire. You'll probably see some walnuts hanging on from years past; they're smaller than the ones you're used to in supermarkets. The ravine to the right is dotted with old oak trees that appear to have escaped the fire, and others that are showing signs of new growth.

WALNUT TREE

# Water Canyon

**LOCATION**: Chino Hills State Park

**DISTANCE**: 4 miles round-trip

**TYPE**: Out and back

**TOTAL ELEVATION GAIN**: 250 feet

**DIFFICULTY**: Moderately easy

**SEASON**: December to March

**FEES ETC.**: $8 day fee. Camping and equestrian facilities available.

**MAPS**: USGS Prado Dam

**TRAILHEAD COORDINATES**: N 33°55.197′ W 117°41.958′

**CONTACT**: Chino Hills State Park (951-940-5600, www.parks.ca.gov/?page_iD=648)

It can be hard to find a small, private spot to hang out with nature in the 14,000 acres of Chino Hills State Park. Most of the park's rolling hills are segmented by wide dirt roads, humming with bikers. Then there's single-track (when there's a track at all) Water Canyon Trail, stream fed, reserved for hikers, and silent but for the frogs and birds. As a trail to nowhere—it peters out toward the back of the canyon—it's seldom visited by anyone but the local wildlife.

That said, Water Canyon and its surroundings took a hard hit in the 2008 Triangle Complex Fire. Once shading the canyon through much of its length, the oak, sycamore, willow, and native walnut trees suffered intense burning. Many trees died, but others are showing green leaves or new crowns of growth. It's still a quiet place with an otherworldly ambience, and watching its post-burn recovery while savoring the solitude is worth the visit.

The hike is at its best late winter, when the little stream murmurs alongside the trail and before the abundant milk thistle grows above ankle level, creating a thorny nuisance to hikers. The trail involves moderate bushwhacking. Long sleeves and pants are advisable because of the plentiful nettle and remains of the previous year's thistle. As with the Hills for Everyone Trail, getting into the park can be an obstacle in itself. At this point, because of state budget cuts, the backcountry area of the park is open only Friday through Sunday, and the park closes for two days for each quarter-inch of rain. That means the park might be closed for well over a month at a time in winter.

## GETTING THERE

Take the Soquel Canyon Road exit from CA 71 in Chino Hills north of the Riverside Freeway (91). Head west from the exit for 1 mile and turn left on Elinvar Drive. At 0.2 mile, Elinvar ends; forcing a left turn onto Sapphire Road. Make an immediate right turn onto Bane Canyon Road, the dirt road into the park. After 2.5 miles, look for the small picnic area on the left with space for a few cars. If the spots are full, continue on Bane Canyon as it veers right for 0.1 mile, up to a large parking lot, equestrian area, and the historic buildings left from the days when this was Rolling M Ranch.

## THE TRAIL

The trailhead to Lower Aliso Canyon Trail is at the small picnic area. (Don't let the names confuse you; this is a different Aliso Canyon than the one in Aliso and Wood Canyons Wilderness Park.) You'll follow a flat, wide dirt road through pasture that is almost entirely covered with non-native plants. The dominant vegetation is mustard, growing taller than your head. In late winter and very early spring, it puts on a pretty show, a sea of yellow that goes on and on, but it dries and turns gray quickly. Milk thistle, which you can identify by the attractive green leaves set off by a web of white lines, is also common along here, along with wild radish, with its four-petaled flowers in lavender and white.

Both mustard and radish are edible plants; the leaves of the mustard plant are a rather spicy green vegetable, and the black seeds from which it gets its name can be used to make the

SOMETIMES YOU HAVE TO SHARE THE TRAIL WITH ALL KINDS

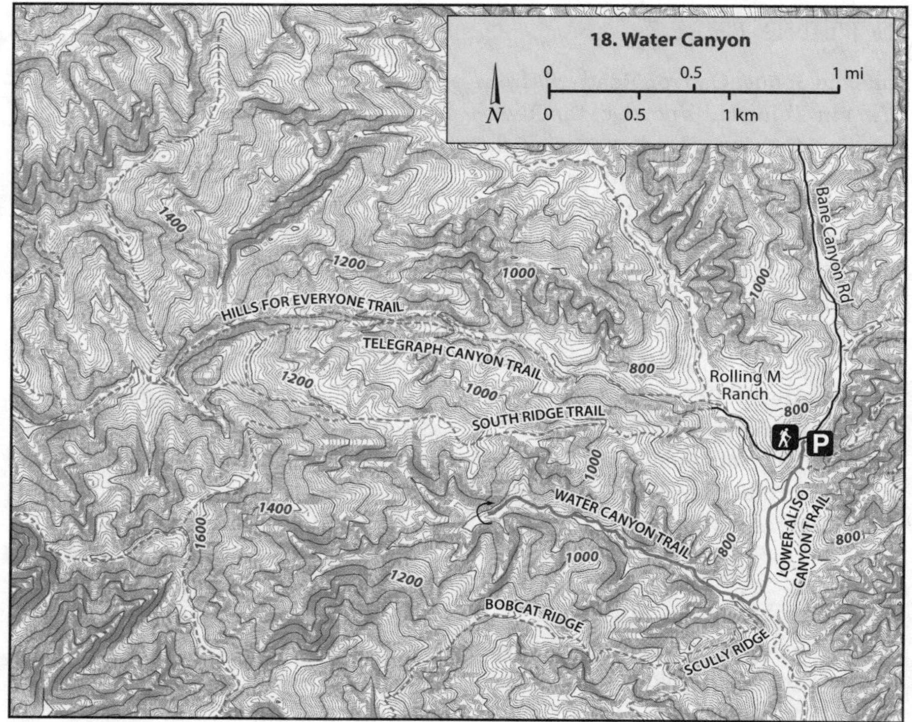


condiment. The root of the wild radish is woody and largely unusable, but the seed pods, when young and green, have a sharp, sweet radish flavor. And the seeds of milk thistle have been used in folk medicine for 2,000 years for treatment of liver and gall bladder problems.

But in the backcountry of Chino Hills, their propensity for drying early in the year makes them dangerous fuel for wildfires. Chino Hills, which provides a crucial wildlife corridor from the Santa Ana Mountains to open space in Los Angeles County, has a long ranching history, and the land suffers from both overgrazing and too-frequent fires that gave these pests a chance to take over.

At the start of Lower Aliso are a couple of giant sycamores that are first starting to put out green leaves after the fire. This is also an area of comely elderberry, growing into graceful, rounded trees rather than the more typical scruffy shrubs. These have made a quick post-burn comeback.

After 0.6 mile on Lower Aliso, you'll cross a small bridge over a stream; soon after, there's another stream crossing, and then a T junction. Lower Aliso heads left; you'll turn right on Scully Ridge Trail and 500 feet later, come to the faint trail at the mouth of Water Canyon.

On my most recent visit, some unexpected company was visiting this area—a dozen or so cattle that had trampled their fence at an adjoining ranch and entered where the grass looked greener. It happens from time to time at Chino Hills, especially after rain softens the earth that holds the fence posts.

The mini-herd followed alongside—at a mutually respectful distance—for a while, and then posted themselves at the Water Canyon Trailhead, a bucolic but stubbornly unmoving reminder of the area's past.

Water Canyon was closed for many months after the fire, and the lack of hikers has allowed what was already a faint trail to disappear altogether at times. During the first part of the trek up canyon, you'll find the best footing on the south side of the creek. After a quarter of a mile, look for a narrow, overgrown foot trail on the north bank, about 30 feet from the creek, cutting through the mustard and thistle.

The willows here are growing fast, but many of the oak and walnut trees were still black two years after the fire. Several groups of leafy oak trees still stand on the south bank, provid-

NEW PRICKLY PEAR PADS GROW FROM A BURNED PATCH OF CACTUS

ing a shaded place for rest. Watercress grows not just in the stream but in the large muddled areas adjacent to it. Elderberry adds greenery everywhere —and so does nettle. The pain and swelling that result from touching the leaves is more than a reaction from having a sharp little hair under the skin. The stinger also contains a histamine, creating skin irritation, and acetylcholine causing the burning sensation. Yet nettles (once they are safely gathered, before blossoming and using protective gloves) can be boiled into a nutritious green like spinach; cooking solves the stinging problem. The plant also has been used in folk medicine to treat asthma, coughs and colds, urinary problems, arthritis and rheumatism, and even, when mixed with wine, impotence. Nettle is sold commercially (stinging qualities removed) as an herbal remedy.

Small frogs sing out in wild chorus along the creek, and you're likely to see some of them along the path. The snags of the blackened trees have become favored perches for birds. Farther into the canyon, a couple of large sycamore trees hold the nests of red-tailed hawks. On one visit, a huge golden eagle sailed past, startlingly close.

At 0.8 mile into the canyon, a big patch of prickly pear cactus grows on the north slope adjacent to the footpath. About half of this was burned, but calling the drooping, gray sections dead would be a mistake. New green pads already are growing from them.

When you've walked 1 mile into the narrowing canyon, it widens out, as though to give you a private space. Although the trail grows even fainter, you can walk farther at this point into an area of low, rolling hills. You'll probably have this entire little world to yourself, but as you work your way down to a shadier area at the canyon's bottom, the thick growth of nettles becomes a bothersome impediment.

# Oak Canyon Nature Center

**LOCATION**: City of Anaheim open space

**TOTAL DISTANCE**: 2 miles

**TYPE**: Loop

**TOTAL ELEVATION GAIN**: 300 feet

**DIFFICULTY**: Easy

**SEASON**: February to May

**FEES ETC.**: None but a $2 donation is requested. Good for children. No dogs allowed. Open daily until sunset, but the parking lot closes at 5 p.m.

**MAPS**: USGS Orange

**TRAILHEAD COORDINATES**: N 33°50.340′ W 117°45.411′

**CONTACT**: Oak Canyon Nature Center (714-998-8380, www.anaheim.net/ocnc)
City of Anaheim Parks Division (714-765-5155, www.anaheimcityparks.com)

Oak Canyon Nature Center is a tiny, underappreciated gem wedged between housing tracts and a golf course in Anaheim Hills. Known mostly for its educational programs for children, this tiny municipal wilderness packs remarkable color, shady serenity, and variety into an easy 2-mile hike. I also saw my first classic hanging beehive in an oak here, a huge thing the size of a toddler.

Timing for this hike is important. Visit from early March to mid-April for an eye-popping array of flowers along its sunny canyon wall, then descend to the cool oak woodland along a scenic stream. If you want a shorter hike on a hot day, the canyon bottom stays delightfully shady.

## GETTING THERE

Exit the Riverside Freeway (CA 91) in Anaheim Hills at Imperial Highway. Turn south on Imperial Highway 0.25 mile to the light at Nohl Ranch Road. Turn left on Nohl Ranch and drive 1.8 miles, just past the golf course on your left, and turn left on Walnut Canyon Road. Drive to the end of the road, to the parking lot for the Oak Canyon Nature Center. Parking and entry are free.

## THE TRAIL

From the parking lot, enter the trail to the interpretive center on your right. Across from the building, pick up the Nature Trail by climbing the small set of wooden stairs and turning left. Follow the paved interpretive loop lined with common local plants, especially sugarbush, a less-common cousin of lemonadeberry. In early spring, the flowers are especially sweet-smelling; later, the berries, soaked in cold or hot water make a pleasing lemonade-flavored

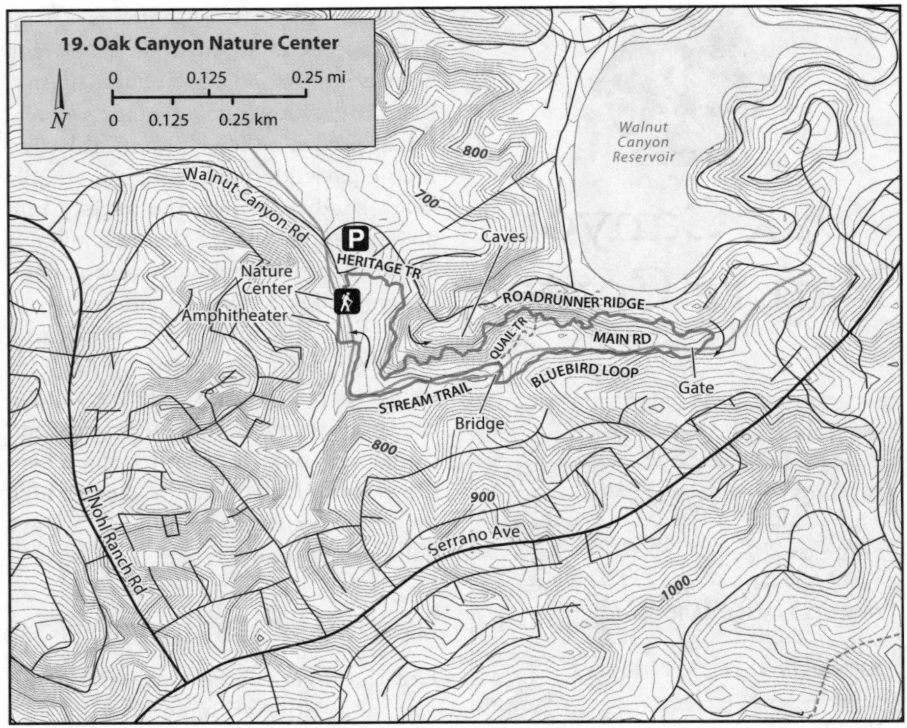


drink. The loop also takes you past a small butterfly garden with plants that regularly attract the fluttering insects. As the end of the horseshoe-shape trail, turn left into another loop of the trail. After about 30 feet, you'll reach the head of Roadrunner Ridge to the left.

A gentle climb takes you to the upper part of the slope on the south wall of the canyon. Here begins a meander through a garden of wildflowers so dense and varied, every turn brings another profusion of color. There are at least four different kinds of phacelia here, including thick stands of Parry's phacelia in a deep, rich purple. Three kinds of lupine can be found along the path; most striking are the fuchsia-colored blossoms of stinging lupine. Blue dicks, or wild hyacinth, which grows sparsely in most places, cover extensive sections here. The corm of the wild hyacinth, nutlike in flavor, was a favorite of early Native Americans. The trail also is lined with chia, a less-common but striking sight in Orange County, with its small, bright blue-purple flowers in rounded heads. Native Americans gathered the edible seeds for their high nutrient and oil levels and made a minty drink by soaking the seeds in water. The trees along here are native walnut; in spring, you'll see the pale green catkins and perhaps some withered leftovers of last year's nuts, dark brown and about an inch in diameter.

At a couple of points, you'll pass trails to either side, but continue straight. After you go three-fourths of a mile, there's a short, steep climb made easier by railroad-tie steps. The trail then gently descends until, after you have

CREEK-SIDE PATH IN OAK CANYON NATURE CENTER

BEEHIVE

hiked one mile, you're at the main road. It's worth checking the power pole here; red-capped acorn woodpeckers are frequent visitors.

Turn left; there's a chain-link fence 100 feet away. Go around it to the left, and 20 feet farther, pick up the Bluebird Loop trail on the right. You immediately come to a fork; bear right, ducking under a spreading sycamore branch and over a fence post across the trail. Watch out for poison oak; it grows in profusion along the ground and in some places hangs down from the trees, dangling down at face level. You'll come to various forks in the trail; keep bearing right, staying along the year-round stream. This section of the canyon is always shaded and densely green. The trail takes you under the graceful oaks, hundreds of years old, that give the canyon its name. The stream is a continual companion along the way, sometimes giving way to small cascades, otherwise slowing into ponds in which waterfowl paddle, including wood ducks. After walking 0.4 mile, you'll come to the main road. Turn right here. About 100 feet farther on, you'll come to a wooden bridge; growing next to it is a huge thicket of wild grapes.

Cross the bridge to the Stream Trail and turn left. If you look closely at the ground along this stretch, you might see wild peony, a beautiful little flower that droops down, in a deep wine color. Native Americans ground its roots into a powder that was used for sore throats; a tea made from the root was used as a treatment for stress and depression.

The trail will continue along the creek, across another bridge, then take you past an amphitheater and back to the interpretive center.

CATERPILLAR OF THE WHITE-LINED SPHINX MOTH

# Historic Dam–Santiago Creek Loop

**LOCATION**: Santiago Oaks Regional Park

**TOTAL DISTANCE**: 3.4 miles

**TYPE**: Loop

**TOTAL ELEVATION GAIN**: 400 feet

**DIFFICULTY**: Moderate

**SEASON**: December to June

**FEE ETC.**: $3 daily; $5 weekend. Leashed dogs allowed.

**MAPS**: USGS Orange

**TRAILHEAD COORDINATES**: N 33°49.292′ W 117°46.480′

**CONTACT**: Santiago Oaks Regional Park (714-973-6620, www.ocparks.com / santiagooaks)

The main attraction at Santiago Oaks Regional Park is the historic dam that represents an ingenious bit of 1800s engineering. But this little park, only 430 acres, packs in other pleasures: an old orange grove, a variety of flowers, and an easily accessible creek winding through a pleasant grove of trees both native and planted. And, if you go in May or June, there should be entire hillsides of bush mallow, a large shrub with pale lavender, cuplike flowers growing all along its branches. Like matilija poppies and many other vivid wildflowers, bush mallow is a fire follower, a plant that sprouts up after a wildfire gives it the right set of growing conditions.

More than 90 percent of the park was affected by fire in 2007. You'll see burn evidence not only in the hills of mallow, but in the scorched trees. The park is popular with local equestrians; you're almost certain to find horses amiably sharing the multi-use trails with you. This hike takes you on a complicated but relatively easy loop to see many of Santiago Oaks' charms.

## GETTING THERE

Take Katella Avenue east from the Costa Mesa Freeway (CA 55). Katella turns into Santiago Canyon Road; at 3.1 miles from the freeway, turn left into Windes Drive. After 0.7 mile, you'll reach the park. Just past the ranger station, the parking lot is on the right.

## THE TRAIL

The first sight in the park is the old grove of Valencia orange trees, growing next to the parking lot. This is a remnant of the farms that once blan-

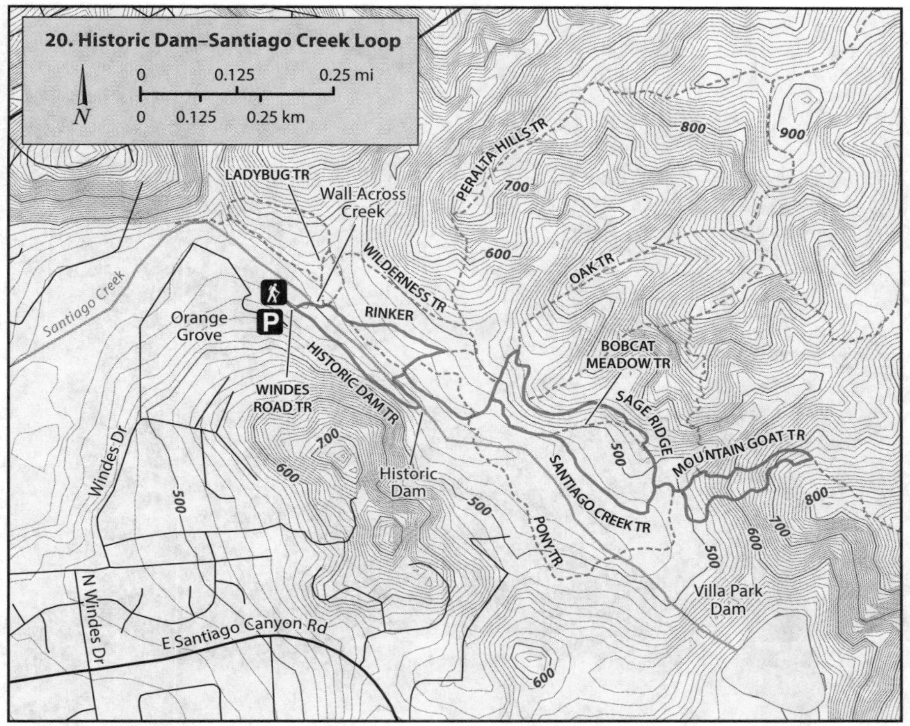


keted the county. It's one of a handful of orange groves left in the county. They did, as it happens, create a tree museum here.

From the parking lot, head back down to the main road, Windes Road Trail, and make a slight right onto Historic Dam Trail. Some 500 feet farther, the trail will make a jog to the left. Two hundred feet beyond this, you'll go down some steps and continue to the right along the creek-side trail. After a fifth of a mile, you're at the historic old stone dam.

This is an appealing spot. Water spills gently over the center of the low stone wall into the pool below. But the dam's small size above ground doesn't reveal what a smart bit of engineering it was. This dam wasn't created to hold back water; it was built to bring water to the surface. In 1872, a clay dam was constructed, going down to bedrock, blocking the flow of underground water so that it would have nowhere to go but up to the surface for agricultural and domestic use. After that dam was damaged by a flood, this structure of stone and concrete was built in 1892.

About 50 feet back from the dam, turn left, going toward the water and a wall of rock. Just to the left of the clearing is another trail that you take to the left. At a quarter of a mile from the start, go up a flight of wooden stairs, and then go right on Santiago Creek Trail. The creek, found along trails in several parks and preserves in the county, was named by the Gaspar de Portola expedition in 1769 in honor of St. James (San Iago.)

THE HISTORIC DAM

At a fork in the trail where there's an information kiosk, turn left. At 0.4 mile, where you see a marker for Bobcat Meadow, continue straight onto Oak Trail. Five hundred feet farther, turn right onto Sage Ridge Trail. This is a place where the fire damage is particularly obvious, with many scorched trees. In April, this area is abloom with wild morning glory; you might also find Catalina mariposa lilies, elegant-looking white flowers. You'll pass Grasshopper Trail and continue straight to where you can see the much bigger, newer Villa Park Dam. This is an area where the hillsides are covered with bush mallow, which blooms in later spring.

The hike gets a little tricky to follow here, but you're unlikely to get lost in this area of the park. At worst, you can always head downhill toward the trees to pick up Santiago Creek Trail again. At 0.8 mile, make a left onto Bobcat Meadow Trail. Then, 259 feet farther along, pick up Santiago Creek Trail again, heading left and uphill to Mountain Goat Trail. Turn left onto Mountain Goat at 0.9 mile. The trail will take you to a lookout point over the newer reservoir and the canyon beyond.

Complete the Mountain Goat Loop heading downhill onto Santiago Creek Trail, toward the entrance of the park. There are some particularly colorful flowers along here in mid-spring, including bright purple vetch. At 2.6 miles from the start, you reach a juncture; turn right on Sourgrass Trail. Go about 250 feet to Rinker Grove Trail and make a left. This is one of the most charming trails in the park, under a mixed grove of eucalyptus, pin[illegible] oak trees.

After a third of a mile along this tra[illegible] turn right, once again joining Santiago Creek Trail. You'll cross over a small wooden bridge; in springtime, you might see tadpoles in the creek below. The trail lets out into a seeming dead end, next to the backyards of neighbors' houses. The trick is to cross the creek here by going down a small shoulder of boulders and across a concrete dam. On the other side of the creek, the trail forks. Turn right, returning to the entrance of the park and the grove. Turn left to return to the ranger's station.

# Peters Canyon Loop

**LOCATION**: Peters Canyon Regional Park

**TOTAL DISTANCE**: 4 to 5 miles

**TYPE**: Double loop

**ELEVATION GAIN**: 500 feet

**DIFFICULTY**: Moderate

**SEASON**: November to June

**FEES ETC.**: $3 day parking. Leashed dogs allowed.

**MAPS**: USGS 7.5-min Orange

**TRAILHEAD COORDINATES**: N 33°47.027′ W 117°45.723′

**CONTACT**: Peters Canyon Regional Park (714-973-6611, www.ocparks.com/peterscanyon)

This narrow slice of semi-wilderness is wedged, too tightly at points, between upscale housing developments. One trail gives a better view of the backyard pools and built-in barbecues of the adjacent McMansions than of the natural landscape. Still, the park has several unusual and scenic features and, choosing carefully from its more than 6 miles of hiking trails, hikers can maximize its pleasures. Peters Canyon is popular among the neighborhood's walkers and runners—with its areas of willows, cottonwoods, and a little eucalyptus forest—and a good place for bird watching, especially along the upper reservoir. This hike will take you through a charming marsh area (if only those houses weren't such a presence across the street), into the eucalyptus forest and around the reservoir.

You can maximize the pleasures of Peters Canyon by visiting late enough in winter for the first flowers to be blooming, but early enough to hike the charming Willow Trail, which is closed from March 15 to September 15 to allow birds to breed undisturbed.

## GETTING THERE

From the Santa Ana Freeway (I-5), take Jamboree Road east 5.2 miles to Canyon View, which will be marked with a sign to Peters Canyon. Turn left on Canyon View 0.1 mile to the park entrance on your left.

## THE TRAIL

Pick up Lake View Trail next to the ranger's station. After 0.2 mile, you'll reach Willow Trail, a shortcut through a small black-willow forest that provides nesting habitat for the endangered least Bell's vireo. After the birds have raised

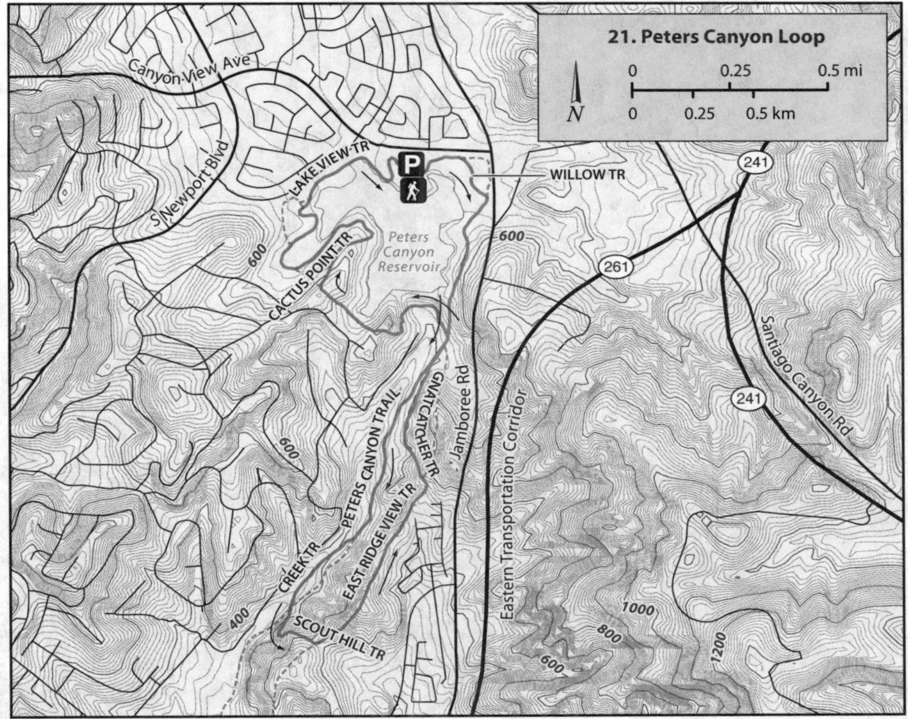


their young, they migrate to Mexico for the winter, allowing the trail to reopen during those months. Willow Trail, a fifth of a mile long, meets up with Lake View again; turn right. (If Willow Trail is closed, you just continue on Lake View Trail to the same point.) About 500 feet later, the trail reaches a pleasant vista point for looking out over the reservoir. A quarter-mile beyond, Lake View Trail veers off to the right; continue straight onto Peters Canyon Trail, the main road in the park. Along the way, meadows are dotted with lupine, bush sunflower, and California poppy.

Once part of a Spanish colonial rancho, Peters Canyon was a hangout of one of the last groups of wolves in Orange County. The land was sold to James Irvine in 1897, and then leased to several farmers. Among those was James Peters, who planted the eucalyptus trees that still forest the lower part of the canyon. Those and his name are the only remnants of that era. In 1899, part of this parcel of land was given over to a nine-hole golf course, the first in Orange County. And in the 1930s, Irvine built the dam that created the upper reservoir, inundating the golf course.

Perhaps the most interesting incarnation of Peters Canyon was its use as training grounds, called Camp Commander, during World War II. Soldiers fought in mock battles with those from an army post 2 miles away. In 1992, the Irvine Company donated the Peters Canyon land to be turned into a county park.

After 0.8 mile on Peters Canyon Trail, turn right onto Creek Trail, the park's most endearing path, leading you along the year-round creek fed by groundwater. Sheltered by eucalyptus and black

EUCALYPTUS FOREST

cottonwood trees, this riparian habitat has the atmosphere of a southern marsh. A boardwalk allows you to stay dry crossing the creek and the mucky parts of the trail. The half-mile path loops back to Peters Canyon. Turn right and about 100 feet later, you'll find the signed trailhead to Scout Hill Trail to the left.

Climb Scout Hill through the forest of graceful eucalyptus, something you don't see in most wilderness areas because the trees are an import from Australia. They have become a major part of the cultivated landscape of California.

The tree was introduced during the Gold Rush, when the crowds of newcomers arriving from more forested areas were dismayed by the practi-

cally treeless landscape of California sage scrub and chaparral. Tall, fast-growing eucalyptus—it could reach 40 feet within three years—was seen as the perfect answer, providing shade and beauty and, so the plans went, far more. In Australia, the trees were vital to construction, furniture-making, and shipbuilding. The railroad industry saw it as a promising wood to build railroad ties.

But the sapwood in the young of California couldn't match the q of the old-growth forests in Austra cracked and warped easily; the railr ties threw their tracks off. Many of th uses planned for the wood never came to fruition. But the eucalyptus made a formidable windbreak for farmers, and is still appreciated today for its scent and decorative elements.

Eucalyptus remains common in the Orange County landscape, but less so than it used to be. Windbreaks were cut down when agricultural fields gave way to development and various pests that attacked the trees killed off many of them and prompted cities to uproot others; they suck up large amounts of water and are called "gasoline trees" by firefighters because they can explode in a fire, and as a result are seldom planted any more.

The eucalyptus trees on Scout Hill Trail are smaller than their counterparts elsewhere, but they provide a quiet, forest-like environment. Scout Trail ends after a half-mile at East Ridge View Trail. Turn left to begin your return to the park entrance. The views are expansive here, though they largely take in big swaths of tract housing, but in springtime you're also passing hillsides thick with lupine and bush sunflower. At 0.8 mile, fork left onto Gnatcatcher Trail, which returns you to the main Peters Canyon Trail. Turn right here.

After a quarter of a mile, you have a choice. You could continue the way you came, up Peters Canyon Trail, or add a mile to your overall distance by turning left on Lake View Trail and walking the path around the lake back to the parking lot. It's a pretty trail with nonstop views of the reservoir and excellent birdwatching, especially if you detour off it to take Cactus Point spur loop to your right.

# Horseshoe Loop

**LOCATION**: Irvine Regional Park

**DISTANCE**: 2.2 miles (including a trip to the zoo)

**TYPE**: Loop

**TOTAL ELEVATION GAIN**: 100 feet

**DIFFICULTY**: Very easy

**SEASON**: December to June

**FEES ETC.**: $3 daily, $5 weekends. Leashed dogs allowed. Good for children. Many recreational facilities. Horse rentals available.

**MAPS**: USGS Orange, Black Star Canyon

**TRAILHEAD COORDINATES**: N 33°47.972′ W 117°45.309′

**CONTACT**: Irvine Regional Park (714-973-6835, www.ocparks.com/irvinepark)

In Irvine Regional Park, hiking tends to be what you fit in while visiting the park, rather than the hike being the point of the visit. Set in a bowl of Santiago Canyon among the foothills, this multi-use park, the oldest county park dating back to the late 19th century (when it was named Orange County Park), is laden with amenities, and its flat areas are covered with picnic areas, playgrounds, and playing fields. There's also a small boating lake, pony rides, a miniature railroad, and a tiny zoo that's most likely the only place you'll encounter a mountain lion in Orange County. But the groomed central area is ringed with a set of pleasant trails. This hike loops around the usually dry, rocky wash of Santiago Creek—if you want to see it flowing, come within a week or two of heavy rain—offering a surprisingly picturesque vista and ending with a walk through a dense oak-and-sycamore woodland as well as a side trip to the zoo.

In addition to its other amenities, Irvine Regional Park offers horse rentals on its backcountry trails. Call 714-538-5860 for details. With the sage scrub and the wide, rocky wash, these areas of the park have a particularly Old West ambience. You'll feel more a part of it on a gentle trail ride.

## GETTING THERE

Take the Jamboree Road exit from the Santa Ana Freeway (I-5) east for 5.6 miles until you reach Chapman Avenue/Santiago Canyon Road. Continue straight, staying in the right lane, for 0.4 mile. Jamboree Road turns into Irvine Park Road, veering left to the park entrance. After paying the fee, take the first left for 0.5 mile to Parking Lot 3 on your right.

One fun note about this area: If you didn't stay to the right on Jamboree, but

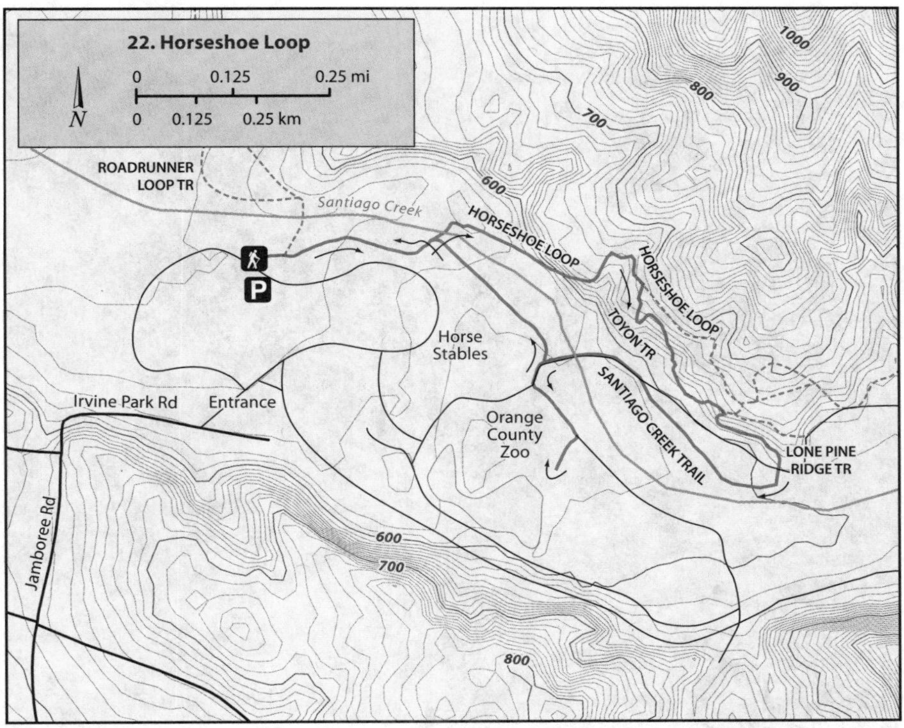


instead made a left onto Santiago Canyon Road, it would be worth noting the crosswalks. Immediately across from the park along this road is the horsy community of Orange Park Acres, whose riders make regular use of the regional park. The crosswalks have a low button for pedestrians and a high one marked with a horse symbol for equestrians.

## THE TRAIL

Cross the road from the parking area and immediately pick up the posted, gravel-and-dirt Santiago Creek Trail to the right. Within 100 feet, you'll reach a Y. Go left on the wider dirt trail. At 0.2 mile, just short of the equestrian center, turn left onto Horseshoe Loop Trail. The trail leads you across the rocky streambed of Santiago Creek. Climb the bank on the other side of the creek as the trail bends to the right.

You're hiking through an area of coastal sage scrub; California sagebrush is the dominant plant here. The plant was once known as "cowboy cologne" because cowboys who reached a town would rub themselves with the fragrant plant to erase the odors of the cattle drive. Not a true sage, it nonetheless smells like one.

Though you're just a few hundred feet from the developed part of the park, the rise to your right blocking the view below and the hills to your left give the trail a more countrified feel. What you probably will hear along this section are the raucous cries of peacocks; the park is full of the brilliantly colored, exotic birds, which seem to especially like hanging out near the stables.

A HORSE AND RIDER MAKE THEIR WAY UP HORSESHOE LOOP TRAIL

At 0.4 mile, the trail begins a short, rocky climb to an overlook point. You can look back at the creek and probably see a horse and rider slowly crossing the creek bed. Below you, horses might be training in the ring. Hills surround the park in every direction. The trail turns left here and then right again, bringing you at two-thirds of a mile to a clearing with a bench under a small shelter, another overlook point. From the shelter, take the narrow trail at the (non-functioning) water fountain back toward Horseshoe Loop. But at 30 feet, before you reach Horseshoe, make a right onto Toyon Trail. At first the single-track trail brings you down a rocky, rutted descent, then evens out. Follow the trail for a quarter-mile, then make a right onto Lone Pine Ridge Trail, which descends for 500 feet and ends at the park road.

Cross the road and almost immediately pick up the lightly trodden Santiago Creek Trail through a grassy, wooded area. The trail will cross a smaller, paved loop road at 0.1 mile, and continue on the other side. Here, on the grassy, single-track trail, you enter a dense, cool woodland of sycamore and old oak trees, with the creek to your left.

At 1.4 miles, you reach another paved road. Turn left here, crossing the creek bed.

You could immediately turn right onto a paved bike trail to return to your car, between the creek on the right and the equestrian center to the left. The paved trail will curve around to the left and brings you back to the junction of Santiago Creek Trail and Harding Loop Trail. Make a shallow right onto Santiago Creek Trail to return to the parking lot.

Or, after crossing the creek, you might want to make a left on that bike trail for a short visit to the Orange County Zoo, a good place to learn more about native fauna. You'll walk for 350 feet around the back of the zoo to your right, then turn right onto a short, marked path that brings you to Parking Lot 10 and the zoo entrance. The animals here are local (with a few exceptions) wildlife that have been injured or for some other reason cannot be returned to the wild. For a while, the zoo housed Samson, a black bear from the San Gabriel Mountains that had gotten so comfortable with civilization that he was swiping avocados and taking regular dips in the hot tub at a Monrovia house. Samson died in 2001, but has been replaced. Also here are a mountain lion, a golden eagle, bald eagle, mule deer, coyote, and bobcat.

After visiting the animals, return the way you came back to the creek crossing and then follow the instructions above to your car.

Courtesy of First American Corp. Historical Library

EARLY VISITORS TO IRVINE REGIONAL PARK, THEN ORANGE COUNTY PARK

# The Hanging Tree

**LOCATION**: Irvine Ranch Natural Landmarks

**TOTAL DISTANCE**: 6 miles

**TYPE**: Out and back

**TOTAL ELEVATION GAIN**: 1,400 feet

**DIFFICULTY**: Moderately strenuous

**SEASON**: Year-round

**FEES ETC.**: Free. Closed access; all hikes are docent led.

**MAPS**: USGS El Toro (quad to be renamed Lake Forest), Black Star Canyon

**CONTACT**: Irvine Ranch Conservancy (714-508-4757, www.irlandmarks.org)

Just off Santiago Canyon Road, near the entrance to Modjeska Canyon, lies Hangman's Tree Canyon, its name commemorating the lynching of two followers of the storied bandit Juan Flores in the 1850s. One problem: To the best of historians' knowledge, no one was ever hanged here. It's unknown how the name came about—maybe because Modjeska Canyon is where Flores escaped lawmen with such a daring move that a peak in the canyon is named for him.

When it comes to stories about Juan Flores, sorting truth from the decades of embellishment can be a tricky matter. But this much is true: There is a hanging tree, and it exists a few miles west of the place that carries its name. Another truth: It's a rare wildfire that doesn't bring some interesting find to light amid the destruction. Wildfires reveal hidden archaeological sites, for example, and in the case of the Santiago Fire of 2007, the burning of an area off the Foothill Transportation Corridor revealed a forgotten plaque commemorating the (believed) real hanging tree. As a result, the Irvine Ranch Conservancy offers docent-led hikes to the tree.

## GETTING THERE

Driving directions will be sent after you sign up for a hike.

## THE TRAIL

Following the usual route chosen by docents, this is a somewhat strenuous hike of about 6 miles with two fairly steep climbs, but one with attractions beyond a close-up view of this particularly gruesome piece of Orange County history. The hikes generally meet in the Orchard Hills area, where the con-

THE LIMB USED (SUPPOSEDLY) TO LYNCH MEMBERS OF JUAN FLORES'S GANG

servancy recently started leading hikes themed to the area's agricultural history. The trail meanders around a still-working avocado orchard (they're actually called ranches), then climbs to Loma Ridge in the foothills, a spot with a sweeping perspective of most of the county and beyond. Down the other side of the ridge, it leads to the tree and a plaque that marks it, placed there in the 1960s by a group of horsemen who annually rode through the county's backcountry. Warning: On this out-and-back hike, you'll have to climb the ridge again before descending to the farmland below.

Loma Ridge, part of the Puente formation, was formed under the surface of the water some 5 to 23 million years ago. It's rich with marine fossils, but when the toll road was being built and cut through the ridge, paleontologists found the remains of a mastodon-like animal that lived 10 to 12 million years ago. They believe the mastodon must have been washed out to sea after its death.

The Hanging Tree hike is as much about the story as it is about the walk.

Perhaps the best place to start is with 21-year-old Juan Flores's escape from San Quentin Prison, where he was serv-

MARKER FOR THE HANGING TREE

ing time for horse theft. There are two stories about Flores's origins: One says that he was the son of a San Jose family of humble means; another version of the story describes him as the scion of an affluent Santa Barbara family.

Flores made his way south to Orange County (then part of Los Angeles County), where he became the leader of a gang of Mexican bandits who called themselves Las Manillas (the handcuffs). Some versions of the legend describe Flores and his gang as Mexican resisters of U.S. rule in Alta California, or at least as men who sought to portray themselves that way; others paint him as a violent thug and horse thief, albiet an inventive one. It is said that some of his men used Dripping Cave, now in Aliso and Wood Canyons Wilderness Park (see chapter on the Wood Canyon loop hike), as a hideout.

But it was a more urban crime that set off the undoing of the gang—the ransacking of three stores in San Juan Capistrano and the killing of a shop owner. Sheriff James Barton and several deputies rode down to what is now Orange County when word first came that Flores had been seen in town.

Barton and his men stopped for breakfast at the rancho of Don Jose Sepulveda in south Santa Ana, leaving their weapons in an outbuilding. Sepulveda warned the men against continuing their quest, since they were badly outnumbered by the 25 or so men in Flores's gang. Another, more apocryphal, telling adds the story of a comely young woman, an ally of Flores's, who was at the rancho at the time, and who might (or might not) have tampered with the lawmen's weapons. More historical accounts say that's impossible because she had been in San Juan Capistrano during the ransackings.

The sheriff ignored Sepulveda's warning. He and his men were ambushed in an area not far from where today's Irvine Spectrum shopping center is located. Barton and three of his men were killed, but two managed to ride back to Los Angeles.

Enraged, Gen. Andres Pico—brother of Pio Pico, the last Mexican governor of California—rode out with a far bigger posse, more than 100 men, and caught up with the gang in Modjeska Canyon. Flores and several of his men rode up to what is now Flores Peak, located in Tucker Wildlife Sanctuary, but were cut off from escape by the cliff. Flores and two of his followers made a daring escape attempt by riding (or sliding) down the 200-foot cliff. The other men were captured, and after a couple of days, so were the three who had gotten away. Locked up overnight, they managed to get themselves untied and escaped again.

When he heard about the escape, Pico, who was traveling with the two men who remained in captivity, reportedly said, "Here's two who won't get away," and ordered them hanged on the spot, from the stout branc[illegible] sycamore.

Today, that ancient sycamore is among several lining a narrow, seasonal creek bed. The branch from which the men were hanged is nearly a foot in diameter, growing almost horizontally from the trunk, and it's easy to imagine that you can make out the vertical lines of the ropes that were tied around it. But it's hard to picture anything much bigger than a rodent being hanged from the limb these days. Whether from the spreading of the branches over time—common with sycamores—or the buildup of the bank it overhangs or both, the branch stretches only a few feet above the ground.

Flores himself was arrested some days later; he was hanged on St. Valentine's Day of 1857 at the site of what is now the towering headquarters of the Los Angeles Unified School District.

One continuing legend says that Flores buried some of his loot on the peak that now bears his name. Local kids still go up there occasionally to look for the (almost certainly mythical) treasure.

# Limestone Canyon

**LOCATION**: Irvine Ranch Natural Landmarks

**TOTAL DISTANCE**: 6 to 8 miles to the Sinks round-trip, depending on the docent-led tour; 6 miles to Box Spring round-trip; 5 miles to Dripping Springs round-trip

**TYPE**: Out and back

**TOTAL ELEVATION GAIN**: 400 to 800 feet

**DIFFICULTY**: Moderate

**SEASON**: November to June

**FEES ETC.**: Free. Closed access, hikes are docent led. Occasional Wilderness Access Days when the public can explore without a docent.

**MAPS**: USGS El Toro (quad to be renamed Lake Forest)

**CONTACT**: Irvine Ranch Conservancy (714-508-4757, www.irlandmarks.org)

One of the most visually "oh-wow" spots in Orange County is the Sinks, on land managed by the Irvine Ranch Conservancy and accessible only via docent-led spots. Also called the "Miniature Grand Canyon of Orange County"—a bit of hyperbole, perhaps—the Sinks is a steep gorge formed by a landslide within the past million years. Impressive at any time, it's particularly dramatic by moonlight, and the conservancy conducts regular night outings there.

Many of the docent-led hikes continue around the other side of the Sinks for an even more striking view, past a *mortero*, or bedrock mortar used by Native Americans hundreds of years ago to process acorn meat into meal, and on to Box Spring, a rare year-round water source under shady oaks.

A third hike leads to Dripping Springs, a fern-covered grotto. Even on the hottest days, hikers suddenly feel markedly cooled when they come within range of the springs.

To sign up for hikes, go to the website www.irlandmarks.org, click on "Limestone Canyon Wilderness Area" on the map of Orange County, and look for the events that interest you. Click on "Online Sign Up," which will create a registration form.

## GETTING THERE

You will be given directions to a locked parking area along Santiago Canyon Road that is opened for the docent-led hikes.

## THE TRAIL

Although the Irvine Company deeded this and most of its other open-land reserves to Orange County—which

THE SINKS

instantly increased the county's parkland by 50 percent—those lands continue to be managed by the Irvine Ranch Conservancy. That means they will continue to be accessible only via docent-led hikes with occasional public-access days where you can wander the land yourself.

Most Limestone Canyon hikes begin at an old cattle camp along Santiago Canyon Road. Shortly before you reach it, look for an overhang across the road; this is an interesting spot to explore on its own, after your hike. From the cattle camp, most hikes lead through an oak-dotted meadow. On some of the hikes you can see fossil imprints embedded in the rocks. These are from the Vaqueros Formation some 20 million years ago. At the top of the spur, you'll turn right along a ridgeline trail for a good view of the Sinks.

The gorge, carved by a landslide that was caused either by a major storm or fault movement, is part of the Sespe/Vaqueros Formation; the hills behind the Sinks are part of the Puente Formation. The Sespe was formed during the Cenozoic Era, some 20 to 40 million years ago, during a time of lowered sea levels worldwide. The climate was changing from humid to dry.

This geological history is told in the walls of the Sinks. The bottom, whitish rock was laid down during a humid era. Above that is a reddish layer—the color caused by the presence of oxidized iron—that was deposited during more arid times.

On the longer trips, you'll be led around to the other side of the Sinks and through coastal sage scrub and serene oak-studded meadows. Along the way, the docent will surely point out the *mortero*, or bedrock mortar, used by early Native Americans, just a few feet off the trail. You'll turn in at a dense oak woodland just before arriving at Box Spring. This was a favorite area of the Tongva Indians who once inhabited this land. Not only was it a certain source of water year-round, but it drew deer and other animals looking for a drink, making for easy and predictable hunting. Chances are you'll see deer tracks and other animal imprints on your visit, as well as water-loving plants such as cattails and bulrush.

The spring was recently renamed; it used to be called Bolero Spring and there's an amusing story about how it got that designation. For years it was called Aguaje de Chinon, or Curly's Spring, after a ringlet-haired hermit who built an adobe there.

From the 1830s to 1860s, it was common for vaqueros (cowboys of the era) to engage in a cruel sport: They would capture a bear to fight a bull in a corral. During the 1840s, Don Jose Sepulveda, who was planning a fiesta at his Santa Ana rancho, wanted to stage one of these spectacles as entertainment for his guests.

DRIPPING SPRINGS

Usually, bear trapping was done on the land that's now covered by Irvine Lake. On this occasion, though, several men rode into Limestone Canyon. They would set out the carcass of an animal and wait for the bear to seek its meal. Lassoing the animal from their horses, they would keep it from attacking by keeping the ropes taut from different directions.

On this particular ride into the canyon, the story goes, a vaquero nicknamed Bolero (or one who bluffs) who was known as a fine rider with a beautiful but high-strung horse, boasted about the exploits he would accomplish if he encountered a bear. When he arrived at the spring, he found a large grizzly already there. The bear reared up and growled, and Bolero's horse bolted in fear. It was left to the other men to capture the bear because Bolero had to chase after his horse. He was such a target of joking afterward that the spring was named after him.

About that overpass bridge across Santiago Canyon Road that you saw on your way to the hike: It was constructed in 1996 so that a company hauling materials from a dredging project could cross the busy road safely with its lumbering trucks. The agreement was that the bridge would be demolished once the project was over. But in the strange ways of nature, the dark recesses on the underside of the bridge became the favored home and breeding grounds of hundreds of Mexican free-tailed bats—up to 1,500 of them. In a county that has been losing bat habitat and population, the 4-inch-long mammals had adopted an accidental home.

The intervention of a county supervisor in 2005 saved the bridge. On your drive down, look for a safe place to pull completely off Santiago Canyon Road near the bridge and take a look underneath. You'll see guano on the street. If you shine a flashlight into the recesses of the bridge, chances are you'll see the roosting bats as well. Be careful here; it's a narrow road with fast-moving traffic.

In the mid-1800s, Limestone Canyon was known as Cañon Aguaje de Chinon, or the Canyon of Curly's Spring. The canyon's name was changed after Sam Shrewsbury settled there in the early 1860s and established a lime kiln that would never prove very successful. Limestone rocks were heated until they swelled and broke open. The resulting product was called quicklime, which was pulverized and mixed with sand for use as mortar.

We're not the first creatures to experience climate change. The lime that gives Limestone Canyon its name comes from the shells of mollusks dating back 54 to 65 million years ago, during one of the most intense global warming events in the planet's past.

Shrewsbury also brought in domesticated bees; beekeeping operations would become one of the main early industries of the Santa Ana Mountains.

Another favorite Limestone Canyon hike, Dripping Springs begins at the same cattle camp, but then turns in a different direction. You'll climb past rock outcrops that are favored nesting spots for raptors, including red-shouldered hawks and American kestrels. During the last ascent toward Dripping Springs, look up and to the left for Elephant Peak, so named because it resembles the head of an elephant, with the ridgeline below it forming the "trunk."

Watch out for poison oak that grows over the narrow path just before the grotto. You might see stream orchids here and scarlet monkeyflower. Maidenhair fern and moss cloak the seep wall. Water comes directly out of the cliff face; the source is rainwater that accumulates in a fault, then is trapped by an impermeable layer, forcing it to seep out in this location. A large rusty pipe protrudes from the ground; believed to be at least 100 years old, it was used by ranchers to pump drinking water for the cattle.

EARLY DEPICTION OF BEAR ROPING IN ORANGE COUNTY

# Coyote Canyon Loop

**LOCATION**: O'Neill Regional Park

**TOTAL DISTANCE**: 4.5 miles

**TYPE**: Loop

**TOTAL ELEVATION GAIN**: 600 feet

**DIFFICULTY**: Moderate

**SEASON**: November to June

**FEES ETC.**: $3 parking fee. Leashed dogs allowed on some trails. Camping facilities available.

**MAPS**: USGS Santiago Peak

**TRAILHEAD COORDINATES**: N 33°39.168′ W 117°36.042′

**CONTACT**: O'Neill Regional Park (949-923-2260, www.ocparks.com/oneillpark)

Rising from the flat camping area of 3,100-acre O'Neill Park, named for the family that owned the once-vast O'Neill Ranch, this trail takes you through many of the park's lovelier and quieter spots to its vista knoll, with a 360-degree view that extends across the county to a peek of the ocean on the clearest days. It's a much-visited hiking destination that can be reached from several different trails; the usual route is Live Oak Trail. But I find this hike, using the seldom-traveled Coyote Canyon Trail, far more scenic and pleasant, with its varied topography from climbing to level walking, and its changing landscapes. Practically until it reaches the knoll, this route stays on the Live Oak Canyon side of the hills, where the views of undeveloped land go on for miles. It also provides delightful stretches of splendid oak woodland.

## GETTING THERE

From South County: Exit the San Diego Freeway (I-5) at El Toro Road and head east for 8.6 miles. Turn right at Cook's Corner, location of the noted motorcycle bar, onto Live Oak Canyon Road. It's a beautiful drive through sparsely developed land until old oaks on both sides of the road form a canopy over your car. Live Oak Canyon Road turns into Trabuco Canyon Road; travel a total of 4.2 miles to the entrance of the park on the right.

From North County: Take the Chapman Avenue exit from the Costa Mesa Freeway (CA 55), heading east for 15.4 miles and making a left onto Live Oak Canyon Road at Cook's Corner, location of the noted motorcycle bar. Proceed as above.

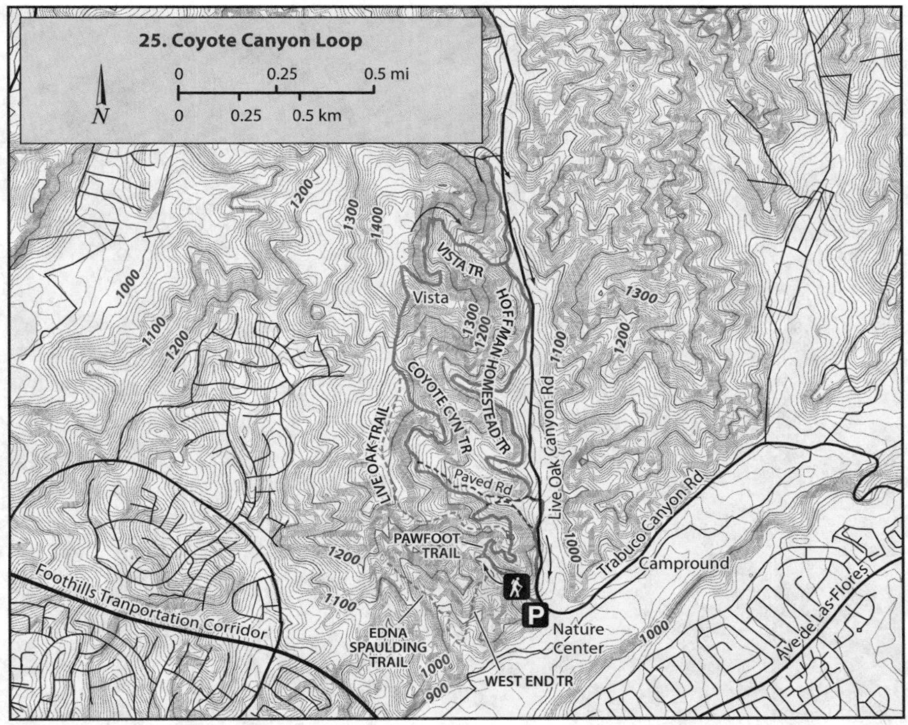


## THE TRAIL

After entering the park, bear shallow right into the day-use area and park in the first lot to your left.

Cross the road to enter the Eagle Grove day-use area and walk up the paved service road 500 feet to the Pawfoot Trailhead. You'll be walking in a wooded area of mostly oak. After you've walked 0.2 mile, you'll cross a paved service road to continue the trail.

After a third of a mile, make a sharp right onto Live Oak Trail. About 150 feet later, pick up Homestead Trail to the right.

You'll climb out of the woodland area into a landscape of thick coastal sage scrub, with plentiful sagebrush, monkeyflower, and in the fall, big stands of goldenbush. By the time you've hiked a half-mile, you already can catch hill and mountain vistas to the east and north. The trail meanders for the next third of a mile, in and out of wooded areas, sometimes climbing, sometimes level, or even going back downhill.

But then you'll make a left onto Coyote Canyon Trail and begin a somewhat steeper ascent. After a fifth of a mile, the trail turns left, continuing uphill another half-mile into an area where, depending on the season, the black mustard might be taller than you are. You'll intersect Live Oak Trail again, a hairpin turn to the left, but you'll continue straight and veer to the right, toward a water tank and a microwave tower.

After a third of a mile, turn right on the small path that brings you up to the knoll for a 360-degree view. To the west, the tract homes look as though they

OAK GALL

are climbing up the hills from Saddleback Valley to join you on the ridge. It's enough to make you all the more grateful for the view to the east and north, of largely open hills and mountains, overlapping in layers to the horizon.

From the knoll you can take the Vista Trail downhill, which is just a short distance farther along the ridge from the lookout point. This is a steep hill that switchbacks make easier to descend. You'll pass numerous stands of prickly pear. On some of them you'll see grayish-white material, the sign of cochineal, used for centuries to make red and purple dyes and even now used for food colorings. (See the chapter on Wood Canyon Loop for more on cochineal.)

After about a third of a mile, you reach the shade of thick stands of oak again. The trail ends at an old dirt service road. Here you have the option of turning left for a quarter of a mile until you reach private property and back. It's a serene walk under the gnarled oaks that gave the canyon its name and near a seasonal stream. Or you can turn right to head back toward your trailhead. The dirt road gives way to a paved road with picnic tables and other visitor amenities along both sides. But you'll veer right to catch the marked beginning of the Hoffman Homestead Trail, which weaves in and out of the oak woodland and is a particularly good trail for finding oak galls among the many scrub oaks—chaparral that look similar to coast live oaks but with their tough, serrated-edge leaves curved like inverted cups and fatter acorns.

The galls, which are round, hard growths, are tissue of the oak that swells in reaction to enzymes released when the gall wasp lays its eggs. The newer galls look like small apples, with a rosy blush; with time, they turn brown. The gall forms a protec wasp larvae, growing to and a half in diameter.

Oak galls enable the para to reproduce, but ground up, t had their uses for humans. Some N American groups made an infusio treat cuts. Processed with other ingr dients, the gall also makes an ink that was used until the mid-19th century. Both the Declaration of Independence and the U.S. Constitution were reportedly drafted with gall ink.

When Hoffman Homestead Trail intersects a paved road, head left down that road just about 100 feet to the paved service road. Turn right and continue down the service road, enjoying the cool canopy of oaks overhead, until you return to the Pawfoot Trailhead (the end of the road) and your car.

PRICKLY PEAR BLOSSOM

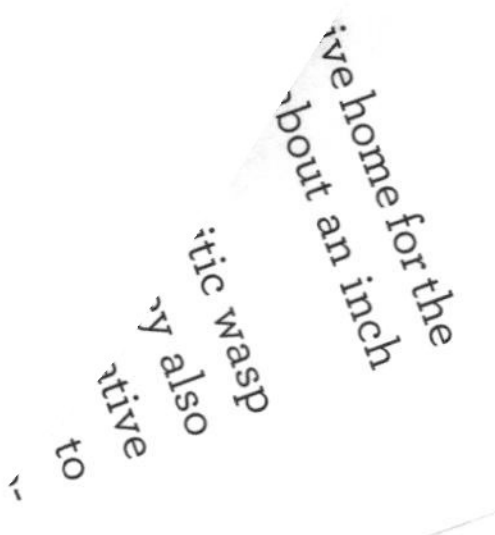

# rabuco

**LOCATION**: O'Neill Regional Park

**TOTAL DISTANCE**: 6.4 miles

**TYPE**: Out and back (or 3.2-mile shuttle)

**TOTAL ELEVATION GAIN**: 200 feet

**DIFFICULTY**: Moderately easy

**SEASON**: November to June

**FEES ETC.**: Free. Leashed dogs allowed.

**MAPS**: USGS Santiago Peak, Cañada Gobernadora, San Juan Capistrano, O'Neill Regional Park county map

**TRAILHEAD COORDINATES**: N 33°36.945′ W 117°37.336′

**CONTACT**: O'Neill Regional Park (949-923-2260, www.ocparks.com/oneillpark)

What a difference a lost blunderbuss makes. In late July 1769, Gaspar de Portola and his men, on the first Spanish overland expedition through Alta California, camped on the bluff above an arroyo, or seasonal creek bed, in what is now the city of Rancho Santa Margarita. There, one soldier lost his *trabuco*, or musket, any soldier's most valuable possession at the time—obviously so, because of how the word *trabuco* caught on. South Orange County has Trabuco Canyon, Trabuco Creek, more than one street named Trabuco, the Trabuco Ranger Station in Cleveland National Forest—and Arroyo Trabuco, where Portola was camping when the soldier had his unlucky experience. This hike will take you to their campground.

The more recent story of Arroyo Trabuco is more heartening—or at least half-heartening. The arroyo, a 6-mile finger that juts from the main section of O'Neill Regional Park, was crossed by two giant arterials that loom overhead—the Foothill (241) Toll Road and Santa Margarita Parkway, all part of the master-planned community of Rancho Santa Margarita. As mitigation for this construction, thousands of oak and willow trees were planted in the arroyo. Splendid sycamores spread majestically throughout.

As a result, Arroyo Trabuco stands out as an example of suburban nature planning done right, with stretches of sheltered, wooded retreat from surrounding suburban encroachment.

## GETTING THERE

Exit at Oso Parkway off the San Diego Freeway (I-5) in Mission Viejo. Turn east on Oso Parkway and drive 2.7 miles to Antonio Parkway. Turn left on Antonio, 2.8 miles to Avenida de las Ban-

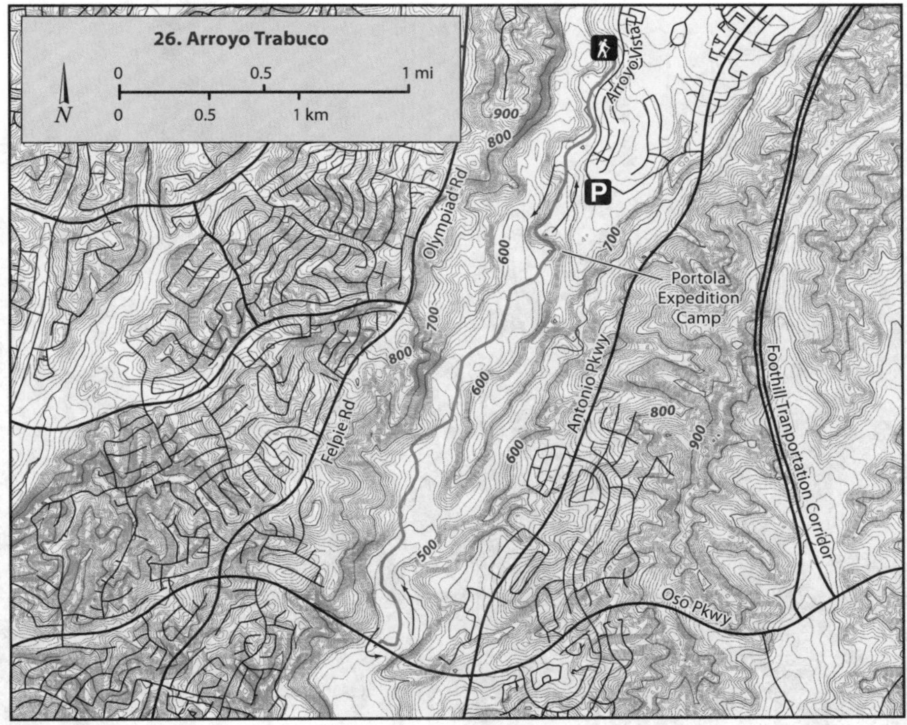


deras. Turn left on Banderas for 0.3 mile to Arroyo Vista. Turn left on Arroyo Vista, driving 0.6 mile to Paraiso. There is plentiful street parking on Arroyo Vista at the trailhead.

## THE TRAIL

The roar of cars on the new roads over parts of the arroyo doesn't make for an unspoiled nature jaunt, and sections of the more than 6-mile-long arroyo are less than charming. So this hike bypasses the more problematic parts, beginning nearly 3 miles from the main entrance of O'Neill Regional Park and traversing the more atmospheric woodland and riparian areas, with multiple creek crossings. Depending on how rainy the winter has been and when you hike, you might end up wading some lengths of the creek. Hike this in the spring, from early March through June, to enjoy the stream washing over its rocky bed. Hiking sandals or river sandals are a good choice for this outing because your feet will definitely get wet. If you want a shorter hike, do this as a shuttle to Oso Parkway, leaving one car in the neighborhood off San Rafael Drive a quarter-mile west of the arroyo.

The trailhead along Arroyo Vista is right across from Paraiso and clearly marked. Head left on the dirt and gravel trail through a meadow area; you'll see the creek bed below you to the right. After three-fourths of a mile, a plaque on a low stone mound to the left and a shed-like wood structure mark the fateful spot where Portola and his men camped on July 24 and 25, 1769. A gun was later found, reportedly in the Trabuco Can-

ARROYO TRABUCO

Courtesy of the Orange County Archives

EARLY PHOTOGRAPH OF THE TRABUCO ADOBE

yon area; it is on exhibition at Bowers Museum, labeled as being circa 1760, but no one knows if it's the lost trabuco.

The wooden shed at this spot shelters the ruins of the Trabuco Adobe, built in 1810 as an outpost of Mission San Juan Capistrano. In 1818, the adobe was used by the padres and Indians to hide the mission's valuables when a boatload of pirates arrived from Buenos Aires. Later, it served as the headquarters of Rancho Trabuco.

Across from this, a rock-strewn trail leads down toward the creek; soon after, you will come to the first of numerous creek crossings, heading down-creek. Here and at other crossings, it's fun to search for newts and tree frogs that inhabit the arroyo. Juvenile steelhead also have been found in recent years.

At times the trail will lead uphill into yellow-flowered thickets of black mustard, but most of the next 2.5 miles will take you through forested meadows and riparian areas. Especially dramatic are the many spreading sycamore trees. In spring, their large, pale-green leaves gently filter sunlight; in fall, the leaves turn an autumnal gold. In either season, look for clusters of dark-green leaves high up in the sycamores. This is mistletoe, a semi-parasite. Though the leaves of the plant photosynthesize, the mistletoe lacks roots; it embeds strands in the sycamore's branches and sucks water and nutrients from the tree.

Giant reed, or *Arundo donax*, grows liberally in patches along the creek. Despite eradication efforts in the arroyo, this invasive plant from Europe is a persistent pest. In most streambeds, giant reed grows in tall, straight clusters, its stems looking similar to bamboo. This is the same plant used for the reeds in oboes, but it was first brought to this country in the 1890s as a windbreak. Some people make them into walking sticks—despite their hollow middles, they're stiff and fairly strong—which seems to be their only useful role in southern California.

Under the wooded canopy of the arroyo, the reeds bend over, forming archways over the trail and cave-like shelters along the way. After 3.2 miles of walking, the Oso Parkway overpass bridges the arroyo overhead. You can turn around here and head back to the car (or walk up to your car off Oso Parkway if doing this as a shuttle).

# Red Rock Canyon

**LOCATION**: Limestone Canyon and Whiting Ranch Wilderness Park

**TOTAL DISTANCE**: 4.4 miles

**TYPE**: Out and back

**TOTAL ELEVATION GAIN**: 500 feet

**DIFFICULTY**: Moderately easy

**SEASON**: Year-round

**FEES ETC.**: $3 parking fee daily, $5 weekends. No dogs.

**MAPS**: USGS El Toro (quad to be renamed Lake Forest), Limestone-Whiting park map

**TRAIL COORDINATES**: N 33°40.904′ W 117°39.870′

**CONTACT**: Limestone-Whiting Ranch Park (949-923-2245, www.ocparks.com/whitingranch)

For a tiny bit of New Mexico in Orange County, take this undemanding and picturesque trail. Imposing red-rock crags eroded by wind and water into dramatic formations and framed against a blue, blue sky are the goal of this hike through one of the newer county parks. But to paraphrase Ralph Waldo Emerson, hiking is a journey, not a destination. On the way to and from the red rocks, you'll pass through welcoming woodland, see oak trees that have managed to push their roots into vertical sheets of rock, and cross numerous creeks. The 500-foot elevation gain is so gradual that you'll barely realize you're ascending most of the way.

Easily accessible—the trailhead is right next to a shopping center—Limestone Canyon and Whiting Ranch Wilderness Park encompasses close to 5,000 acres, although half of those—the Limestone Canyon land—is still off limits to the public except through docent-led hikes.

This hike is Whiting Ranch's classic. The shade and creeks that remain at least a little damp through most of the year make it a convenient escape at any time of year.

## GETTING THERE

Take the El Toro Road exit from the San Diego Freeway (I-5), heading east toward the mountains. Drive for 4.5 miles to the light at Portola Parkway; turn left. At 1.8 miles, just after passing one of the numerous shopping centers along the way, turn right at Market Street, then make an immediate left into the small parking lot. The trailhead is at the end of the parking lot, where there's a round patio with a towering metal sculpture; you can pick up a county trail map here.

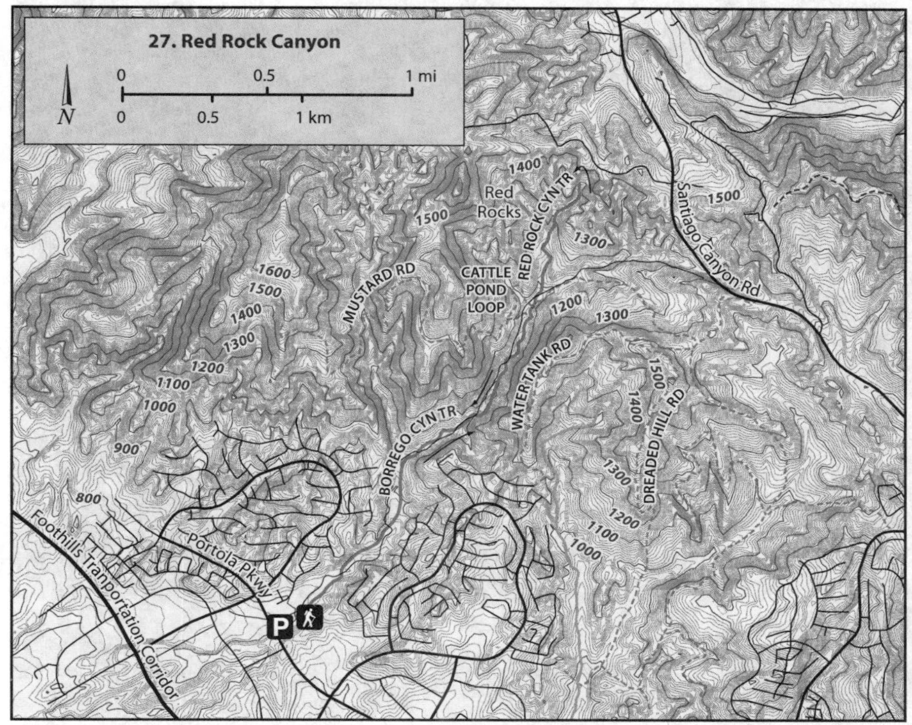


## THE TRAIL

You'll start out on Borrego Trail, and looking at it on the park map, you'll be tempted to groan. For close to a mile, the trail follows a thin finger of open space squeezed between residential neighborhoods. Prepare to be pleasantly surprised. From the moment you descend from the patio area that marks the beginning of the trail, you're immediately steeped in oak woodland thick enough to soften, if not always mask, the houses on the ridgelines above.

Despite the suburban surroundings, be aware that this is mountain lion country. In 2004, one biker was killed and another severely injured by a cougar. There have been several sightings in the Foothill Ranch area, though not all of them have been confirmed.

Flowers always seem to get an earlier-than-usual start here. Even in December, I've seen plentiful wild cucumber—at this stage, profusions of small white flowers on a climbing vine—morning glory, white nightshade, fuchsia-flowered gooseberry, and the lavender of canyon pea. There are a couple of large patches of white-flowered currant—deeply veined leaves on stems growing about 5 feet high, with clusters of delicate white blossoms. Hikers and bikers share the trail amiably; in fact, I sometimes suspect that the cyclists here have attended an "Etiquette on Wheels" class. Instead of the usual "On your left!" warning, they sing out, "Good morning!" to alert you to their presence and then ask after your well-being as they pedal by. Borrego Trail is one-way for bikers; they can ride into the park,

BIKERS IN THE OAK WOODLAND

but have to walk their bikes back. Most choose instead to ride a loop over to another area of the park and return on Portola Parkway.

The 2007 Santiago Fire burned most of the park, but although you'll see blackened or singed trees, the canyon is filled with a variety of robust flora. Most of the oak trees and laurel sumac are sprouting with abundant new leaves. The stream that weaves its way to both sides along your path waters thickets of blackberry and wild rose.

At a quarter-mile, you'll cross a small bridge. There are numerous creek crossings, though, so wear appropriate footgear—or just prepare to get a little wet during the winter and spring. At 0.6 mile, you reach a crossing thick with watercress and cattails. The trail gets more wild looking after 0.8 mile as you begin to leave the houses behind.

At 1 mile, you go through an area where a sheer rock wall rises from the other side of the creek bed. At the top of this wall, you'll see at least one hardy

RED ROCK CLIFFS

oak tree that has managed to wedge its roots in and around the rock to grab a precarious perch for itself.

Borrego Trail ends at 1.6 miles; turn right on Mustard Trail. Some 500 feet along this trail, you reach small Cattle Pond Loop, a reminder of this land's ranching past. And just 25 feet past Cattle Pond, turn left onto hikers-only Red Rock Canyon Trail.

You begin to climb into a sunnier area with a combination of sage scrub and riparian vegetation. Suddenly and dramatically, the red cliffs appear before you, about a half-mile ahead. At times you'll cross the ephemeral stream; other times, you'll walk in it to trace the route that continues somewhat more steeply uphill. Prickly pear cactus and yucca replace the trees on the hillsides.

The banks on either side of you begin to show red color from iron, a harbinger of the rocks that are still in your view. At 2 miles, the trail grows steeper as the canyon narrows into a gorge and you begin to hike close to the smaller outcroppings of red rock, eroded by water into a badlands formation. It's just another 500 feet before you come face-to-face with the more spectacular crags. The drier, barer terrain here could have you believing—if you look only in certain directions—that you're in Sedona.

The sandstone red rocks are part of the Sespe Formation, the same as the dramatic Sinks gorge just a few miles away on the Irvine Ranch Land Reserve. (See the Limestone Canyon chapter.) The silt, sand, and conglomerate that make up the formation were deposited in layers during a period in which the sea level dropped worldwide, some 48 to 28 million years ago. In some areas of the rock, you can see white sandstone at the bottom before the iron-rich red sandstone begins. The layering is easy to discern throughout the rock, but especially in the lines of small, rounded cobbles embedded in the outcropping.

The trail ends at 2.2 miles in a sheltered area among the cliffs.

# Starr Ranch Sanctuary

**LOCATION**: Dove Canyon

**TOTAL DISTANCE**: 1 to 3 miles

**TYPE**: Out and back, loop

**TOTAL ELEVATION GAIN:** 600 to 800 feet

**DIFFICULTY**: Moderately easy, good for children

**SEASON**: November to June

**FEES**: Varied donations requested. Family days are free.

**MAPS**: Cañada Gobernadora

**CONTACT**: Starr Ranch Sanctuary (949-858-0309, www.starrranch.org)

Tucked in a handsome canyon, accessible only via a gated community, private Starr Ranch Sanctuary toils away at impressive environmental research and education with only a handful of Orange County residents knowing it exists and even fewer knowing that the public can gain limited access to hike and participate in ecology programs there. You can join pre-planned adult camps to learn about and participate in field research; put together a field trip for schoolchildren; sign up for its twice-yearly Family Nature Days; or assemble your own group and arrange for a guided hike.

## GETTING THERE

The sanctuary, behind the gates of suburban Dove Canyon, shares Bell Canyon with Caspers Wilderness Park. It also is adjacent to Cleveland National Forest. You will be given directions and permission to enter through the Dove Canyon gate after you arrange your visit.

## THE TRAIL

Bell Canyon is named for a six-ton rock that had the extraordinary quality of ringing out when struck with another rock, in a musical tone that resonated against the canyon walls. This bell-like ring reportedly could be heard from as much as a mile away. Pre-mission Acjachemen Indians used Bell Rock for religious ceremonies. But after spending thousands of years in the same place, the rock became a target for treasure hunters who dug around it in the first half of the 20th century (the rock rang only faintly after that), and a homesteader arranged to have it moved in 1936 to Bowers Museum in Santa Ana, where it is today. If you go to see it, take

AN OLD RANCH BUILDING SERVES AS THE SANCTUARY'S FIELD LABORATORY

note of the little indentations in the surface—those were hammered into the rock as part of fertility ceremonies for young Native American women. Also at the Bowers is the Maze Stone from Starr Ranch, a boulder bearing a mysterious, labyrinthine petroglyph.

During the ranching days of the region, part of the sanctuary land was owned by Josiah C. Joplin, who planted an olive grove in the 1870s that you can still see as you drive into the sanctuary.

The sanctuary's name comes from the family who bought it in two parcels during the late 1930s and early 1940s. Eugene Starr was a wealthy oil man and avid hunter who purchased close to 9,000 acres through the Bell Canyon area. There he built a hunting lodge as well as an icehouse, cowboy quarters, and other work buildings, many of which are still on the ranch today. He also planted citrus and other trees that are still in the large meadow at the center of the ranch. The Starr family left the ranch to a foundation to carry out charitable and educational activities. In 1973, the foundation donated close to 4,000 acres to the National Audubon Society to create the sanctuary, which remains under the society's auspices. The southern part of the ranch was sold to the county, creating Caspers Wilderness Park.

Today, the sanctuary offers a range of sights and experiences. You drive past old orchards, through beautiful natural areas touched throughout by picturesque Bell Creek. The old ranch houses have been kept up; one is used as a laboratory, another to house the directors of the sanctuary, and a third for the interns who come there to work.

The ranch is one of the best places to see California bunch grasses, especially purple needlegrass, which used to cover the county's open meadows but now are rare. Years of ranching, when annual grasses like oat were introduced, have wiped out much of the perennial native grass.

THE NATIVE GRASSLAND OF STARR RANCH SANCTUARY

The shorter of the ranch's two main hiking trails shows off one of its interesting experiments with eliminating invasive plants. The 1-mile Lookout Trail makes a quick 600-foot ascent to a high meadow with views back to Bell Canyon and across to Cleveland National Forest. Beautiful though the vistas are, one of the most interesting points along the trail involves two adjacent patches of land. One patch is filled with aggressive artichoke thistle, which has taken over entire hillsides in some areas of the county; the adjacent patch is filled with native purple needlegrass. The ranch has been experimenting with the thistle, a persistent pest, by whacking very young plants to ground level, killing them without using pesticides. The control patch shows what the land would look like without the attack of thistle.

The 2-mile Loop Trail moves in and out of oak woodland, with mild up-and-down grades. Along the trail are spots that have been sown with gypsum, with bait placed in the middle to attract animals. The gypsum shows the animals' prints in clear detail, while motion-sensitive cameras photograph the visitors. Mountain lion prints are common. The trail returns on the ranch's main dirt road, which is actually its prettiest trail.

The ranch also conducts extensive research on birds, water quality, and on the effects that habitat restoration have on wildlife, which the sanctuary has in abundance. In my brief visits there, I've seen foot-long lizards, a fox, and a group of nine deer browsing in the old orchard. But for those interested in going a step beyond watching the sights along the trail, Starr Ranch offers the chance for children and adults to train and act as wildlife biologists for a day or a week. It also runs weekly "Junior Biologist" summer camps for children.

# Dick Loskorn–West Ridge Loop

**LOCATION**: Ronald W. Caspers Wilderness Park

**TOTAL DISTANCE**: 3.5 to 5.5 miles, with possible 1.2-mile out-and-back add-on.

**TYPE**: Loop

**TOTAL ELEVATION GAIN**: 400 to 800 feet

**DIFFICULTY**: Moderately easy

**SEASON**: December to April

**FEES ETC.**: $3 weekday parking, $5 on weekends. No dogs allowed. Camping and equestrian facilities available.

**MAPS**: USGS Cañada Gobernadora, Caspers Wilderness Park map

**CONTACT**: Caspers Wilderness Park (949-923-2210, www.ocparks.com/caspers)

Adjacent to Cleveland National Forest and Starr Ranch Sanctuary, 8,000-acre Ronald W. Caspers Wilderness Park has a more wild and remote feel than many other county recreation areas. It's also the rare county wilderness to offer overnight camping and equestrian facilities.

This modest loop trail offers a wealth of varied habitats within its 3.5 miles—loads of flowers, many of them not all that common, cactus gardens, big vistas, and enchanting woodland filled with ancient oak trees with huge, twisting limbs.

Children enjoy this hike, with its giant oaks and creeks to splash in, but keep them close to you. This is mountain lion country. There were two attacks on young children during the 1980s, and the park was closed to children for 10 years afterward.

This is an especially lovely hike in winter and spring, when creeks are running and wildflowers are in riotous bloom. You might want to bring a wildflower guide for this one; there's a chance you'll find several types of lilies on the Dick Loskorn Trail and scarlet monkeyflowers at the creek crossings.

You can do the 3.5-mile loop or, skipping the woodland section, expand this into a 5.5-mile hike up to the opposite East Ridge Trail, with another set of spectacular flowers and views. This is one of my favorite routes, and truth be told, I usually finish it by taking a little jaunt up through the Oak Trail anyway, to enjoy the cool woods as a finish to the hike, making it a total of 6.7 miles.

## GETTING THERE

Take the Ortega Highway (CA 74) exit from the San Diego Freeway (I-5). Drive

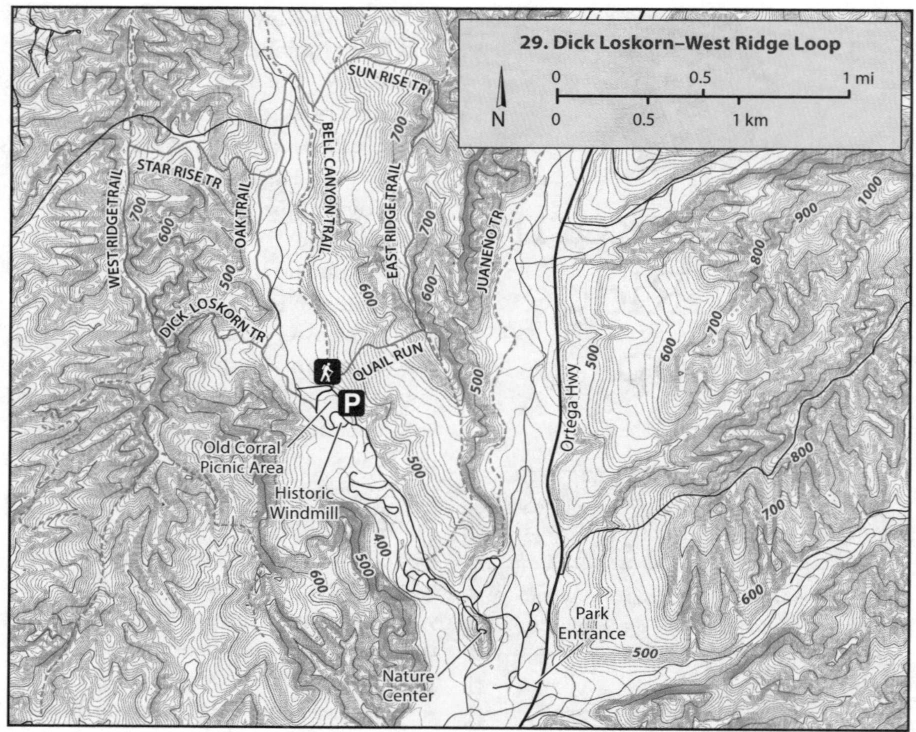


east 7.6 miles to the entrance of Caspers on your left. After paying your fee at the kiosk, head straight into the park for 1.4 miles and turn left, parking in one of the few spots right across from the old windmill and in front of the group picnic area. If the spots are full, there's another, much larger parking lot just a couple hundred feet farther down the park road.

## THE TRAIL

There are several access points to the Nature Trail, a loop that can be rather confusing. To find the trailhead, walk a couple hundred feet away from the road and then when you come to the little structure housing the restrooms, turn right, going past the side of the building another couple hundred feet. There you'll find a clear marker to the Nature Trail, which starts you out on a journey through an idyllic landscape of prickly pear cactus, Matilija poppies, and rocks strewn with such casual grace, they look like the work of a landscaper.

For hundreds of years, this canyon was the home of Native Americans. Bell Canyon is named for a six-ton rock that rang out when struck with another rock. (See the chapter on Starr Ranch Sanctuary.) The rock is now in the courtyard at Bowers Museum in Santa Ana.

Most of Caspers Wilderness Park was once part of Starr Ranch. The northern part of the ranch was deeded to the Audubon Society and became the sanctuary that's the subject of another chapter in this book. In 1970, the Macco Corporation entered into escrow to purchase the southern part of the property, planning to build an amusement park. But the venture fell through and three years later, the Orange County Board of Supervisors decided to buy the land for a public park, naming it Starr Viejo Regional Park. In 1974, Ronald W. Caspers, a supervisor who had advocated the park purchase, was lost at sea with members of his family, and the park was renamed for him.

After a little more than a tenth of a mile, find the marker for the Dick Loskorn Trail and head left. It's a gentle climb on a bike-free, single-track trail that turns steeper as you go. In spring, the Loskorn Trail is strewn with colorful flowers, including the hairy petals of the weedii mariposa lily and the even rarer Catalina mariposa lily. The trail begins to wind along the canyon edge, providing views of the white sandstone bluffs. The trail ends at the West Ridge Trail, where you'll make a right onto the wider, rolling ridgeline at the park's western edge, with views for miles. The ridge trail has a completely different set of flowers growing along its edges.

After three-fourths of a mile, you'll reach the well-marked Star Rise Trail; turn right down the trail, which is often in bad shape in its steepest sections after rainfall. Here, the plants change yet again to bushier chaparral.

In a half-mile, at the bottom of the hill, you'll reach the junction with Oak Trail. To complete the shorter loop, turn right into its cool recesses.

This isn't your usual oak woodland. The limbs of the trees here are tortuously gnarled and heavy, reaching out at all angles. The trunk of one oak is close to 5 feet in diameter.

You'll pass in and out of this sheltering woodland and cross the creek several times. At 2.2 miles, turn right onto Nature Loop. Stay on this loop as it curves left, ignoring the Dick Loskorn Trail off to the right, until you make your last big creek crossing at 2.6 miles. A tenth of a mile later, you reach the Old Corral picnic area where you left your car.

To hike the longer loop, ignore the Oak Trail and stay on Star Rise as it curves to the left for a half-mile. Then make a sharp right onto Bell Canyon Trail for a few hundred feet, and a left onto Sun Rise Trail.

You'll climb through prettily flowered territory to East Ridge Trail, known among wildflower aficionados for its beautiful finds. You'll also have vistas over a different area of the park, with Ortega Highway below and mountains climbing up from its other side. Enjoy the views and the flowers

Aviva Meyers

GNARLED OAK

THE OLD RANCH WINDMILL

for a mile, then turn down Quail Run, a half-mile descent that takes you to the trailhead of the Bell Canyon Trail. Turn left to walk a few hundred feet down the main park road, returning to your car.

On your way out, you might want to stop at the interpretive center as well, a mile back toward the front gate of the park. A sign will direct you to a short road to the right leading up to the center, one of the prettiest in the county park system with a small museum and an overlook that takes in much of the park. A feeder draws all sorts of birds; in spring, swallows plaster their nests into the corners of the eaves at the overhang leading into the museum, allowing you to watch them tend their young from an unusually close vantage.

# Vernal Pool Loop

**LOCATION**: Santa Rosa Plateau Ecological Reserve

**TOTAL DISTANCE**: 5 miles

**TYPE**: Loop

**TOTAL ELEVATION GAIN**: 250 feet

**DIFFICULTY**: Easy; gentle terrain

**SEASON**: February to May

**FEES ETC.**: $3 donation. Dogs strictly prohibited.

**MAPS**: USGS Wildomar

**TRAILHEAD COORDINATES**: N 33°31.335′ W 117°16.435′

**CONTACT**: Santa Rosa Ecological Reserve (951-677-6951, www.santarosaplateau.org)

Some hikes are inherently more satisfying than others—packed with vistas, flowers, animals, history, variety, and unique features that make every footfall a pleasure. This loop around a section of the Santa Rose Plateau Ecological Reserve and past its largest vernal pool is like that. But timing makes all the difference. In March or April, the pool—about 25 acres when full—will usually still have water, and the wildflowers along the prairies bloom with eye-candy variety and abundance. Come summer, the pool and most of the flowers are gone. This is a delightful trek for children who can handle the distance; if not, a short, flat hike just to the vernal pool and back still provides plenty of thrills.

The plateau is actually in Riverside County, a few miles past the San Mateo Canyon Wilderness of Cleveland National Forest. Part of the foothills of the Santa Ana Mountains, it is close enough and remarkable enough to be a regular visiting spot. Aside from the alluring flower show, the main attraction is the large vernal pool that, in the right season, will be filled with tadpoles—and the snakes hunting them. You might also get a glimpse of the rare fairy shrimp with one of the strangest life cycles on earth. Looping down from the pool, you can visit historic adobes from the land's earliest ranching days and see expansive meadows of graceful native grasses that are rare finds in the Orange County region these days.

## GETTING THERE

From I-15, take the Clinton Keith Road exit in Murrieta. Drive southwest on Clinton Keith Road for a total of 7.4 miles. You'll pass the Santa Rosa Plateau Ecological Reserve visitor center at 4.1 miles. Shortly before the marked

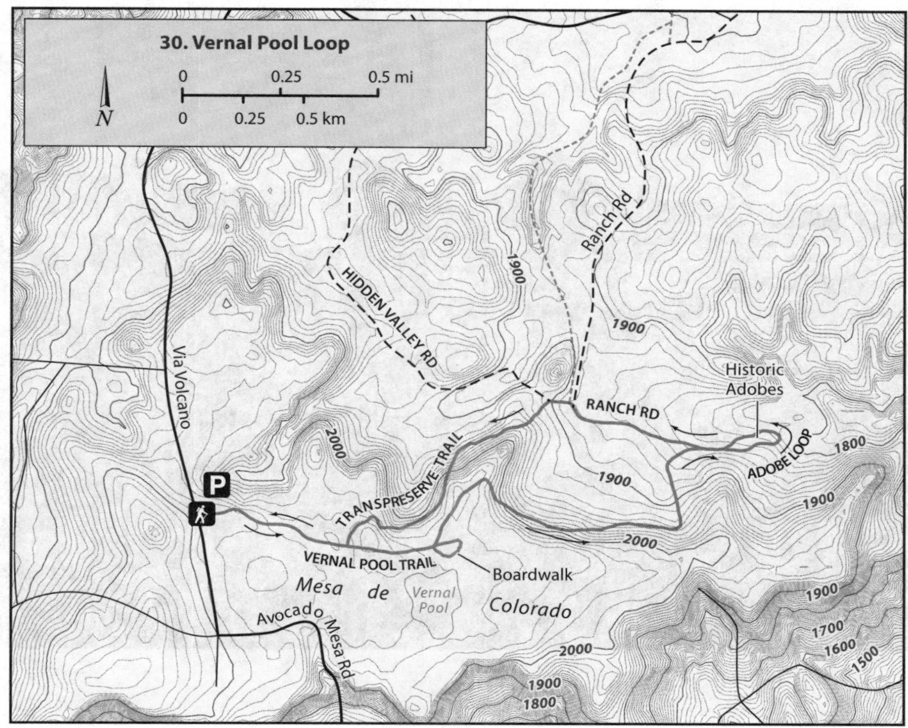


trailhead, the name of the road will change to Via Volcano. Park on the dirt lot next to the trailhead. On weekends in spring, the trailhead is usually staffed with helpful docents bearing maps and printed information about the flowers and animals you might see.

## THE TRAIL

If it's still winter or the season has been exceptionally rainy, drive a little past the trailhead to view the two smaller vernal pools from the road before parking. At the trailhead, drop the $3-per-person fee into the iron ranger. And be certain not to bring your dog, leashed or otherwise.

Then take the Vernal Pool Trail across the fields. If you're here in April, chances are you'll see a bumper crop of fuzzy, black caterpillars with orange markings, destined to become checkerspot butterflies. The variety of flowers along the trail can amaze even veteran hikers: red maids, yellow beardtongue, checkerbloom, the sapphire of eriastrum, the amethyst color of delicate lupine. Bright-yellow Johnny jump-ups, resembling pansies, and California golden poppies blanket entire meadows.

At a half-mile, continue straight past two trails on your left, including the Trans-Preserve Trail, which later on will return you to this spot. In the distance to the left, you can see a couple of the glorious Engelmann oaks this area is known for—similar to California live oaks but especially large, with deeply twisted, spreading limbs and bark like that of a gray alligator. Growing along a band that stretches from Pasadena to Baja California, these are considered

LARGE VERNAL POOL

the most endangered of the oak trees. They grow only in coastal foothills at least 20 miles from the ocean at elevations of 500 to 4,000 feet. The mesas that made up much of their habitat were also ideal for construction and fires consumed others; now, the Santa Rosa Plateau has one of the largest remaining stands of these oak.

Five hundred feet farther, you'll reach the large vernal pool. In a good rain year, it might still be full in mid- to late spring, but even in a parched year, there's usually water and wildlife in April. As the water recedes, wildflowers pop up around its borders. You'll see dense patches of goldfields, a short, deep-yellow daisy-like flower, mixed with blue-eyed grass and fuchsia-colored red maids. In other words, this is a great place to bring a wildflower guide.

At 0.7 mile, take the Boardwalk Loop Trail to the right. This little spur, a fifth of a mile long, takes you across one end of the pool for a close-up look at the wildlife.

Some 90 percent of California's vernal pools have disappeared, and only 5 percent of southern California's pools remain. The preservation of the Santa Rosa Plateau and its pools began with The Nature Conservancy buying more than 3,000 acres of the most sensitive land; other parcels were added over time and there are plans to create an unbroken wildlife corridor with the Cleveland National Forest.

Vernal pools are, as their name implies, seasonal ponds, usually only a foot or so deep, formed by winter rainwater that collects in depressions where underlying rock and soil are fairly impervious to water. On the Santa Rosa Plateau, it's the basalt from ancient volcanic flows that keeps the water on the surface. Once the rainy season ends, the pools slowly disappear through evaporation and percolation at the rate of about 1 inch per week.

Chances are you'll easily spot snakes slithering through the shallows; these are two-lined garter snakes, hunting for tadpoles, which are also easy to see. Harder to spot are the fairy shrimp, feathery creatures about a half-inch long (the Santa Rose Plateau species) or up to an inch long (vernal-pool fairy shrimp). You'll want to get your face close to the water to make them out—the boardwalk makes that easier—and look for the tiny creatures about halfway between the surface and the bottom of the pool. But it's their strange life cycle more than their appearance that makes the fairy shrimp almost as otherworldly as its name.

The shrimp spend most of their lives as cysts, which look like tiny eggs perhaps a hundredth of an inch in diameter. These aren't eggs, though; they contain live embryos that are in a state similar to suspended animation. The embryonic shrimp survive the dry summer when there is no water in the vernal pool; they can survive many dry years in succession. They also can be frozen for months, placed in a vacuum for 10 years, even heated to temperatures that approach the boiling point of water, and still revive. There have been cysts that were dated to be 10,000 years old that nonetheless hatched after they were placed in water.

All that long survival as an embryo is followed by a very short life span. Once the pool refills and the cysts hatch, the shrimp live 40 to 50 days, maturing to adulthood, mating—and filling the pond with cysts that will be all that's left of the shrimp once the pool dries again.

After you have viewed your fill along the boardwalk, turn right toward the adobes. At 1.1 miles, the trail begins its descent amid a colorful display of red monkeyflowers and a flower that resembles the canyon pea but bright fuchsia in color, rather than the pale lavender you see along Orange County trails. This is the San Diego pea flower.

As you descend, you look out across a rolling meadow to distant mountains, including Mount San Gorgonio and Mount San Jacinto, which might still be wearing their caps of snow. At one point, 1.4 miles from the start of the hike, you might find chocolate lilies just off the trail to your right, bell-like flowers 2 to 3 inches in diameter that actually look as though they have been spun from a fine milk chocolate. You'll also see purple sanicle, its blossom forming small maroon-colored balls. Raptors often ride the thermals overhead.

At 1.7 miles, you'll reach Ranch Road. Make a right here. You're in a basin dotted with old oak trees as well as manzanita and meadows filled with purple needlegrass, a native bunch grass that has been pushed out by invasive annual grasses throughout much of southern California. The needlegrass has survived here in part because the ranching families who lived here from the mid-1800s through the early 1900s, on what was then called Rancho Santa Rosa, were wise stewards of the land, never grazing more cattle than the property could sustain and removing the cattle when it was time for the grass to sprout.

Still left from the rancho days are two small adobe buildings dating back some 150 years, the oldest standing structures in Riverside County. The Dear family in particular, which owned the ranch in the late 1800s, was known for its hospitality and held huge May Day parties in the area where you're standing. Hundreds of people arrived from many miles away—not an easy trip in pre-car days—to attend these legendary gatherings.

After examining the adobes, take the short Adobe/Nature Loop around the adobe area. It will lead through an oak woodland studded with flowers. About a quarter of a mile along the way, look to the right to find padres shooting stars, a brilliantly colored little flower in purple and yellow that grows on a plant only a few inches high. There are also plentiful buttercups, with their shiny yellow petals, and more chocolate lilies.

The trail opens out to another vista across the grasslands to the mountains, then closes in on a dense oak woodland along the Nature Trail, bisected by a picturesque stream that's home to pond turtles and newts. At the end of this mini-loop, 3.2 miles from the start of the hike, are some wooden posts that are heavily pocked by acorn woodpeckers. This is a common hangout for the strikingly marked black-and-white birds with red-topped heads.

Turn right on Ranch Road, heading back in the direction you came from, passing the Vernal Pool Trail. After a quarter-mile, Ranch Road veers to the right; you'll continue straight on a connector to Hidden Valley Road, and turn left 100 feet farther on the Trans-Preserve Trail. The trail climbs through oak woodland, grasslands, and flowers—most notable are deeply colored purple vetch and pale fringe-pod. At 4.3 miles, the trail levels out, and at 4.5 miles it returns to the Vernal Pool Trail. Turn right here to return to the trailhead.

ENGELMANN OAK, A STANDOUT IN ITS FIELD

# III.

# SANTA ANA MOUNTAINS HIKES

# Big Mo Trail

**LOCATION**: Coal Canyon, Chino Hills State Park

**TOTAL DISTANCE**: 5.7 miles

**TYPE**: Out and back

**TOTAL ELEVATION GAIN**: 600 feet

**DIFFICULTY**: Moderate

**SEASON**: December to March

**FEES ETC.**: Free; long walk to trailhead

**MAP**: USGS Black Star Canyon, Chino Hills State Park map

**TRAILHEAD COORDINATES**: N 33°52.293′ W 117°41.050′

**CONTACT**: Chino Hills State Park (714-879-3471, www.parks.ca.gov/?page_iD=648)

An exception to the words of the old Joni Mitchell song: In one corner of Orange County, they took down a parking lot and put up Paradise. Well, not exactly, but close enough. In 2003, exit ramps off the Riverside Freeway (CA 91) at Coal Canyon were closed and the asphalt paving beneath the underpass torn out to make a wildlife crossing connecting Chino Hills State Park with the open lands of the Irvine Ranch Land Reserve and Cleveland National Forest. It was the culmination of years of planning that included the public purchase of Coal Canyon, where the ramps had been intended to serve a planned 1,500-house development.

Though access is a pain—the distance to and from the mouth of the canyon is almost as long as the hike itself—Coal Canyon itself is a contained and private place with a variety of thick green vegetation and flowers after some heavy rains. In fact, this is a hike you want to do in the midst of a good rainy season; the goal is a wonderful little grotto with a tiny, ephemeral waterfall at the far back wall of the canyon.

## GETTING THERE

Take the Green River Road exit off the Riverside Freeway (CA 91) in Corona. On the south side of the freeway, turn west on Green River Road for 1 mile, where you'll see a widening of the road to the right; usually you'll see other parked cars. If you reach the entrance to the golf course, you've gone a quarter-mile too far. The trailhead coordinates are at the parking lot.

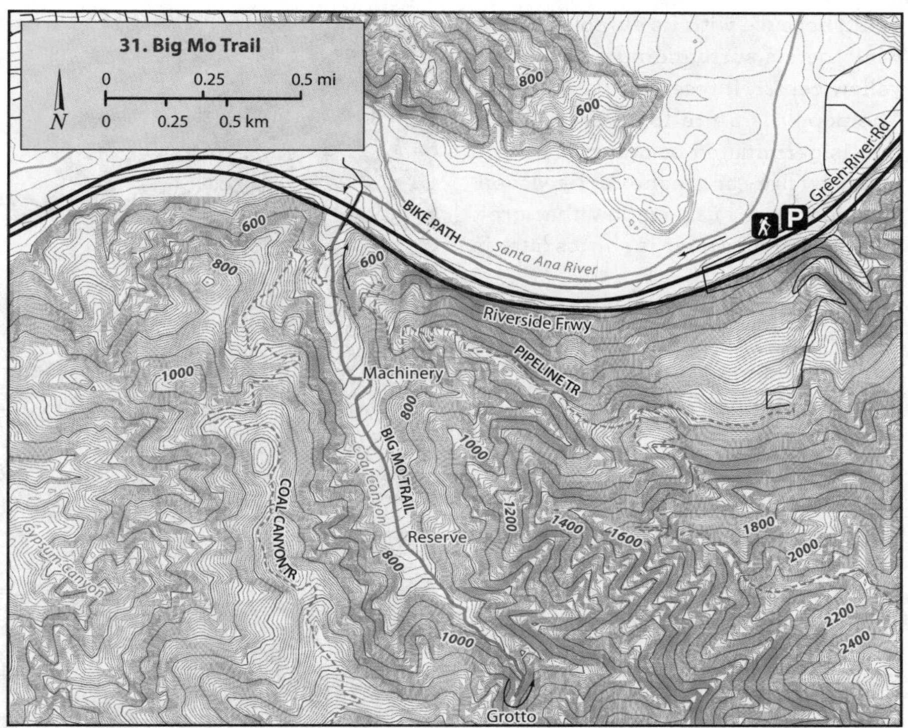


## THE TRAIL

Head downhill toward the entrance to the golf course for a quarter of a mile. There, you'll see the entrance to the paved bicycle path between the freeway and the Santa Ana River. The roar of the freeway to your immediate left is irritating and unavoidable. A river project has torn out most of the graceful, large trees to the right.

After a mile on the bike path, you'll reach the entrance to Coal Canyon, with a kiosk to your right and the freeway underpass to your left. Turn left and follow in the footprints of the wildlife. You might see a motion-activated camera that records the movement of animals, although vandals often rip them out. Once on the other side of the freeway, you'll see a fragment of paved road ahead at a high chain-link gate that's almost always left open.

You begin on Coal Canyon Trail, but that quickly veers off to the right and heads uphill to the Tecate Cypress Ecological Preserve (see the chapter on the Coal Canyon Trail hike). You stay left on the flatter dirt-and-gravel Santa Ana River Trail (unmarked at this juncture). At a Y-juncture at 1.5 miles from the start, Pipeline Trail heads uphill to the left; you fork to the right onto Big Mo Trail. In late winter or spring, thickleaf yerba santa should be in bloom, a plant with dusty-looking grayish leaves crowned with clusters of tubular pale-lilac flowers.

There are several stands of matilija poppy, also known as "fried egg" plant, because with its aureole of huge white petals surrounding a prominent yellow center, it resembles a fried egg. The poppy is a fire follower—a flower that is germinated or otherwise set in bloom by fire—as are the cuplike lavender blooms of bush mallow that grow along the stems of large shrubs later in spring.

Isolated from the rest of Chino Hills State Park by the freeway, and named for a coal mine that operated in the canyon from 1876 to 1878 (the coal here and in adjacent canyons was of inferior quality), Coal Canyon escaped the devastating 2008 wildfire that consumed almost all the rest of the park's flora. But in 2002, the canyon was hit by a fire that badly damaged its stand of Tecate cypress, killing a 200-year-old tree named Big Mo. (Learn more about the cypress in the chapter on Coal Canyon Trail.) This trail is named for that tree.

You can certainly hike Big Mo later than March, but it's more pleasant if you pick a cool day. As a steep box canyon, Coal Canyon is cut off from the breezes on those three sides, and by Chino Hills on the fourth. Unless the rainy season has been unusually generous, the little waterfall you're seeking will be dry. In addition, the sometimes overgrown trail seems to shelter more than its share of rattlesnakes. At least I've had two encounters there, and now do my hiking in the canyon before the snakes come out in spring.

Rattlers aside, the wildlife watching in Coal Canyon can be rewarding. Gopher snakes race across the path and coast horned lizards blend in with the pale dirt trail. The lizards are increasingly difficult to find and have become a federal "species of concern." Hawks and turkey vultures are common sights, and this is known as one of the best places to catch a sight of golden eagles on a lucky day. The canyon is also home to the rare coastal banded gecko.

LITTLE WATERFALL AT THE END OF BIG MO

Continue following Big Mo Trail, passing a large hunk of rusted machinery at 1.8 miles as the trail makes a slow hairpin turn.

At the 2.2-mile mark—just less than a mile from when you crossed through the underpass—a sign notes the boundary of the ecological reserve. From this point on, the trail virtually disappears; but 50 feet short of the reserve sign is an informal path leading down to the creek bed to the right. Take this and begin working your way upstream. Even after heavy rains, this wash is usually dry—at first. Though the streambed is rocky, you can usually find some sandy areas to walk for the first 0.3 mile. Then the creek narrows, along with the canyon walls. The streambed is rockier as you work your way to the back of the canyon amid thick shrubbery, including the tubular pink flowers of chaparral currant, an uncommon find on Orange County hikes. You begin to find water trickling through the creek bed.

At 2.8 miles, at the dudleya-dotted rock wall that marks the canyon's end, the creek makes a hairpin turn to the right, then right again into the little grotto. It's like a secret rock room with a spray of water spattering from the rock lip 20 feet above to the rock below.

# Coal Canyon Trail

**LOCATION**: Chino Hills State Park

**TOTAL DISTANCE**: 7 to 10 miles

**TYPE**: Out and back

**TOTAL ELEVATION GAIN**: 900 to 1,800 feet

**DIFFICULTY**: Strenuous

**SEASON**: October to June

**FEES ETC.**: Free. Long walk to trailhead. No dogs allowed.

**MAP**: USGS Black Star Canyon

**TRAILHEAD COORDINATES**: N 33°52.365′ W 117°41.166′

**CONTACT**: Chino Hills State Park (714-879-3471, www.parks.ca.gov/?page _iD=648) Department of Fish and Game (858-467-4209, www.dfg.ca.gov/lands)

The 31 acres of ridgetop land at the meeting point of Coal, Fremont, and Gypsum canyons used to be known as the Tecate Forest. But it's hard to call something a forest when few of the trees are taller than your waist, mere babies a few years old that sprouted after a 2002 fire, followed by another in 2006, wiped out most of the mature cypress. This somewhat arduous climb takes you through abundant wildflowers to the Tecate Cypress Reserve, which contains one of the four stands remaining in the United States and the northernmost in the world, to see these rare trees making a comeback. This also takes you to a great vista point where you can peek into nearby canyons and pick out landmarks across much of the Los Angeles area.

## GETTING THERE

Take the Green River Road exit off the Riverside Freeway (CA 91) in Corona. On the south side of the freeway, turn west on Green River Road for 1 mile, where you'll see a widening of the road; usually you'll see other parked cars. If you reach the entrance to the golf course, you've gone a quarter-mile too far.

## THE TRAIL

There are a few routes for getting to the rare Tecate cypress; Coal Canyon is the most accessible of them. Accessible is, of course, a relative term. As with the Big Mo hike in this book that also enters Coal Canyon, getting to the trailhead means parking 1.3 miles away and walking alongside the roar of the freeway. Put on some earbuds for the noisy stroll along the Santa Ana River.

Head downhill toward the entrance

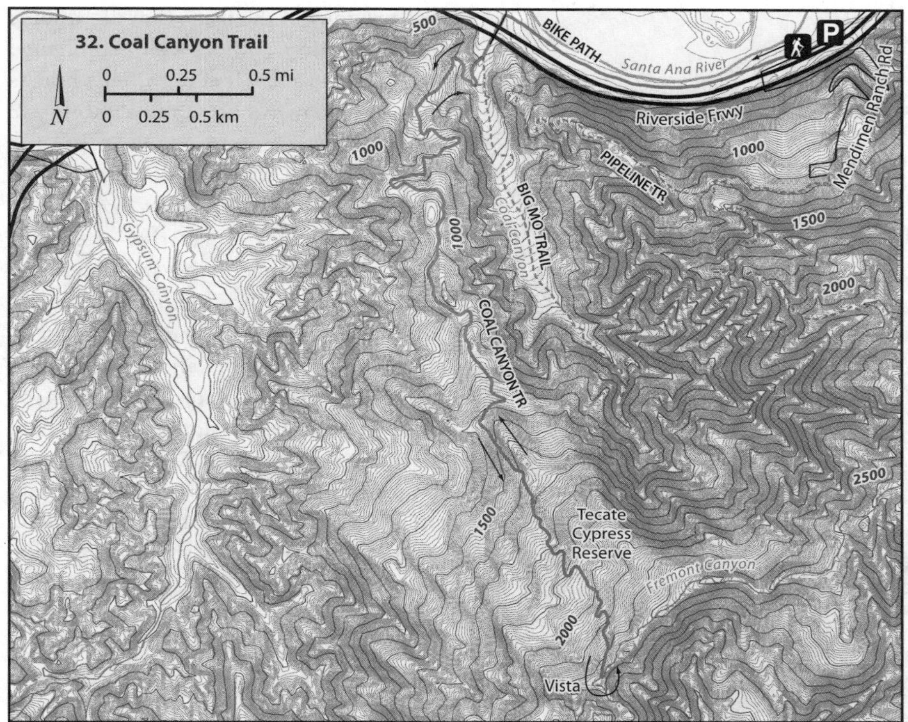


to the golf course for a quarter of a mile. There, you'll see the entrance to the paved bicycle path between the freeway and the Santa Ana River, which will take you a mile farther along this noisy and generally uninteresting area.

At 1.2 miles, turn left into the old underpass. The original exit ramps to Coal Canyon were closed down and the underpass paving ripped out to make a wildlife corridor for animals to travel between the Cleveland National Forest area and Chino Hills State Park. (See the chapter on Big Mo Trail.)

As you enter the park through a large chain-link gate, you'll see three trails. Stay on the paved portion, which veers to the right. The pavement quickly ends and you'll cross the usually dry creek bottom, then ascend on posted Coal Canyon Trail, a well-maintained fire road.

And you'll climb. And climb.

But as you do, you'll also quickly gain vistas that extend into Coal Canyon and beyond to Riverside County. In springtime, you'll pass an entire slope filled with stands of matilija poppy, a fire-following wildflower also known as "fried egg" plant because of its prominent yellow center surrounded by large white petals. Roadrunners might speed across your path and raptors are likely sights in the canyons around you. As you gain altitude, look along the rockier sections of the trail for seams of coal, which was mined in the area during the 1800s.

One million years ago, a naturalist told me, the southwestern United States was covered with Tecate cypress. Now, this group of trees grows within a preserve run by the California Department of Fish and Game. The 2002 fire, caused

YOUNG TECATE CYPRESS TREES ELBOWING FOR SPACE

by sparking from a power line, wiped out all but a few of the cypress here; among those to perish a 200-year-old granddaddy nicknamed Big Mo. ("Big" next to other Tecate cypress, that is; Mo was about 30 feet tall.)

But this evergreen species—which looks like a short, plump version of the familiar Italian cypress—evolved to survive fire. In fact, it needs fire for reproduction. Burning opens its tight, round cones to disperse the seed and give rise to a new generation. All along the upper part of this trail, you'll see hundreds of the progeny of the trees that died, some mere seedlings, others well-established young trees a few feet high. This hike is an exercise in awe for nature's ability to adapt and regenerate.

At 10 miles with a, 1,800-foot elevation gain, it's also just plain exercise.

The question is whether the trees will have a chance to re-establish themselves. A 2006 fire, caused by a controlled burn in the Cleveland National Forest that got out of hand, also hit parts of the Tecate population. The tree needs at least 30 years or more to mature and produce viable seeds. Fires in the near future could have a disastrous effect.

At 2.2 miles from the Coal Canyon Trailhead, you'll see the metal gate that marks the boundary of the Tecate Cypress Ecological Preserve. Before the fire, a large Tecate cypress stood immediately ahead, marking your entry into a rare habitat. That tree is gone now, but as you continue climbing, you'll see the young evergreen trees crowded along the trail and spread out among the slopes on both sides, looking robust and bright green. Tecate cypress sprouts quickly until it reaches 10 or 15 feet in height; then its growth slows considerably.

You'll also walk among dense thickets of yerba santa, with its tubular, lavender flowers. The name means "holy herb"; yerba santa was used by Native Americans and early settlers for rheumatism, to heal bruises, and as an expectorant and treatment for other lung ailments and is sold these days as an herbal remedy.

At the point where you enter the reserve, you've climbed 900 feet. It's an additional mile and a half (and another 900-foot elevation gain) to a nearly bare overlook where the three canyons meet,

A MORE MATURE TECATE CYPRESS THAT ESCAPED THE FIRES

for extraordinary views that stretch easily to Pasadena, Santa Monica, and San Clemente Island.

Close up, to the southeast you can see the handsome, rugged length of Fremont Canyon, part of the vast Irvine Ranch Land Reserve property that is scheduled to be donated to the county as of this writing. Immediately beneath you as you look toward the ocean is Gypsum Canyon, where the Irvine Company is planning a large housing development. To the north, you can easily make out the observatory on Mount Wilson, with La Cañada Flintridge and Pasadena below. A little west of there, you can spot downtown Los Angeles, and farther west, Santa Monica. The views of Orange County are practically all-encompassing and the ocean clearly visible, with both Santa Catalina and San Clemente islands off in the distance. The snowcapped mountains of the inland ranges appear strikingly close.

A couple of larger cypress trees grow here; they appear to have escaped the fire because of the relative dearth of brush.

You've earned your view—and the easier return trek downhill.

# Black Star Canyon and Falls

**LOCATION**: County easement; Cleveland National Forest

**TOTAL DISTANCE**: 5.5 to 10.2 miles round-trip

**TYPE**: Out and back

**TOTAL ELEVATION GAIN**: 300 to 1,200 feet

**DIFFICULTY**: Moderate to very strenuous

**SEASON**: November to June

**FEES ETC.**: No fees. Leashed dogs allowed. First part of trail is a public easement surrounded by private land. No trespassing off-trail through this section.

**MAPS**: USGS Black Star Canyon

**TRAILHEAD COORDINATES**: N 33°45.873′ W 117°40.685′

**CONTACT**: Trabuco Ranger Station (951-736-1811, www.fs.fed.us/r5/cleveland)

As picturesque and filled with interesting features as Black Star Canyon is, those recommendations can't possibly live up to its colorful if infamous history and the current wild tales about the canyon being frequented by the Ku Klux Klan and haunted by mysterious beings that appear in the night wearing hooded black robes. In 1831, there was a bloody armed conflict between white trappers and Native Americans—believed not to have been the local Indians but men from outside tribes—who had stolen their horses. Most of the Indians in the fight were killed. In 1899, an ugly murder took place over money owed for a horse trade. The early Spanish settlers told stories of a banshee with the head of a horse, called La Llorona, or The Wailer, quite possibly because of the winds that howl through the canyon, which is named for the coal mine that operated here in the late 1800s.

You can take an easy stroll through this alluring and easily accessible canyon to an overlook, or opt for a choice of two more strenuous outings described below with particular goals in mind. In this case, the shorter of the two is the more difficult: a torturously slow, bushwhacking and bouldering push along the creek to a 40-foot waterfall, by far the most challenging hike in this book. Or you can climb 1,200 feet on a 10.2-mile round-trip outing to the remains of a Native American village and the ranch where the murder took place. Be careful to stick to the trail during the first miles, before you enter Cleveland National Forest territory. Some hikers have been harassed by private land owners, who are fed up with the late-night partying and trespassing. Most people never experience a problem,

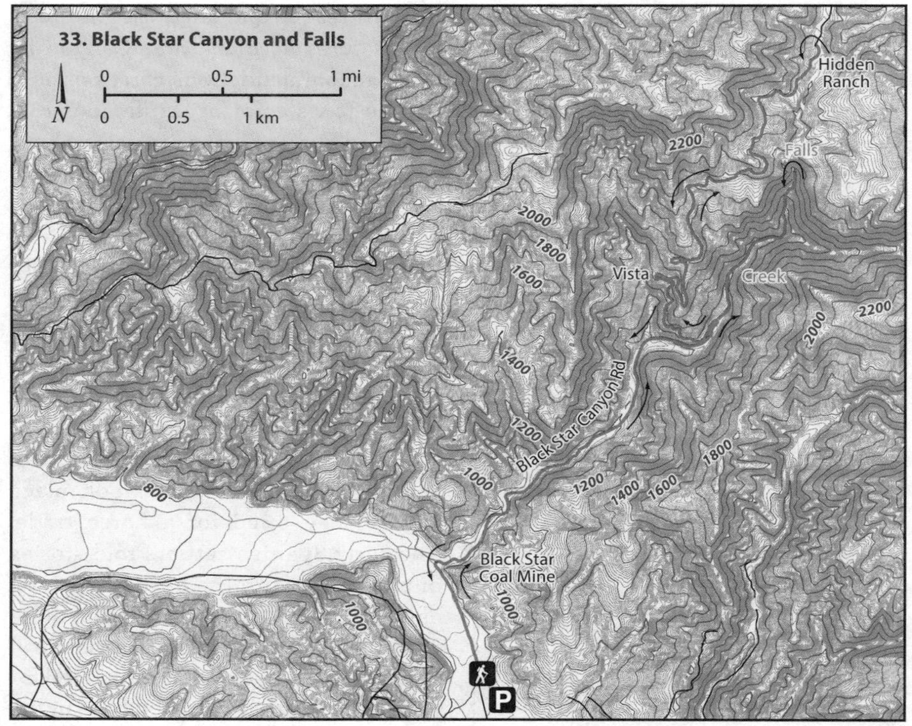


but if you do, simply remind the property owner courteously that this is a public easement and that you will do no harm.

## GETTING THERE

From South County: Taking the El Toro Road exit from the San Diego Freeway (I-5), head east 13.3 miles (the name of the road will change to Santiago Canyon Road) to the entrance of Silverado Canyon. Turn right on Silverado Road, and almost immediately make a left onto Black Star Canyon Road. After 1.1 miles, pull off into the informal parking area on the right side of the road, just before the gate.

From North County: Take the Chapman Avenue exit from the Costa Mesa Freeway (CA 55) east for 10.7 miles (Chapman Avenue becomes Santiago Canyon Road) to Silverado Canyon Road. Turn left and proceed as above.

## THE TRAIL

Walk through an open stretch on a paved road. Much of this lower area is owned, as of this writing, by the Irvine Company, which offers occasional docent-led hikes through its property but was planning to hand title to the county. The Black Star area is expected to be the first part of the larger 20,000 acres involved in the transfer to become an open-access park.

At 0.6 mile, the road makes a sharp right turn into a picturesque wooded area. The road is dirt with patches of pavement for the next couple of miles. Just as you make the right, you're in the vicinity of the old coal mine, but it's on private property and not visible from the road.

You'll pass through coastal sage scrub and under oak trees; the riparian area below the road provides good birdwatching on a sunny day. As you move farther into the canyon, you'll walk on nearly level terrain under groves of graceful eucalyptus planted by private property owners and see alders growing along the creek.

At 2.4 miles, the road makes a hairpin turn to the left. This is the place where, if you're planning to get to the waterfall, you exit the main road—not straight ahead on the narrow footpath, but down to the creek bed on your right. The next stretch, three-quarters of a mile long, entails thrashing your way upstream. This is easier if the creek is low or dry—but in that case, there won't be much of a waterfall to see. If you're here during a time of full creek

John Smith in cooperation with Naturalist For You

BLACK STAR FALLS, WITH WATER FALLING FROM A MINE SHAFT TO THE LEFT OF THE FALLS

BEDROCK MORTARS AT THE NATIVE AMERICAN VILLAGE

flow, within weeks after good rains, you should come equipped with heavy pants, long sleeves, and tough (preferably waterproof) boots for the rocks and bushes ahead. Gardening gloves or a poison-oak block for your hands can be good ideas, too.

For the next three-fourths of a mile, and more time than you'd generally count on for such a short distance, there will be several unavoidables in your life: bushwhacking, poison oak, rock scrambling, bouldering, and stream-crossing (or occasional wading). There is, at times, a lightly trodden, much-overgrown path on the side of the creek—usually on the left—that makes things slightly easier as you work your way upstream. Plan a minimum of three hours for just the 1.5-mile creek-side (or mid-creek) haul to the falls and back to the trail. Slow though progress might be, it gives you more time to appreciate the beauty of the stream as it rushes over many small cascades and to look for California newts and black-bellied salamanders or listen for the song of the canyon wren. This hike is filled with pleasurable sounds and sights no matter how far you decide to go.

Remember that, unlike climbing a hill, the return is as challenging as the way in, with all the same obstacles. If you begin to tire, turn around. Closer to the falls, the boulders can be some 10 to 15 feet high and slippery.

Shortly before you reach the falls, a spring drips year-round in an area of perennial pools. Stream orchids and Humboldt lilies might be found near the stream in late spring to summer.

The waterfall crashes down over multicolored rock. Lower down and to the left of the main falls, water also pours from an old mine shaft into the pool below.

If you were looking for a less strenuous outing, you could return to your car at the hairpin turn, rather than going down to the creek. Or you could continue on Black Star Canyon Road for another quarter to half a mile as it leaves the shaded area and begins climbing into an open, sunny area of sage scrub to overlook areas with vistas across the nearby hills.

Another option is to continue climbing for 2.7 miles past the hairpin turn—5.1 miles from the trailhead—to the area of Hidden Ranch, on a preserve, where the Native American village was located. Dress lightly for this exposed hike, and make sure you've got a sunhat and sunscreen protection. Bring plenty of water.

You'll ascend 1,200 feet, to just over a 2,000-foot elevation, by the time you're 4.6 miles up the road; then there's a very gradual descent for the next half-mile to Hidden Ranch.

A sign marks the site of the Tongva village. Do not disturb the site, which is protected as a California historical landmark, but you can amble around and see a rock dotted with numerous bedrock mortars or *morteros*. Avoid stepping on the rocks in order to preserve the mortars and the lichens growing there. There's a much-passed-around story about Spanish conquistadors marching up the canyon and massacring the entire village; this is a myth that sprang from the true story about the stolen horses and the trappers. According to an account of the confrontation, a group of frontiersmen agreed to retrieve the horses for the owners. They ambushed the horse thieves at a temporary camp downhill from the village. The Native Americans fought back but were outgunned by the white men. A few of the thieves managed to escape.

The killing of James M. Gregg in 1899 would have a lasting impact of its own. Shot by the owners of the ranch, he was taken via wagon down the long bumpy road and then to a doctor's house in Orange, where he died. Though the gunman admitted his role in the affair, and a first jury convicted the defendants, the judge inexplicably ruled that there had not been enough evidence. The case was dropped, but the judge, J.W. Ballard, was voted out in the next election, largely over his unpopular decision.

Many people say no matter which stories are true, the canyon has a dark and foreboding air about it. I find it one of the more serene and inviting spots in the county, but you can judge for yourself as you trek back to the canyon's bottom.

# Fremont Canyon

**LOCATION**: Irvine Ranch Natural Landmarks

**TOTAL DISTANCE**: 2 to 15 miles round-trip

**TYPE**: Out and back or loop

**TOTAL ELEVATION GAIN**: Varies

**DIFFICULTY**: Easy to very strenuous

**SEASON**: November to June

**FEES ETC.**: $3 daily, $5 weekends for access through Irvine Regional Park. Closed access, hikes via docent-led tours.

**CONTACT**: Irvine Ranch Conservancy (714-508-4757, www.irlandmarks.org)

One of the most visually arresting, environmentally sensitive, and simply gorgeous places in the county, Fremont Canyon is known as the canyoneer's canyon, with a wild, rugged character. Yet in this canyon with the huge, rounded boulders also grow beautiful old woodlands and carpets of colorful wildflowers in spring and late winter. It provides habitat for a number of rare species, including the Tecate cypress.

The tours offered here by the Irvine Ranch Conservancy can be brutal: 15-mile cardio hikes with total elevation gains of 3,500 feet, accomplished in less than four hours. One of the most popular hikes is a more moderate 5-miler to the old coal mine, with a 1,000-foot elevation gain. Or you can hunt for seams of coal on a path with vistas of Irvine Lake. Parts of the canyon—including a boulder-rimmed vernal pool—extend into the Cleveland National Forest, where there is open, though not easy, public access.

## GETTING THERE

You will be given driving directions when you sign up for a program via the conservancy's website. Tours begin in an area accessed via Irvine Regional Park.

## THE TRAIL

Though most of the activities offered at Fremont Canyon are of the strenuous sort—think 16-mile bike rides over steep terrain—there are possibilities for everyone. A new listing there was for an easy photography hike. Hikes begin under a canopy of oak at the mouth of the canyon. You'll also see introduced trees such as eucalyptus, pine, and ash.

Irvine Ranch Conservancy

LOOKING INTO FREMONT CANYON

In earlier years, Fremont Canyon was a popular haunt of grizzly bears. In fact, early Native Americans did not set up villages or settlements in Fremont Canyon because of its grizzly population.

Parts of Fremont Canyon are on publicly accessible land, but most of it is managed by the Irvine Ranch Conservancy. The Irvine Company gave 20,000 acres of its preserved lands to the county parks system in 2010, but the county contracts with the conservancy to preserve and restore the lands and to lead public programs on them. Since the change in ownership, the number of offerings in the canyon has fallen off, which is a shame. Because of the canyon's many steep trails and rugged nature, hikes there aren't for everyone. Still, it's worth stalking the online listings on the conservancy's website to sign up; Fremont is as beautiful and wild looking as it gets in the county.

One hike particularly worth joining is the coal-mine hike, which brings you to a surface mine, quite different from the tidy adits you see in other canyons of the Santa Ana Mountains. The Fremont coal mine, like those in nearby Black Star and Coal canyons, pulled low-quality coal, called lignite, from the ground. Miners scraped off the surface rock and other materials that covered the coal rather than tunneling into the ground for it.

The mine operated from 1864 to 1912, providing fuel both for the short-lived silver-mining operations in Silverado Canyon and for railroads in the Los Angeles area. Coal also was shipped as far away as San Francisco. A large pile of the stuff remains at the canyon's mouth, near the parking area—a testimony to this coal's poor burning qualities: The pile is still there even after several fires in the canyon.

Coal forms from fossilized plants buried rapidly in swampy conditions and then covered by sediment, so that no oxygen is available to break it down. The cleanest-burning coal forms in fresh-water swamps. There are various signs that Fremont Canyon's coal formed in an estuary with brackish water—remember that most of Orange County once lay under a shallow bay.

Another moderately difficult hike of about 6 miles climbs to a vista point for viewing Irvine Lake, which was created in the 1930s by the construction of Santiago Dam. The dam is an imposing presence at the bottom of the canyon; the lake, tucked amid hills, is a privately managed, stocked fishing destination.

On the trail up toward the lake—on the opposite side of the canyon from the coal mine, which is still visible from that distance—you can easily make out seams of coal. Dudleya grows thick along the road cuts. In spring, one entire hillside along the way becomes a purple carpet of lupine and other wildflowers.

Lizard Rock is, logically enough, the lounging grounds for the granite spiny lizard. The canyon's dense woodlands and many rock caves provide habitat for bat populations in Orange County, with 11 different species.

The wide canyon bottom is enchanting, with ancient sycamores spreading along the ground and oak trees that have pushed their roots into and over rock that looks almost as though it

THE VIEW OF IRVINE LAKE FROM FREMONT CANYON

has been painted with watercolors in shades from beige to black. According to Robert Glass Cleland's book, *The Irvine Ranch*, the caves deeper in the canyon's recesses were regularly used by outlaws, and at one point, a group of horse thieves was hanged at one of the trees at the mouth of the canyon, their ears cut off as evidence of the deed. The spectacular inner canyon area, with its twists and turns, is off limits to hikers.

A more challenging, 10-mile hike with an elevation gain of 1,800 feet heads up toward the Tecate cypress reserve, near where Fremont Canyon meets Coal Canyon. (See the chapter on the Coal Canyon Trail for more information about this rare conifer in Orange County.)

Two other plants seldom seen in Orange County grow in this area—chaparral beargrass and pitcher sage, with its particularly striking-looking blue flowers.

# Maple Springs Road

**LOCATION**: Cleveland National Forest

**TOTAL DISTANCE**: 4.6 miles (with up to 12 miles added on if you wish to ascend to Modjeska Peak)

**TYPE**: Out and back

**TOTAL ELEVATION GAIN**: 600 feet

**DIFFICULTY**: Easy (unless you brave the climb to the peak)

**SEASON**: November to June

**FEES ETC.**: Leashed dogs allowed.

**MAPS**: USGS Corona South

**TRAILHEAD COORDINATES**: N 33°44.868′ W 117°34.999′

**CONTACT**: Trabuco Ranger Station (951-736-1811, www.fs.fed.us/r5/cleveland)

There's a delightfully perverse quality to Silverado Canyon. Much of Orange County was once bucolic; now it's a 3-million-person metropolis. In contrast, Silverado was a bustling silver-mining town some 130 years ago with seven saloons, three hotels, two blacksmith shops, and a collection of brothels. Now it's a community of independent-minded people who fiercely cherish their rustic way of life.

This is a relatively easy walk along the lower part of Maple Springs Road in upper Silverado Canyon, along a creek that runs most of the year and amid beautiful and hard-to-find flowers and plants. The vistas stretch across endless hills without a house to be seen. At points along the creek, check dams create pools just begging you to slide in on a hot day. You can walk as long or short a distance as you please. This hike takes you 2.3 miles in on the road, to Lost Woman Canyon, and back. The paved road ends at a spring 4 miles past the trailhead; at that point, it turns to a winding dirt road that, if you're in the mood for a 4,000-foot-elevation gain, will take you all the way to Modjeska Peak, the second highest peak in the county. Together with Santiago Peak, the goal of another hike in this book, it makes up the county landmark called Old Saddleback. Keep an eye out for cars making the trip up to the peak.

## GETTING THERE

From South County: Taking the El Toro Road exit from the San Diego Freeway (I-5), head east 13.3 miles (the name of the road will change to Santiago Canyon Road) to the entrance of Silverado Canyon and turn right. It's a charming drive along Silverado Canyon Road,

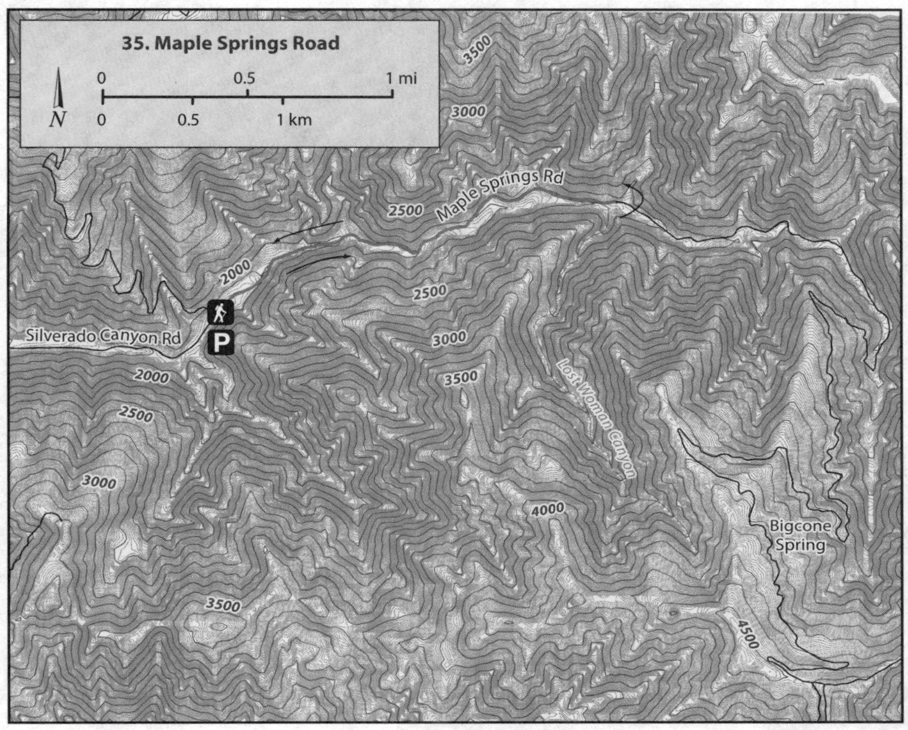


with its older cottages, creek crossings, and a handful of local businesses. About 0.8 mile after you pass the large church on the right side, you'll pass an open area with steep canyon walls to the right. This is known as the Holz Shale, a paleontologist's delight, with a wealth of late Jurassic marine fossils including ammonites. It's on private land. The road grows steeper and narrower as you drive deeper into the canyon; after 5.5 miles, you reach a small parking area and the entrance to Cleveland National Forest. If all the spots are taken, you can find a couple of places to pull off the road after entering the national forest.

From North County: Take the Chapman Avenue exit from the Costa Mesa Freeway (CA 55) heading east for 10.7 miles (the name of Chapman Avenue changes to Santiago Canyon Road after 4.3 miles) to Silverado Canyon Road. Turn left and proceed as above.

## THE TRAIL

At the forest boundary, the name of the street changes to Maple Springs Road. Though the road is paved in this section, there's still a carefree ambience here of having left civilization behind. You'll cross shaded, limpid Silverado Creek several times. Look for the bigleaf maple trees, with their deeply lobed leaves looking like giant hands, along the sides of the road. The tree is seen only in scattered spots south of the San Francisco Bay Area. The trees don't grow as large as their eastern

CALIFORNIA THISTLE

cousins, but they have the same seed-containing wings—the kind kids like to send spinning in the air like helicopters. Bigleaf maple also can be used to make maple syrup.

There are many little informal pathways off the road leading to the creek on either side. At 0.8 mile, a path to the left leads 50 feet or so to a clear, cold pool of water in the creek, sheltered by oak trees. Silverado Creek has water later in the year than most area creeks, even in late May during a particularly dry year. A third of a mile beyond this, you'll see an opening on the side of the road to the right, looking something like a circular turnaround. A path from this down to the creek leads to another spot for picnicking, contemplation, or a cool dip. Be careful of the plentiful poison oak. Some people prefer to do this hike via the creek itself, with its abundance of wildlife; in that case, plan for a much shorter hike because of the rocky creek bottom—and for wet feet. You also can make this into a sort of loop hike by taking the road in one direction and the creek the other way.

In the earlier 1800s, the canyon was known as Cañon de la Madera (Timber) for its tall trees, especially conifers at higher elevations, valued for their long, straight trunks, ideal as the beams for the roofs of adobe houses.

But in 1877, two hunters discovered silver in the canyon's upper reaches.

Courtesy of First American Corp. Historical Library

EARLY WOMEN MINERS

*The Los Angeles Star* reported the discovery, setting off a silver rush. The gold rush had recently played out, and times were tough in Los Angeles. Mining began the next year, after the rainy season. Soon, thousands of miners were camped out along picturesque Silverado Creek. But the area wasn't easy to mine. Seismic shifts meant that a vein of ore might be seen for a hundred feet or so, and then suddenly disappear. By 1883, the mines were nearly abandoned. One, the Blue Light Mine, continued to operate sporadically into the early 1900s.

This entire area is still pocked with mine shafts on the dirt paths above Maple Springs Road. They're fun to see but dangerous to enter, and the Forest Service has been working on sealing off the entrances.

Along the path you'll see other plants that are rare finds. There's a gooseberry with berries four times the size of those in coastal sage scrub, and a particularly beautiful thistle, looking like a large, pale-pink pincushion. California thistle is one of the two native thistles found in Orange County.

The farther you venture along the road, the more dramatic the vistas grow across the expanse of Cleveland National Forest, until you reach Lost Woman Canyon, named, dubious legend has it, for a teacher from the local one-room school who went off to explore the beauty of the upper canyon. Despite numerous searches, she was never found. When the wind whistles through this canyon, it's said to sound like the wailing of a woman pleading for aid—the lost schoolteacher.

If you decide to keep venturing up the roadway, you'll come across areas scorched by the 2007 Santiago Fire, but you'll also find bigger views, big-cone Douglas fir, and more and larger bigleaf maple.

# Fisherman's Camp and San Mateo Canyon Trails

**LOCATION**: Cleveland National Forest

**DISTANCE**: 7.4 to 7.8 miles round-trip

**TYPE**: Out and back

**ELEVATION GAIN**: 900 feet

**DIFFICULTY**: Moderately strenuous

**SEASON**: November to June

**FEES ETC.**: Advance permits required for camping

**MAPS**: USGS Sitton Peak

**TRAILHEAD COORDINATES**: N 33°31.938′ W 117°23.586′

**CONTACT**: Trabuco Ranger Station (951-736-1811, www.fs.fed.us/r5/cleve land); El Cariso Office (951-678-3700)

The first part of this wildflower-studded hike follows a popular trail to a restful but once-busy campground in Tenaja Canyon. From there, a climb and descent takes you to San Mateo Canyon, with its sparkling creek and endless views of mountains and meadows. But amid this undeveloped land is a very human surprise.

## GETTING THERE

Take the Ortega Highway (CA 74) exit from the San Diego Freeway (I-5), heading east. Drive 23.4 miles and turn right on South Main Divide/Killen Trail Road. You'll drive 17.8 miles along here, first on a good road with scenic outlooks (on the left, you might see hang gliders soaring) to a one-lane, barely paved stretch with many blind turns. You'll pass the parking lot for the off-roading area to your left, and at 16.2 miles, the Tenaja Falls Trailhead on your right. Continue 1.5 miles past the Tenaja Falls parking area to a tiny, unmarked turnout to Fisherman's Camp Trail. There's room for two cars here, but only with one parking behind the other, a troublesome arrangement. If another car is parked here, backtrack for 500 feet to a slightly larger parking area along the road.

## THE TRAIL

From the tiny parking area, you immediately plunge into oak woodland. Some 900 feet ahead, the scenery opens up to a vista of Tenaja Canyon and the mountains beyond, completely unspoiled and usually utterly quiet. Here, you'll sign in at the small wooden box.

You're hiking in the San Mateo Canyon Wilderness Area, the wildest part of the Trabuco district of Cleveland

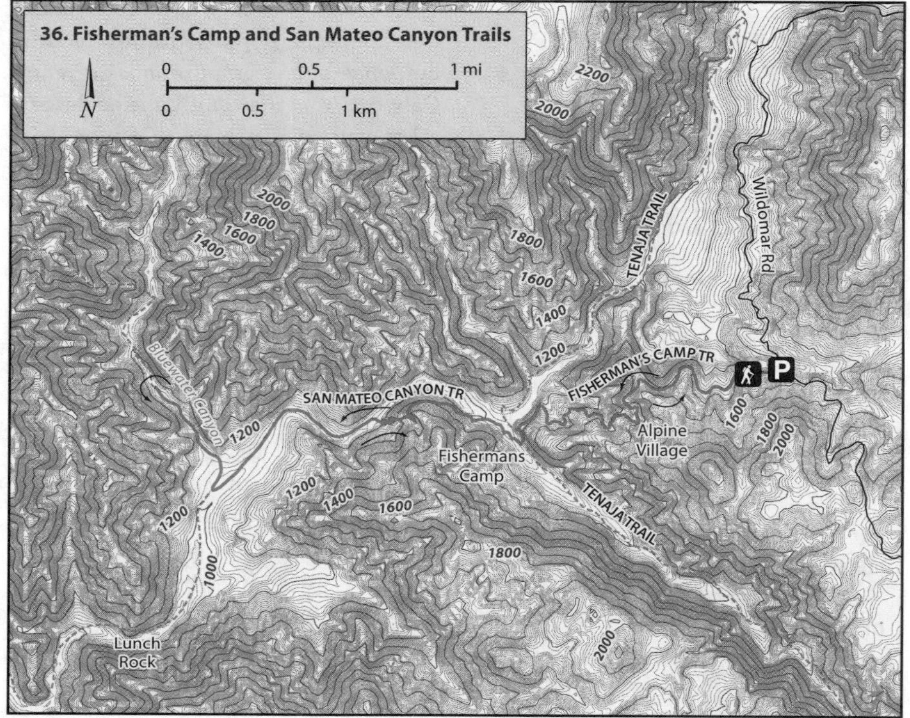


National Forest. Bikes are prohibited here, and signs of civilization are practically nil. It also offers some idyllic camping spots for people who want to get away from developed campgrounds and rows of RVs. You can set up a tent in the midst of the wilderness—Fisherman's Camp is a perfect place for tyros to try out backpacking—as long as you obtain an overnight permit from the Forest Service and respect the ban on campfires. Because the farther recesses of the wilderness are too distant for most day hiking, a backpacking trip is the perfect way to explore this area at length.

You'll descend along gentle terrain on a ledge leading you down into Tenaja Canyon. In spring, there are too many wildflowers to list. Many of them, like splendid mariposa lilies and deerweed, will be familiar from the common trails in county wilderness parks. Others, such as San Diego sweet pea, with its hot-pink color, and purple larkspur, are rare treats. The low-growing flowers that are greenish-white in color and star shaped, are more dramatic in name than in looks—Fremont death camas. As the name implies, the entire plant is poisonous and has at times been fatally mistaken for wild onion. The monkeyflower here, in addition to the usual peach, red, and bright yellow, grows in a handsome copper color.

One of my favorite points along this trail is a distinctly unwild feature 0.8 mile from the sign-in station: a hidden village of miniature ceramic houses and other figures. No one knows how long it's been there, who put it there, or why. It was discovered by a team of Sierra

Club volunteers who were searching for vandalized trail markers (more about that later). Most hikers call it the Alpine Village because of its Tyrolean theme. At first the "village" was kept up immaculately, with the plants around it clipped to show off the houses. Lately, it's appearing a little more worn, though hikers who know about it will stop by occasionally and clean it off. In any case, it's an appealing little twist on the nature-vs.-civilization theme. We flee to the wildest spots we can find to get away from civilization and then delight in finding an imaginative fragment of civilization in the wild. There's another one of these in the wilderness, with a ceramic-bunny theme, along the road above Devil's Canyon. In ways, they're an old-fashioned version of geocaching.

To find the Alpine Village, look for the saddle around a sharp bend where you are ascending very slightly, a change in the otherwise downhill route. Peer into the drainages to your left until you see one with a faint trail and follow that into the drainage for about 10 feet, behind the bushes that hide a small grotto from the trail. Here, on the right side, the village is set up on separate little ledges within the secret hideout.

Give the village a quick dusting if it

Joel Robinson / Naturalist For You

FREMONT'S DEATH CAMAS

needs one, and then head another 0.6 mile downhill—a total of 1.5 miles from the start—to reach Fisherman's Camp, a hospitable, stream-divided clearing amid the mountains with a large sandy area perfect as a tent pad.

Across the clearing from where you came, two trails head uphill in different directions. A small white marker with black hand-lettering directs you to the San Mateo Canyon Trail to the right.

There used to be metallic trail markers, but vandals hacked down and hid many of them. These replacement markers are the thoughtful gift of a backpacker who often camps alone in the wilderness area for extended periods. Sometimes, troublemakers will remove his signs, too, or switch them around; then he makes things right again.

You'll head steadily uphill at this point in an area of scrub oak, and farther along, blue-flowered ceanothus, for 0.6 mile. At 2.1 miles from the start, the trail begins a series of switchbacks downhill in an area of sage scrub on the other side of the knoll.

At the bottom of the hill, at 2.5 miles, you reach an oak woodland and then almost immediately a ferny, shady riparian area that's damp even in late spring, to the point where cattails and California bulrush block your trail. Poison oak is plentiful here. Five hundred feet farther, a sandy trail takes you to the creek, easily crossed by rock hopping.

You'll find another of those helpful little white markers, showing you the way as you continue on level ground along the creek bank on San Mateo Canyon Trail.

Walking on this narrow ledge above San Mateo Canyon, you can see the creek below you and beyond it a grassland meadow. The only sounds are the creek and the breeze ruffling the grasses, and the most numerous hiking companions are probably butterflies. You'll cross several small drainages until at 3.0 miles, you enter another

THE ALPINE VILLAGE ALONG FISHERMAN'S CAMP TRAIL

THE VIEW ACROSS THE SAN MATEO CANYON WILDERNESS

woodland, decked in season with the fragrant pink flowers of California wild rose. The trail might be a little overgrown here, though still easily passable. Most of the trail maintenance in this area is performed by Sierra Club volunteers and the helpful backpacker.

At 3.2 miles, cross a rock streambed and find the marker where Bluewater Trail meets San Mateo Canyon. You have a choice here. Turning right, you enter Bluewater Canyon on a faint trail that follows a small creek. There are several small pools and an unusual flower called California thread-torch. It's well named. Threads of bright-orange grow upward, tangling together as though this were an Olympic torch. Continue in this quiet canyon for a half-mile before turning around.

Your alternate route is to pass Bluewater Trail entirely and head left, continuing on San Mateo Canyon Trail for another 0.7 mile to an area of deep pools along the creek that invite you to take a dip, and a large, flat rock known as Lunch Rock. San Mateo Creek surprised biologists several years ago. Steelhead trout were found in 1999 near the mouth of the waterway by a college student who was fishing, after the trout had been marked off as extinct in the creek. The find led to explorations of other southern California creeks where the fish had been believed long gone, and to encouraging discoveries in some of them.

This is the turnaround point. The hiking beyond Lunch Rock is even more beautiful and wild but laborious, with overgrown trails, rock scrambling, and some wading through the creek.

# Tenaja Falls

**LOCATION**: San Mateo Wilderness, Cleveland National Forest

**TOTAL DISTANCE**: 1.6 miles (plus optional half-mile add-on)

**TYPE**: Out and back

**TOTAL ELEVATION GAIN**: 250 feet

**DIFFICULTY**: Easy; add-on makes it mildly strenuous

**SEASON**: December to April

**FEES ETC.**: Sign-in at trailhead. Primitive backpacking allowed with advance permits.

**MAPS**: USGS Alberhill, Sitton Peak and USFS San Mateo Canyon Wilderness topographic map

**TRAILHEAD COORDINATES**: N 33°32.947′ W 117°23.675′

**CONTACT**: Trabuco Ranger Station (951-736-1811, www.fs.fed.us/r5/cleveland); El Cariso Office (951-678-3700)

This is a short hike to a big waterfall, with five tiers totaling nearly 160 feet. If it's been a rainy winter, go in late March or early April to see plenty of colorful wildflowers even in this dry corner of the San Mateo Wilderness; in drier seasons, go soon after the rains. The problem is that there's nowhere to see the entire falls at once. This trail takes you to the top of the waterfall with views along the way of the upper portion. In case you would also like to see the inspiring view at the bottom, I've added a half-mile optional foray along the creek bottom that involves considerable bushwhacking, rock hopping, foot wetting, and poison-oak dodging. It's challenging, but beautiful if you've got the patience. It's easier to do this part of the hike in January, before the poison oak has spread (it's still there, in the form of a few bare stems), but then you miss the wildflowers.

## GETTING THERE

Take the Ortega Highway (CA 74) exit from the San Diego Freeway (I-5) heading east into Cleveland National Forest. Drive 23.4 miles to South Main Divide/Killen Trail Road and turn right. You'll drive 16.2 miles on this road, passing a popular hang-gliding spot on the left, and several miles later an off-roading area. The road turns extremely narrow and winding and is thinly paved; keep an eye out for approaching cars and exercise care around the many blind turns, until you reach the small marked parking area on the right for the Tenaja Falls Trail.

## THE TRAIL

Even from the little parking area, you begin seeing a profusion of wild-

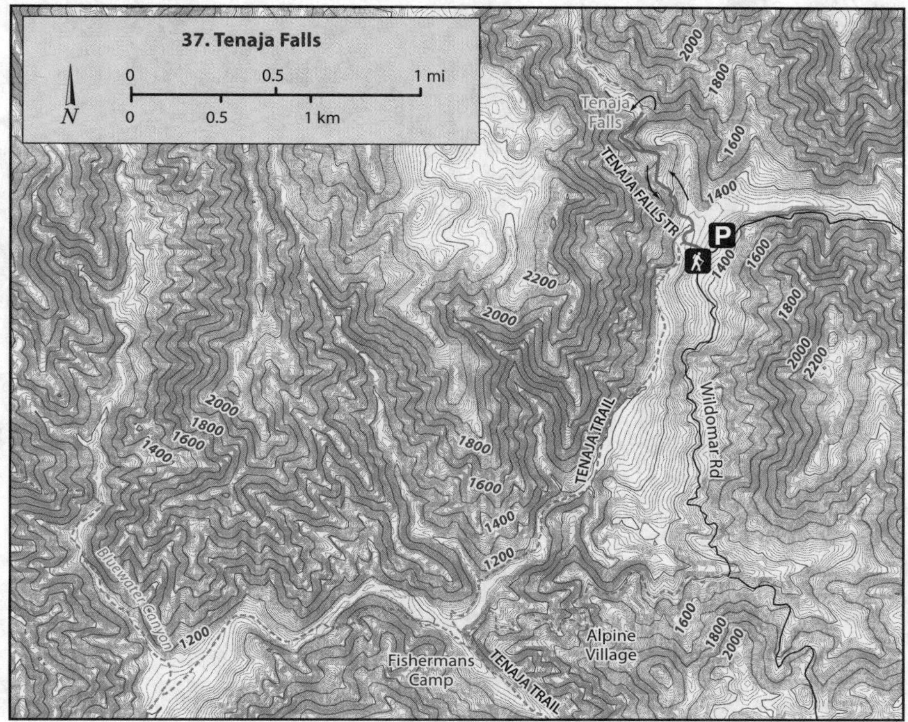


flowers in an array of colors: purple nightshade and Canterbury bells, the burgundy of wild peony, the azure of blue-eyed grass, pink owl's clover, and red monkeyflower.

You'll follow a short trail on a gradual downhill slope, the chaparral on both sides decorated with pea flowers and wild hyacinth. At 440 feet, go around the gate and begin watching out for poison oak. At one-tenth of a mile, stay straight to remain on the trail, avoiding the larger trail forking along the stream to the right. You'll need to cross San Mateo Creek here. There's a concrete ford but in times of good waterfall flow, the depth can be a good 8 to 12 inches or more. You can find a drier crossing by following the trail that forked off to the right for about 200 feet to a set of large rocks spanning the creek.

Now head uphill. There are fewer flowers as you do and the trail turns rocky, but as you ascend you'll see brilliant red and bright-orange monkeyflower, as well as big bushes of yellow bush beardtongue. The flowers, with their snapdragon shape, are a bright yellow when they first bloom, then fade over time to lemon color and then to cream. Thanks to local flower expert Bob Allen for the following explanation of how the beardtongue got its name: From the throat of the flower's corolla, a rudimentary stamen called the staminode protrudes as though the flower were sticking out its tongue, and has bristles at its tip—thus the beard.

At 0.5 mile, an opening on the side of the trail gives you your first view of Tenaja Falls, a long but generally thin stream of water sliding over polished

TENAJA FALLS

granite. Views continue over the next quarter-mile until you reach the top of the falls and the giant old oak tree, where there are pools of clear water and the creek that feeds the falls. It's a popular picnic spot.

From here, though, you can't see the falls itself very well; for a better view, cross the creek and follow the informal trail for about 400 feet until you gain more perspective on the falls. Watch your step and avoid trying to get closer to the falls, where the rocks are glassy and slippery. You might see people climbing down the rocks for a more encompassing look but the better idea is to resist such a treacherous venture.

If you're in the mood for a longer hike, follow the creek upstream along Tenaja Falls Trail before turning around. If you hunger for better views of Tenaja Falls, head back downhill for a half-mile and look for easy openings to descend the slope down to the stream at your left. If this is spring, be on your guard for poison oak growing extensively all along the creek, which flows about 250 feet from the trail. Turn left, working your way back upstream by a combination of rock hopping, bushwhacking, and picking up what overgrown trails you can by the sides of the creek. California newts are common finds in the creek.

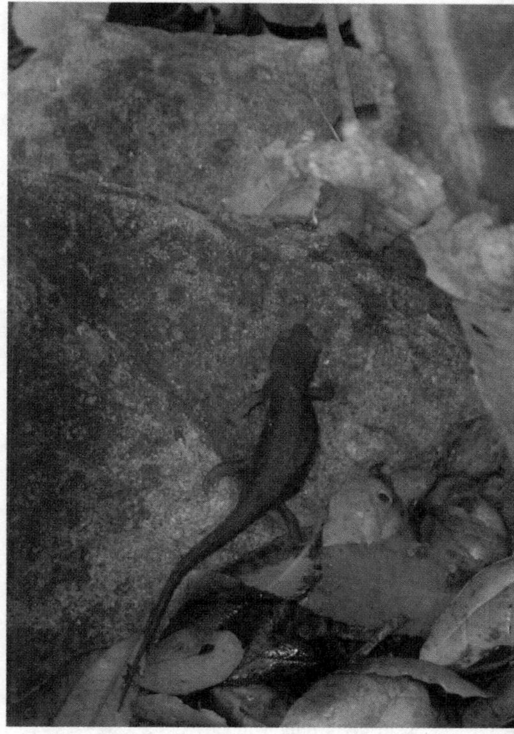

CALIFORNIA NEWT

No matter which path you take, the growth is dense and the progress slow. Within a quarter-mile or so, you're rewarded with a far more awe-inspiring view of the falls from the bottom. Return to the main trail; at this point you're only about 1,000 feet from the parking lot.

# El Cariso Nature Trail

**LOCATION**: Cleveland National Forest

**TOTAL DISTANCE**: 1.4 miles

**TYPE**: Loop

**TOTAL ELEVATION GAIN**: 100 feet

**DIFFICULTY**: Easy

**SEASON**: January to May

**FEES ETC.**: Good for children.

**MAPS**: USGS Alberhill

**TRAILHEAD COORDINATES**: N 33°39.061′ W 117°24.756′

**CONTACT**: Trabuco Ranger Station (951-736-1811, www.fs.fed.us/r5/cleveland); El Cariso Office (951-678-3700)

If you've never hiked the Santa Ana Mountains before, you might want to start with El Cariso Nature Trail, a short interpretive trail that has plenty of interesting sights, many of them helpfully labeled and explained. It will introduce you to some of the plants that you're unlikely to see at lower elevations and is easy enough to make a good family hike, even for the preschool set.

Late winter and early spring are the best times to hike this trail in order to view the flowers.

## GETTING THERE

Take the Ortega Highway (CA 74) exit from the San Diego Freeway (I-5) in San Juan Capistrano. Head east on Ortega 23.2 miles to the El Cariso Fire Station on the right; if you reach South Main Divide, you have traveled too far. You can park in the lot at the visitors' center with interpretive displays; there's also a ranger station here.

## THE TRAIL

The trailhead begins behind the visitors' center, next to the fire station. As you climb, one of the first plants you'll come to, on the right, is an eastwood manzanita, with oval leaves and reddish bark that peels over time. In early spring, the manzanita has small ,white flowers that resemble lily-of-the-valley; these give way to edible fruit that looks like small apples—the word *manzanita* means little apple. Some people claim that a tea made from the leaves can treat urinary problems and relieve poison-oak rash.

In this early section of the trail, you'll also find sugarbush, a chapar-

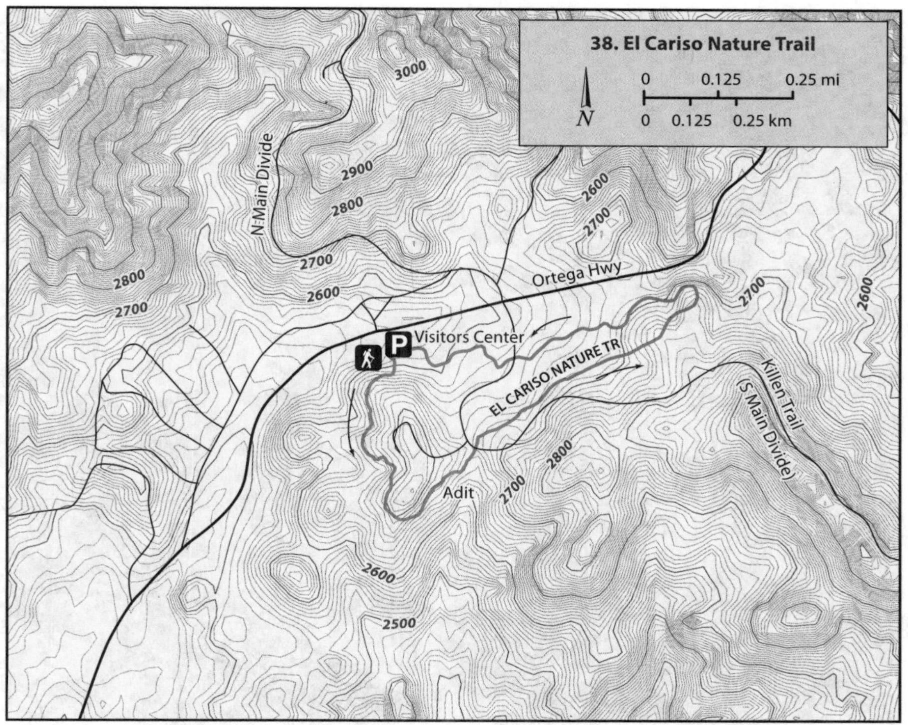


ral plant like lemonadeberry but with sweet-smelling flowers that grow in a vertical cluster along one side of the branch. Holly-leaf redberry is another plant far more common in the mountains than in foothill or coastal areas. California wild peony has a deep-burgundy blossom; purple Canterbury bells also add vivid color.

There are carpets of miner's lettuce, low-growing plants with rounded leaves, which do indeed taste like lettuce and were used by early miners as a source of vitamin C.

At 0.4 mile, the trail takes you to an abandoned adit; there are many of these throughout the Santa Ana Mountains, colorful reminders of the mining craze in these mountains during the late 1800s. Silver, tin, and lead were among the minerals sought; coal mines operated in the northern canyons of the mountain range. Though it's dangerous for people to enter the mines, they make useful homes for some animals.

The rocks in this area are colored spectacular shades of purple, red, and orange; adding to the color scheme are yellow and blue-green lichens. Because many lichens are sensitive to air pollution, the sight of abundant lichens usually means fairly good air quality. The lichens are a partnership of two plants, fungus and algae living in symbiosis. The fungus collects and stores moisture; the algae use the moisture to manufacture food.

At 0.7 mile, the trail crosses South Main Divide, a paved road. The land is more exposed here, offering nice views

ADIT

into the San Mateo Canyon Wilderness. After crossing the road, you pass through a section of Coulter pines, also called penny pines, or most aptly nicknamed, big-cone pines (not to be confused with big-cone Douglas fir in the mountains' higher elevations—which actually has a much smaller cone). The Coulters produce the biggest cones of any pine, up to 16 inches long and 10 pounds, with a distinctively spiny shape; because of this, they've also been called widowmakers. You're certain to see some cones on the ground. These particular trees were planted, although Coulter pines are native to this area.

After the pines, you enter a green area of scrub oak and other chaparral before the trail crosses South Main Divide again at 1.2 miles. From here, it's just 1,000 feet back to the parking lot.

# Chiquito Trail

**LOCATION**: Cleveland National Forest

**TOTAL DISTANCE**: 9 miles

**TYPE**: Shuttle

**TOTAL ELEVATION GAIN**: 900 feet

**DIFFICULTY**: Moderately strenuous

**SEASON**: December to June

**FEES ETC.**: Leashed dogs allowed.

**MAPS**: USGS Alberhill, Sitton Peak

**TRAILHEAD COORDINATES**: N 33°39.092′ W 117°26.867′

**CONTACT**: Trabuco Ranger's Station, Cleveland National Forest (951 736-1811, www.fs.fed.us/r5/cleveland); El Cariso Office (951-678-3700)

This eye-pleasing trail has most of what you expect and want from a hike in the Cleveland National Forest: loads of wildflowers, hushed oak woodlands, big vistas, bare, primitive-looking rock areas, running creeks, and not one, but two waterfalls. Doing this as a shuttle hike allows you to take in all the variety and do a lot more descent than climbing.

The ideal time to hike Chiquito Trail (named for the horse of a 1920s ranger) is after substantial rainfall in the late winter to mid-spring, when the creeks will be full, the wildflowers abundant, and Chiquito Falls rushing with water.

## GETTING THERE

Take the Ortega Highway (CA 74) exit eastbound from the San Diego Freeway (I-5). Drive 19.5 miles east to the candy store; the endpoint of the trip is the parking lot across the street from the store. Leave one car here and in the other car, continue 2.2 miles farther east on Ortega Highway to Long Canyon Road, which bears no street marking. Instead, look for the wooden sign that reads, "Los Pinos Conservation Camp" and "El Cariso Hot Shots Regional Center." Turn left and drive 2.2 miles to the San Juan Trail, at the day-use parking outlet just before the Blue Jay Campground.

## THE TRAIL

You're immediately greeted by flowers on San Juan Trail in springtime. Checkerbloom, with its pink cup-like flowers, mingles with deep-purple nightshade, and the lavender of canyon pea and wild hyacinth, also known as blue dicks.

At the first intersection with Old San Juan Trail, at 1.1 miles, continue straight across; the trail then veers left, down the north side of the slope.

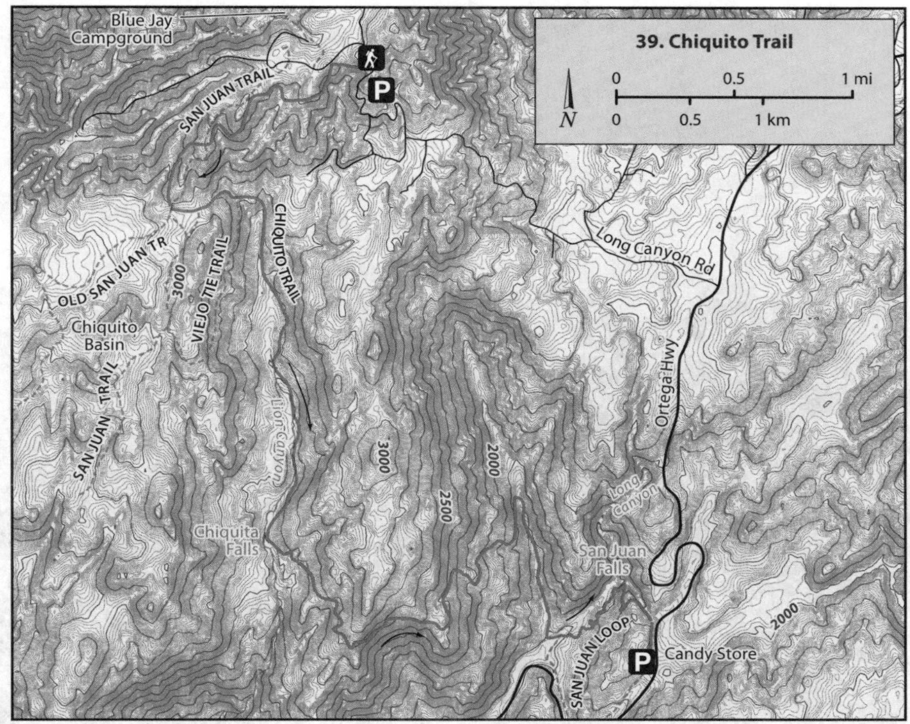


Within a half-mile, you'll reach another intersection with the older trail; again, continue straight across it on a nearly level grade.

At this point, you'll alternate between oak woodland, and sage areas with stirring vistas across the mountains. White sage grows lavishly here, along with its frequent companion, neon-red paintbrush, as well as morning glory and caterpillar phacelia. That last one is an easy flower to identify—tiny white-to-lavender blossoms growing along stems that coil at the tips so that they do indeed resemble fuzzy caterpillars.

The trail in this area is no longer strewn with stones, but there are plentiful bits of embedded rock and tree roots that protrude from the trail, easy to stumble over.

Various small informal paths veer off, but you'll stay on the main path and in the right seasons find more colorful flowers: white ceanothus, or wild lilac, along with burgundy-colored wild peony and purple Canterbury bells.

At 1.5 miles, you'll come to an intersection of trails; continue straight into the oak woodland, the trail decorated by Chinese houses, each flower in the low-growing clusters showing off two colors: a purple-pink lower part and pale-lavender upper. At 1.75 miles, you come out of the woodland into Chiquito Basin, a peaceful meadow isolated by the hills surrounding it. This is known as a particularly fine place to spot large mammals—coyote, deer, bobcats. You'll pass through a sunny area with monkeyflowers of many hues, and the yellow pansy-resembling flower Johnny jump-ups, before reaching the marker

THE SANTA ANA MOUNTAINS FROM CHIQUITO TRAIL

for Chiquito Trail at 2.1 miles. Turn left here onto the trail into perhaps the most charming part of the hike—cathedral-like oak woodland dotted with granite boulders, alternating with flower-bedecked sage scrub.

At 2.8 miles, where a marker notes that Ortega Highway is 7.5 miles away, pass the posted Viejo Tie Trailhead, continuing on Chiquito through a thickly forested area with a creek running next to you.

Shortly after coming out of the oak forest, at 4.4 miles, you'll see what looks like a trail going straight ahead with another trail turning to the left. The trail straight ahead is an informal spur that takes you to the lip of Chiquito Falls, just 50 feet ahead. It's worth a visit, especially in the wettest season, when water blasts its 15-foot granite wall.

Then return to the continuation of Chiquito Trail. You'll begin a moderate ascent as the trail curves around to your right, allowing you to get a fuller if more distance view of the waterfall.

At 5.1 miles, you'll descend down a rocky trail to an area of far-reaching vistas. Ortega Highway is below you. You'll climb again, in an area where plants are sparse, a surprise after the lush flora up to this point. Instead, the trail is decorated by rounded, dramatic boulders, including large areas of handsome pink granite. On my most recent hike through this area, I saw no fewer than five good-

COAST HORNED LIZARD

sized coast horned lizards (good-sized being perhaps 4 inches long) in the area. This species has become rarer along southern California's trails and is now considered a species of concern, as non-native Argentinian ants have pushed out the lizard's preferred food, red harvester ants.

At 5.5 miles, you'll descend again, until at 6.1 miles you find yourself again in shaded oak woodland. You'll reach canyon bottom at 7 miles and immediately cross a narrow creek. You're surrounded by walls of white rock that surround this little riparian area. At 7.6 miles, take a left in the fork in the trail. A quarter-mile later, you'll cross the creek two more times until you reach the intersection with San Juan Loop Trail at 7.8 miles.

You could turn right or left here, but I suggest left, which will take you to your second waterfall, San Juan Falls, at 8.6 miles, and the pretty reflecting pool at its lip. This path also avoids the worst of the traffic noise from Ortega Highway.

From the falls, it's 0.4 mile uphill to your second car at the trailhead of San Juan Loop.

# 40

# Old San Juan Trail

**LOCATION**: Cleveland National Forest

**TOTAL DISTANCE**: 3.3 miles

**TYPE**: Out and back

**TOTAL ELEVATION GAIN**: 650 feet

**DIFFICULTY**: Moderate

**SEASON**: Year-round

**FEES ETC.**: Dogs on leash allowed.

**MAPS**: USGS Alberhill

**TRAILHEAD COORDINATES**: N33°39.068′ W 117° 27.322′

**CONTACT**: Trabuco Ranger Station (951-736-1811, www.fs.fed.us/r5/cleveland); El Cariso Office (951-678-3700)

Not every hike in the more remote-feeling areas of the Cleveland National Forest is a long, strenuous ordeal. The Old San Juan Trail leads you to full-on mountain views, a tranquil grassland studded with many old oak trees and alive with bird calls, and the fun of searching out the bedrock mortars of Native Americans who lived here long before white settlers arrived.

## GETTING THERE

Take the Ortega Highway (CA 74) exit from the San Diego Freeway (I-5) heading east for 21.7 miles. Turn left on Long Canyon Road, which bears no street marking. Instead, look for the wooden sign that reads, "Los Pinos Conservation Camp" and "El Cariso Hot Shots Regional Center." Drive 2.6 miles, through the first part of Blue Jay Campground, to the trailhead on the left-hand side just before the cell phone access area and gate to the farther Blue Jay area. Park at the trailhead.

## THE TRAIL

San Juan Loop. San Juan Trail. Old San Juan Trail. A hiker couldn't be blamed for a little confusion caused by these close-together trails with nearly identical names in the Cleveland National Forest. This hike utilizes the Old San Juan Trail, with its no-nonsense, straight-downhill approach. Just to further complicate things, if the gate to Blue Jay is locked, you can use the newer but longer San Juan Trail just before reaching the campground; a kiosk and small parking area on the left side of the road mark the trailhead. The trail will intersect with Old San Juan Trail at 1.1 miles, at which point you would turn left. The older trail cuts a mile off the hike round-

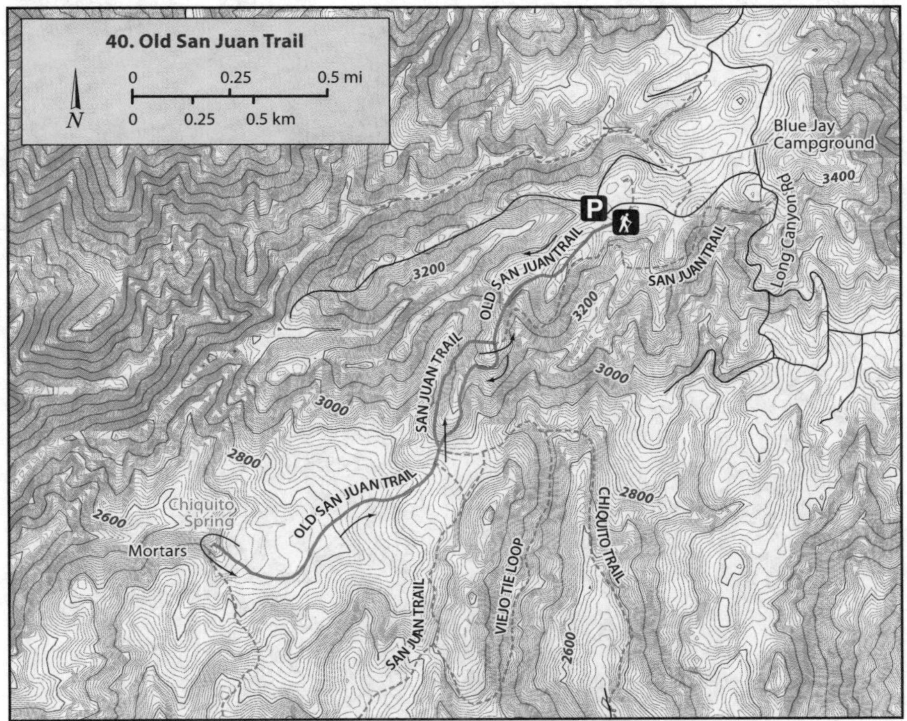


trip, though on the return trip this hike will borrow a small section from the newer trail to avoid the most rutted, rocky climb.

For the first 0.2 mile past the trailhead, you hike through a small, walk-in campground (check out the doorless outhouse) surrounded by manzanita and white sage. By the quarter-mile mark, the landscape opens more. At a fork, a wide, rocky trail heads uphill to the left; you turn right and downhill on the narrower trail. You'll come to two more forks at a quarter-mile and a half-mile; keep heading straight downhill on the main trail, with views across the mountains to the west and south.

At 0.6 mile, you reach the first intersection with the new San Juan Trail, with its more gentle terrain and descent. Consult your inner mountain goat here. The next 0.3 mile on the old trail is rutted, rocky, and steep. The new trail will take nearly twice as long to reach the same spot, but is in better condition with an easier descent.

Assuming you've stayed on the old trail, the two trails will intersect again at 0.9 mile. The newer trail cuts across to the left on an almost-even grade; no matter which trail you took to get here, it's time to use the old trail for the rest of the trip downhill.

The trail continues less steeply and you leave the rocks behind, walking on an eroded dirt path. You soon enter a dense oak woodland that surrounds a peaceful, rare grass meadow, a wonderful place for picnicking, wildlife watching, and spending quiet hours.

As you continue along the path, check in with your surroundings for

BEDROCK MORTAR OFF OLD SAN JUAN TRAIL

little surprises. On a recent hike, soon after a rain, I found the clear imprint of a mountain lion. The nearly bare branches of a straggly, tiny scrub oak were covered with thousands of lady bugs, which also swarmed in mounds underneath. Bright-yellow fungi grew in a layered colony on a downed log. If mycology is an interest of yours, Chiquito Basin is known as a place where mushrooms grow in abundance and variety.

At 1.4 miles, the trail abruptly descends into a slump and back up the other side. Just a little farther on, at 1.5

miles, the trail begins a hairpin turn south, to the left. On the left-hand side of the trail, you'll see one of the small, metal trail markers; this one is pocked with bullet holes. Instead of making the turn with the trail here, go straight ahead on a barely discernible, overgrown footpath in the grass, heading to the creek bed that curves north and west of you. The trail grows even more confused as you head west, with several fainter tracks around it. After heading west halfway to the line of trees, you'll want to head north (right) to the area of Chiquito Spring, named for the ranger's horse that drank from it. Here it might seem as though your search for the bedrock mortars is stymied. Look across the creek bed to the northern side. On the mild slope, set back some 50 feet from the creek, you can spot two sections of buff-colored rock outcroppings. There's a relatively easy, angled path into the creek bed and up on the other side at N 33°38.273' W 117°28.316'.

Hunt around the rocks on the other side for the bedrock mortars used to crush the abundant acorns into a meal. They're located on several different rocks among both outcroppings. The coordinates for the rock area are N 33°38.295' W 117°28.317'. Expect abundant poison oak in this area.

On your return, when you reach the first intersection, turn left on the newer San Juan Trail to avoid the steep climb on more unstable footing of the old trail. By this time, the sun will be higher and the shelter of the shady, scenic north slope will be especially welcome. Within a half-mile, you reach the higher intersection; this time, you turn left up the old trail.

As always from this area, as you begin your descent down Long Canyon Road from the Blue Jay and Falcon campground areas, check to the southwest for those sudden, stunning glimpses of glimmering ocean beyond the layers of unsullied mountains.

LADYBUG SWARM

# Upper Hot Spring Canyon

**LOCATION**: Cleveland National Forest

**TOTAL DISTANCE**: 2.4 to 3 miles round-trip

**TYPE**: Out and back

**TOTAL ELEVATION GAIN**: 400 feet

**DIFFICULTY**: Moderately strenuous because of difficult terrain

**SEASON**: December to May

**FEES ETC.**: Leashed dogs are allowed.

**MAPS**: USGS Alberhill, USFS Cleveland National Forest map

**TRAILHEAD COORDINATES**: N 33°39.191′ W 117°27.144′

**CONTACT**: Trabuco Ranger Station (951-736-1811, www.fs.fed.us/r5/cleveland); El Cariso Office (951-678-3700)

When you finally reach those sunny days right after the first big rainstorms of winter, you're aching to get out in the hills that are finally turning green again—just as the county and state parks close because of the deluge. But the trails of Cleveland National Forest nearly always beckon, and this foot-soaking hike in a pristine canyon, with its creek newly flush with water, will lead you to a waterfall and to the realization that the hiking season has indeed started again.

You will be treading on and climbing over lots of rock, both river rock and outcroppings, and there is no way to keep your feet dry. In addition, the crags of rock can be slippery and require caution. Hiking shoes with good tread are recommended for this trail, either waterproof boots or hiking sandals. You might want to bring several lengths of brightly colored ribbon (not green) to mark various forks in the path. Mild bushwhacking is necessary along the creek trail.

## GETTING THERE

Take the Ortega Highway (CA 74) exit from the San Diego Freeway (I-5) heading east for 22.2 miles. Turn left on Long Canyon Road, which bears no street marking. Instead, look for the wooden sign that reads, "Los Pinos Conservation Camp" and "El Cariso Hot Shots Regional Center." Drive on Long Canyon for 2.7 miles to the farther area of Blue Jay Campground, past Old San Juan Trail. If the gate to the farther campground is closed, use the trailhead in the Falcon Campground.

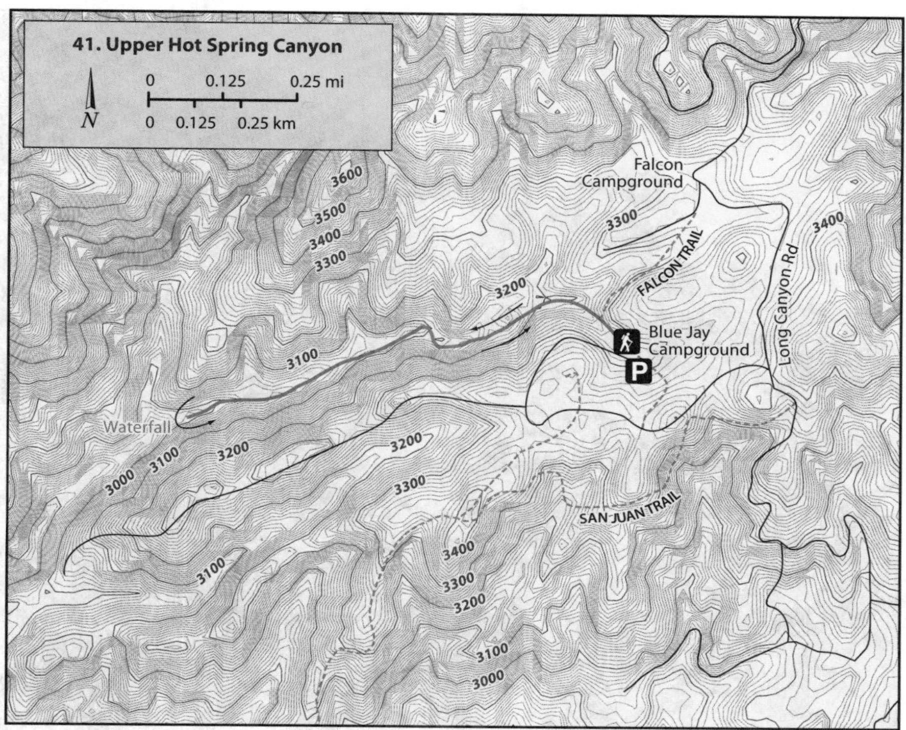


## THE TRAIL

The Falcon Trail will take you to Hot Spring Canyon from one of two trailheads. If the small loop that makes up the farther reaches of Blue Jay Campground is open, I prefer the trailhead there, which cuts more than a half-mile from your trip. But there are often gates across the side road to this less-used campground; in that case, directions from both trailheads are below.

From Blue Jay: On a fairly level trail, you walk through an area of abundant white sage and yucca. Almost from the start, you can hear the agreeable sound of the creek burbling below you to the left. At 750 feet, you'll see a small informal trail heading steeply downhill to the left. Take this for 500 feet to the creek. Cross the creek and head left—southwest—on the faint trail along the streambed, going downstream.

(From Falcon campground: Take the trail a half-mile down to a gully where there is a footbridge. Cross the footbridge to a Y junction. The left-hand side is the continuation of Falcon up to Blue Jay; you want to take the narrow, informal trail to the right, alongside the creek, going downstream.)

In an oak-shaded glen, you'll cross the creek several times until, at a tenth of a mile, you'll come to an area of small cascades and pools; if you have come during the rainiest part of the year, another stream will be joining yours from the south.

At this point, the nature of the trail

THE WATERFALL IN UPPER HOT SPRING CANYON

changes. Though there will be sections of a good dirt path ahead, you'll also spend a lot of your time either picking your way downstream in the creek, or clambering over the outcroppings of vivid if somewhat crumbly, multicolored rock. It's slow going.

Along much of the way in this damp, often-shady canyon, you'll see several kinds of mosses and ferns. Mountain mahogany (not a true mahogany) is common, as are young sycamore trees. Sycamores are generally found near a water source; they can drink up to 400 gallons of water a day.

At 0.4 mile, a small tributary joins the creek from your right (north). At this point, you might want to mark the trail so that on the way back, you remember to cross that drainage and continue on the stream to the right rather than follow a similar-looking stream up a similar-looking side canyon. There will be three more points where streams similarly merge from the north: at the half-mile, two-thirds mile, and 0.9-mile points. You can either memorize or mark these for your return.

One note about Upper Hot Spring Canyon: Some people hike extensively along and above the creek looking for hot springs. There are hot springs, but they are at the far lower end of the canyon, in Ronald W. Caspers Wilderness Park and the subject of Chapter 43 in this book.

At exactly 1 mile, you'll reach the top of the falls rushing through a crack in the rock. You can easily descend to the bottom of the falls, which cascades over two tiers into two pools below. There are more falls farther on, but the descent is treacherous with unstable and sometimes crumbling rock. Instead, return the way you came, remembering to stay with the main stream and to remove any markings you left along the trail. One last sight along the way: As you drive back on the upper reaches of Long Canyon, look to the southwest. You can see the ocean glimmering amid the mountain peaks from some 25 miles away.

# San Juan Loop Trail and Ortega Falls

**LOCATION**: Cleveland National Forest

**TOTAL DISTANCE**: 2.3 miles for San Juan Loop; .3 mile for Ortega Falls

**TYPE**: Loop, plus short spur for San Juan Loop; Out and back for Ortega Falls

**TOTAL ELEVATION GAIN**: 400 feet combined

**DIFFICULTY**: Easy

**SEASON**: January to May

**FEES ETC.**: Leashed dogs allowed.

**MAPS**: USGS Sitton Peak

**TRAILHEAD COORDINATES**: San Juan Loop: N 33°36.770′ W 117°25.611′
Ortega Falls: N 33°37.542′ W 117°.575′

**CONTACT**: Trabuco Ranger Station (951-736-1811, www.fs.fed.us/r5/cleveland); El Cariso Office (951-678-3700)

The San Juan Loop Trail packs a lot into a 2.1 miles journey around the back side of a hill. Loads of wildflowers in the late winter and early spring. A creek cascading among white boulders, an oak woodland, and my favorite, a waterfall. It's short enough for you to complete this hike and then drive 1.6 miles east to the trailhead for Ortega Falls and fit in that mini-adventure as well. One thing I can never figure out about the San Juan Loop is how, although the descent during the first half of the hike is significant enough to require switchbacks in places, the return climb seems short and as though you can't possibly be putting in that much of an elevation gain. Whatever the magic is, I'm on its side.

## GETTING THERE

Take the Ortega Highway (CA 74) exit from the San Diego Freeway (I-5) and head east for 19.5 miles. The trailhead to San Juan Loop Trail is in the large parking lot on the left, immediately across from the candy store. Begin with the trailhead on the east side of the parking lot.

For Ortega Falls: From San Juan Loop Trailhead, drive east 1.6 miles to a large turnout on the left.

## THE TRAIL

The main thing you'll notice for the first quarter-mile of San Juan Loop—and beyond—are the flowers. On bushes, on the ground, they're everywhere, and in such variety that they seem as though they must have been planted. Purple nightshade, which always hangs its head as though to hide its bright-yellow center, wild hyacinth, and California wild peony all decorate the trail. As you

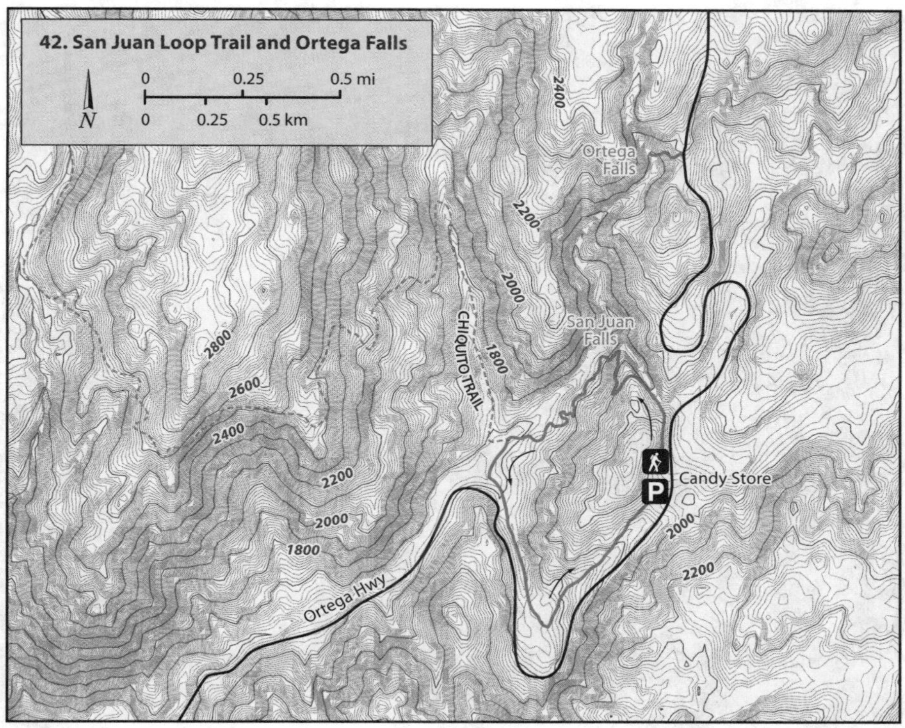


curve left around the back of the hill, the view changes as you come upon the towering buff-colored granite that makes up the walls of Long Canyon, giving it a rugged yet cathedral-like look. At the quarter-mile mark, you'll see a series of several cascades in the creek at the bottom of the gorge, and then, below you, San Juan Falls, a 15-foot drop. Take the spur trail that gently descends to the right down to the creek; some easy rock hopping will take you to the lip of the falls.

After returning to the main trail, you'll walk down a set of rocky switchbacks, listening to the sound of the creek below. Tiny blue butterflies are common in this area in spring. At the 1-mile point (not counting the spur trail), you'll find yourself at the creek bottom, in an area pleasantly dotted with old sycamore trees. The bank of the creek is dotted with dudleya and blanketed with miner's lettuce. You'll also pass the trailhead to the Chiquito Trail—that trail, combined with part of the San Juan Loop, will make up a shuttle hike elsewhere in the book (see Chapter 39, the Chiquito Trail).

Just after you leave the creek, it's time to start watching out for poison oak, which grows abundantly for the next third of a mile. But so do masses of California wild rose with its pink flowers and hypnotic rose scent. On the opposite bank of the creek, you'll see the blue flowers of periwinkle, a plant introduced by early settlers in these mountains that is now considered an exotic pest. At 1.2 miles, a serene oak

ORTEGA FALLS

woodland begins as you follow the gently gurgling creek. Soon after, you begin climbing, still through the oak trees. Visually, this seems like a remote spot; unfortunately, you're also traveling parallel to and under Ortega Highway, and its noisy rush of cars somewhat spoils the illusion.

At 1.5 miles, you'll find yourself across from the camping sites and picnic area of Upper San Juan Campground. Just past this, an unmarked fork in the trail seems determined to confuse you. Bear left and begin a climb up exposed rock, decorated along the sides of the trail by purple nightshade and canyon pea. With no visible trail on the rock itself, and several little side trails heading off at various angles, it's easy to feel as though you're getting lost during this little stretch. Just continue up the rock until you regain the trail. At 2.1 miles, the trail brings you to the west side of the parking lot.

Since you've driven all the way out here, it's worthwhile during the rainy

WILD PEONY ALONG SAN JUAN LOOP

season to drop by—which is almost literally true—Ortega Falls. In the first days after heavy rains, you can usually see a group of cars parked by the short, steep trail down. (It is unmarked, and invisible from the road.) The spot is also popular with climbers who work their way up the nearly sheer rock walls of the canyon.

As short as the trail is, use caution if you bring children. Some scrambling over rocks on the steep paths is required.

There are several informal trails from the parking area down to the falls. The one immediately to the left of the large sign warning about the need for a Forest Adventure Pass will take you most quickly to the base of the falls and with fewer rocky obstacles.

Shortly after beginning that trail, fork right and continue down the steep path amid ceanothus and other chaparral. Unlike the generally vast green expanses of the Cleveland National Forest in winter, you're descending into a closed-in, awe-inspiring canyon of buff-colored granite with sheer walls and many boulders.

Halfway down the trail, it changes from dirt to rock. Thirty feet from the bottom, there's a drop of several feet; this is more easily negotiated going around to the right-hand side of the rock.

You'll see some willow and possibly purple Canterbury bells at the bottom, along with some *Arundo donax* or giant reed, an invasive pest growing up to 20 feet high and resembling bamboo that chokes streambeds throughout southern California. The bare rocks are usually somewhat marred by graffiti, so much so that rangers sometimes stand at the top of the trail looking out for vandals. If you're in luck, you'll arrive not long after the Warriors Society, a volunteer group of bikers, has been down there cleaning off the markings.

Graffiti or no, Ortega Falls, and the creek heading downstream, send cool, white water rushing through the rocks. There are plenty of rounded boulders nearby, perfect seats for indulging in a contemplative sit, listening to the relaxing rush of the falls and the soothing music of water rushing over and around stone.

# San Juan Hot Springs

**LOCATION**: Ronald W. Caspers Wilderness Park

**TOTAL DISTANCE**: 13 miles

**TYPE**: Out and back

**TOTAL ELEVATION GAIN**: 1,000 feet

**DIFFICULTY**: Strenuous

**SEASON**: November to June

**FEES ETC.**: $3 daily, $5 weekends. No dogs allowed. Camping and equestrian facilities available.

**MAPS**: USGS Cañada Gobernadora

**TRAILHEAD COORDINATES**: N 33°32.428′ W 117°33.134′

**CONTACT**: Caspers Wilderness Park (949-923-2210, www.ocparks.com/caspers)

If you get the feeling that someone is intentionally making it hard for you to get to the most beautiful and interesting area of Caspers Wilderness Park, you're not being paranoid. You practically have to jump through hoops—or more specifically hike 13 miles—to get to and from the hot springs at the eastern end of the park and to beautiful Cold Spring Canyon, an emerald ravine so green even well into June that it feels almost like a rain forest. It's not easy to find natural hot springs in Orange County—at least, not without trespassing on private property—and though the trek is long, the rewards both along the way and at the end are worth it. Water that arrives preheated at the surface of the earth is an awe-inducing phenomenon, not to mention a creek that runs with hot water. Adjacent Cold Spring Canyon, dense with greenery, has a dreamy, isolated quality.

Bring plenty of water and some food on this hike. There are some exposed areas, and it's impossible to finish within the earlier morning hours.

## GETTING THERE

Take the Ortega Highway (CA 74) exit from the San Diego Freeway (I-5) in San Juan Capistrano. Head east on Ortega Highway 7.6 miles to the entrance to Caspers Wilderness Park. You'll be charged a fee at the entry kiosk. Proceed straight on the main park road 0.3 mile to the San Juan Meadow group camping area on your right. There is some day-use parking here as well; park here for the trailhead to the Juaneño Trail.

## THE TRAIL

Why are you embarking on such a long journey when there's another gate to the park quite close to the hot springs? Blame mischief-minded visitors who helped themselves to a little informal and illegal hot-tubbing, damaging the area where a resort once treated guests to the sulfur-scented, 122-degree water. As a result, the park has closed the old entrance and installed barbed wire. Until 2014, it also did not maintain the section of San Juan Creek Trail between Oso and Cold Spring Canyon trails, allowing the shortcut to become overgrown and dangerous. Fortunately, a change in park administration brought in staff with a commitment to public access and talent at trail restoration; using this segment to loop back on the return trip cuts close to two miles off of what used to be a 15-mile hike.

San Juan Hot Springs was already a buzzing tourist destination in the 1870s; some 20 years later, a hotel and other buildings were constructed. Early photos show women in long skirts posing at what looks almost like a hamlet. According to Orange County historian Phil Brigandi, the resort was shut down around 1936 by the health department, and for years, efforts were made to add it to the Cleveland National Forest. In the late 1970s, a new owner renovated and restored the run-down spring resort, with several hot tubs located close to Ortega Highway. The spa closed down, and a 1993 fire destroyed most of what was left. You can see the remains of some buildings and an old soaking pool on this hike, as well as several small ponds of bubbling, hot, mildly sulfurous water.

Because almost half of your hike will be along the Juaneño Trail, you'll be

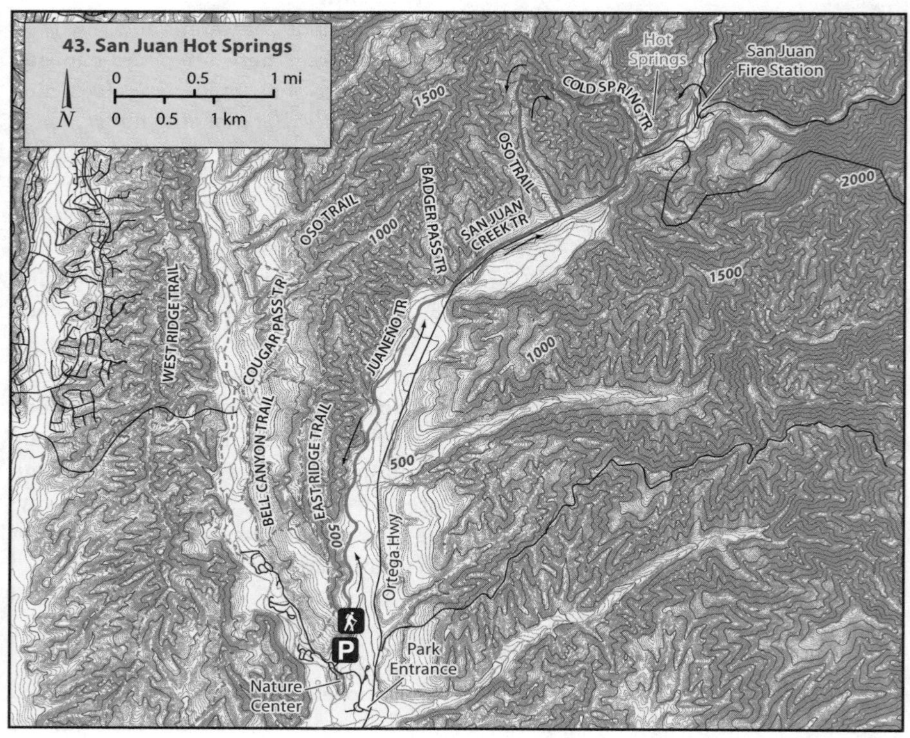

POOL OF HOT, SULFUROUS WATER

grateful for the variety of sights along this path. You'll wander beneath peaceful oak woodlands, along the base of steep bluffs of sedimentary rock and through sage scrub. Several times, the path will take you across the bed of San Juan Creek, which is dry more often than not. In late spring, though, the dry wash is filled with what have to be the most colorful prickly pear cactus in the county—giant patches of cactus laden with large blossoms in shades of yellow, pink, and peach. Non-native Spanish broom flowers in showy yellow all along its stems, an attractive nuisance.

In June, eye-catching specimens of California milkweed also grow along the Juaneño Trail. These are extraterrestrial-looking plants, growing up to 5 feet high, with grayish, fuzzy leaves and big, rounded heads of oddly shaped, lavender or dark-red flowers that have a short season. This is one species of milkweed from the genus Asclepias, named for the Greek god of healing Asklepios because the ancients found so many medicinal uses for it. Milkweed is also the only plant that the caterpillar of the monarch butterfly will eat.

The Juaneño Trail ends at the San Juan Creek Trail. Turn left here and continue for 0.9 mile, ignoring the trailhead to Badger Pass Trail on the left.

Turn left at the posted entrance to Oso Trail. (San Juan Creek Trail continues as a single-track trail here, and is the more direct way to the hot springs, but unless the ranger at the kiosk has told you that the trail has been recently cleared and maintained, steer clear of it. The heavy bushwhacking required and the possibility of losing the trail altogether make any shortcut not worth the effort.)

Oso Trail will climb steadily amid scrub and prickly pear cactus, a 700-foot-elevation gain that offers views westward across that park and back toward Ortega Highway.

After 1.5 miles on the Oso Trail, it continues upward to the left but you'll turn right on Cold Spring Canyon Trail. Here you enter a world unto itself. In the distance to your left, as you descend toward the canyon floor, you'll find unbroken vistas across overlapping layers of blue-green mountains. The canyon flooded during heavy rains several years ago, and a botched trail-repair job carved a wide, rock-strewn trail through it. The canyon is still recovering from that damage, and fortunately more recently, hand-groomed trail restoration is helping that along.

The trail will pull you into the hushed, creek-watered ravine of Cold Spring Canyon, with thick growths of wild grape and chaparral plants including holly-leaf red berry, a large shrub with bright-red, edible berries.

The trail ends after 1 mile, at San Juan Creek Trail. Turn left and begin to climb out of the canyon, past two heavy posts driven into the ground. After 0.4 mile of walking along this trail, look for a large date palm tree to your right. At that point, examine the clearing on the hillside for the small pools of hot water, many set with low rock walls that are beginning to tumble down. Soaking in the tubs or putting your hands on these is prohibited.

Continue downhill on the trail another 500 feet to reach the bottom of the hill and turn right. This will lead you to a fenced area of ruins, including the elegant old soaking pool sitting amid natural pools of water and rushes that

SIGN TO THE OLD HOT SPRINGS RESORT

THE VIEW FROM COLD SPRING CANYON TRAIL

have found a hospitably moist environment. One stone wall dates back about 80 years; old building remains include a pump house and the ruins of a one-room house that once could be rented there. Turning back, look for a large oleander growing at a small stone bridge; this is the hot-water creek. Further exploration to the east of the ruins takes you across San Juan Creek to an old picnic area, shaded by oaks, and a sign to the hot springs. On the way there, take a right hook down the ITO Trail (which stands for Inside The Outdoors, an ecology program for schoolchildren) under cool trees to the creek, which is almost always flowing. Under these trees along the creek was where the modern hot springs operation placed hot tubs, pumping the hot water there from the hillside. Each hot tub came with a small semi-enclosure for privacy, dubbed with such fanciful tropical names as Shangri-La.

It's the perfect spot for a rest and a picnic before the trek back by the same route.

You can shorten the return trip by taking San Juan Creek Trail from Cold Spring to Juaneño, now that the park has carefully restored the old trail. This cuts two miles from the distance, making it 13 miles instead of the former 15 miles. In fact, you could do that in both directions, making this an 11-mile hike, but then you'd miss out on Cold Spring Canyon and what are, to me, the loveliest sights in all of Caspars.

# Trabuco Canyon–West Horsethief Loop

**LOCATION**: Cleveland National Forest

**TOTAL DISTANCE**: 10 miles

**TYPE**: Loop

**TOTAL ELEVATION GAIN**: 2,200 feet

**DIFFICULTY**: Strenuous

**SEASON**: January to July

**FEES ETC.**: Free parking. Leashed dogs are allowed.

**MAPS**: USGS Santiago Peak, Alberhill

**TRAILHEAD COORDINATES**: N 33°41.004′ W 117°30.070′

**CONTACT**: Trabuco Ranger Station (951-736-1811, www.fs.fed.us/r5/cleveland)

You don't have to love flowers to enjoy this hike, but it wouldn't hurt. This demanding loop has many pleasures to recommend it: creeks, forests, thickets of fragrant mountain chaparral, huge vistas that extend both east and west of the Santa Ana Mountains, an abandoned adit. Oh, and did I say flowers? Because of its varied habitat and a large open area that's generously watered by Trabuco Creek and its tributaries, this hike is loaded with them—too many kinds to name. Some of the less-common ones you'll see include chaparral currant, larkspur, bush poppy, and prickly phlox, along with bay laurel, a veritable forest of red-branched, twisting manzanita, and one of the southernmost patches of madrone, a bushlike tree that resembles manzanita. The blue-flowered ceanothus, or wild lilac, along this trail grows especially thick and fragrant. You might want to toss a wildflower guide into your backpack.

If you get an early start, you can climb up the switchbacks before the sun makes it over the ridge from the east, giving you a pleasantly cool ascent. This is one hike where sneakers or trail-runner shoes don't cut it. You'll want a sturdy hiking shoe with protective soles for the long stretches of stone-covered trail. Though you can find plenty to enjoy from January to May, these trails are at their gaudiest in March and April. Then again, the true flower hunter can find the sublime Humboldt lily in bloom here in late spring and summer.

## GETTING THERE

From South County: Exit the San Diego Freeway (I-5) at El Toro Road and head

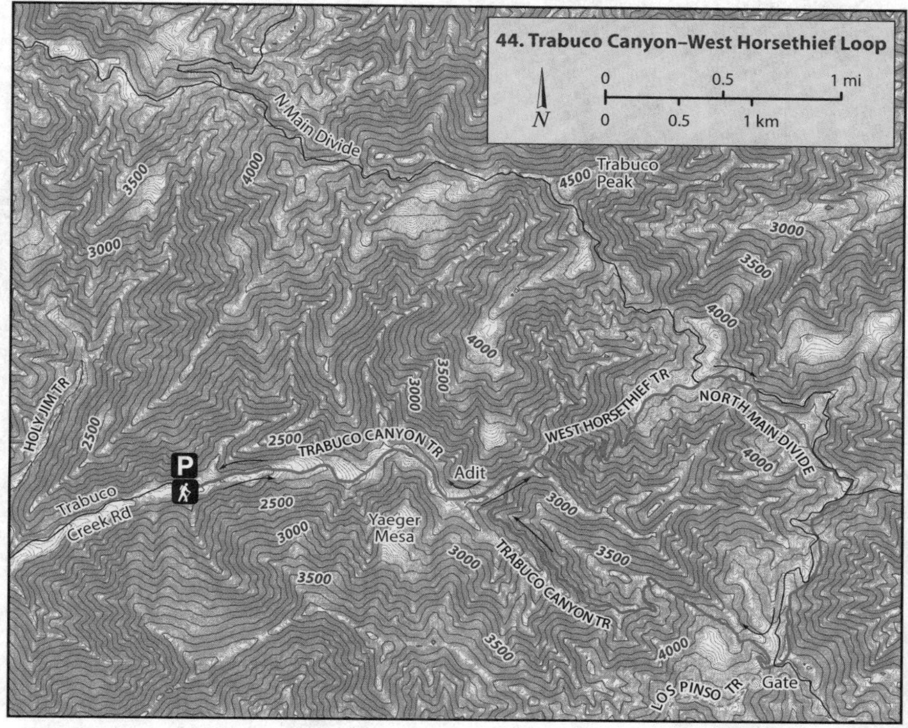


east for 8.6 miles. (The name of the road changes to Santiago Canyon Road.) Turn right at Cook's Corner, location of the noted motorcycle bar, onto Live Oak Canyon Road, which turns into Trabuco Canyon Road. Travel a total of 5.2 miles, past the entrance to O'Neill Regional Park and over the bridge, then make an immediate left onto Trabuco Creek Road, where you see a large dirt clearing to the left. Drive 4.4 miles on this rocky, deeply rutted road, a difficult trip for sedans. The road has a lot of teeth-rattling washboarding and after rains collects pools of water so deep in places that even giant SUVs occasionally get stuck. Timing your hike to be at least a week after the most recent heavy rain will help so that the pools dry a bit. But the drive is as beautiful as it is nerve-fraying, and once you've gotten a couple of miles into the canyon, the road is worth a hike all on its own, following wide Trabuco Creek with its old stone check dams.

You'll see a wide, flattened area for parking with chemical toilets and a visitors' kiosk. This is the entryway to Holy Jim Canyon; you'll continue driving on the road that continues straight ahead for a mile to the Trabuco Canyon Trailhead. Here you'll find a parking area with space for a couple of cars.

From North County: Take the Chapman Avenue exit from the Costa Mesa Freeway (CA 55), heading east for 15.4 miles and making a left onto Live Oak Canyon Road at Cook's Corner, location of the noted motorcycle bar. Proceed as above.

WOODLAND ALONG TRABUCO CANYON TRAIL

## THE TRAIL

The first section of Trabuco Canyon Trail follows the path of an old dirt road to a former campground in the open area ahead, but it has narrowed nicely to give a sense of seclusion, despite the rusted hulk of a car to the right. About 40 feet away, the waters of Trabuco Creek rush downhill and the entire wooded area has a rain-forest feel to it. Look for alder trees, delicate maidenhair fern, the round leaves of low-growing miner's lettuce, and the first of the bay laurels, which have the distinctive smell of the bay leaves from your pantry.

The last wild grizzly bear in the Santa Ana Mountains was killed in Trabuco Canyon in 1908. The grizzly population had been decimated by ranchers who killed the bears to protect livestock. They also were killed by bounty hunters who took advantage of the state's $10 reward for each bear and vaqueros who made it a sport to catch and kill them. (See the chapter on Limestone Canyon.) Known as "Little Black Bear" or "Honey Thief," the old female bear wore out any welcome it had when in 1907 it destroyed 30 bee stands in an area where beekeeping was a popular occupation. A trap was set; Honey Thief was caught but escaped. Hunters tracked the bear for weeks afterward, finally killing it at the mouth of Trabuco Canyon. It was found to be thin and arthritic; the hide was sent to the Smithsonian.

At 0.4 mile, the woods let out into a dry, rocky area where you'll begin seeing a vivid assortment of wildflowers. Among the showiest are larkspur and patches of prickly phlox, deep-lavender flowers whose petals form a sort of windmill pattern, along with thickleaf yerba santa, with its thick, grayish leaves.

You'll find an adit on the left at 1.1 miles. Continue along a path that alternates between loose rock and woodland dirt areas. There will be several drainages to cross above the main creek. At 1.5 miles, an unmarked trail leads right; you'll stay to the left on Trabuco Canyon Trail. Then at 1.7 miles, the Trabuco trail itself veers to the right, but you'll fork left onto West Horsethief Trail.

At 2 miles, you'll begin your ascent up a series of wide switchbacks, your trail decorated by flowers as you go. Along with the usual assortment of sage-scrub flowers, you might see the bright yellow of the common large monkeyflower or the big, four-petaled blossoms of bush poppy. As you reach higher elevations, manzanita and blue-flowered ceanothus will become more common. Look back, down the length of Trabuco Canyon, to see the views of overlapping mountains. At 2.7 miles, ignore the informal trail that heads more steeply uphill. Instead, stay with the main trail. About 1,000 feet later, you enter an area with Coulter (or big-cone) pines as the trail levels somewhat in a flowered forest of manzanita and wild lilac. From here until you reach North Main Divide, the trail will alternately flatten and climb. At a fork at 3 miles, stay to the right.

You'll reach North Main Divide, a wide dirt-and-rock road, at 3.3 miles. Turn right and enjoy expansive views on both sides of the road. To the west are the mountains of Trabuco Canyon; to the east, you can spot Lake Mathews and Lake Elsinore as well as the often snowcapped peaks of Mount San Gorgonio and Mount San Jacinto.

At 4.6 miles, a side road veers to the left; stay on the level and wider North Main Divide through thickets of man-

TRABUCO CANYON

zanita and the shade of conifers. Watch out for occasional cars and motorbikes along the road.

At 5.8 miles—2.5 miles from when you started on North Main Divide—you'll see a large metal gate used to close off North Main Divide to traffic at certain times of the year. Two trails go to the right, neither of them marked at this point; you'll want to take the first trail, before you can pass through the gate, heading downhill on Trabuco Canyon Trail.

You'll pass a gently cascading creek to your left at 6.1 miles. Along this path, you'll travel through a largely woodsy area at first, with oak and more bay laurel. It's along this area that you can often find chaparral currant, with its clusters of showy pink, tubular flowers that give way to edible fruit.

The pathway opens out into a sunny area again, thick with dudleya (the low-growing succulent in a rosette that sends out brilliant red-purple blossoms on slender stalks), white sage, and neon-red paintbrush. At 8.2 miles, you'll reach a stone-littered creek crossing. On the other side of the creek, you'll reach West Horsethief Trail again, completing the loop. Turn left here on Trabuco Canyon Trail to return back through the oak and alder woodland.

# Santiago Peak via Holy Jim Canyon

**LOCATION**: Cleveland National Forest

**TOTAL DISTANCE**: 16 miles

**TYPE**: Out and back

**TOTAL ELEVATION GAIN**: 4,000 feet

**DIFFICULTY**: Very strenuous

**SEASON**: October to June

**FEES ETC.**: Free parking. Leashed dogs allowed, but not advised because of the length and difficulty of the hike.

**MAPS**: USGS Santiago Peak

**TRAILHEAD COORDINATES**: N 33°40.612′ W 117°31.039′

**CONTACT**: Trabuco Ranger Station (951-736-1811, www.fs.fed.us/r5/cleveland)

They call it the talking mountain, not for some legendary story about the spirits that whisper among the winds at its summit. The reality is far less romantic. The tallest point in Orange County, at 5,687 feet, Santiago Peak fairly bristles with communications antennae atop its scraped-bare summit. Still, the views are unparalleled (though Modjeska Peak comes close), stretching close to 100 miles in every direction on the clearest of days. The trail getting there is also loaded with sights, aromas, and history—the shady, stream-fed lower area of Holy Jim Canyon, the climb through mountain chaparral including ceanothus, fragrant even when it's not in bloom, and heavily shaded areas of maple, oak, and big-cone Douglas fir. There are several springs along the way.

Along with Modjeska, Santiago Peak makes up the landmark feature called Old Saddleback, visible from most of Orange County. Some people call it Saddleback Mountain because from afar it appears to be a single mountain.

There are several ways to reach Santiago Peak—for that matter, with a four-wheel-drive and steady nerves, you can drive there from Ortega Highway along North Main Divide—but this is the shortest and most enjoyable way to be able to brag you've climbed the county's highest mountain.

Bring far more water than you normally would even for a long hike—none of the water at the springs should be considered potable—along with food, good hiking shoes, and some extra clothing. It's considerably cooler on the top of the peak than from your starting point. You might want to pack a pair of binoculars for the view at the top.

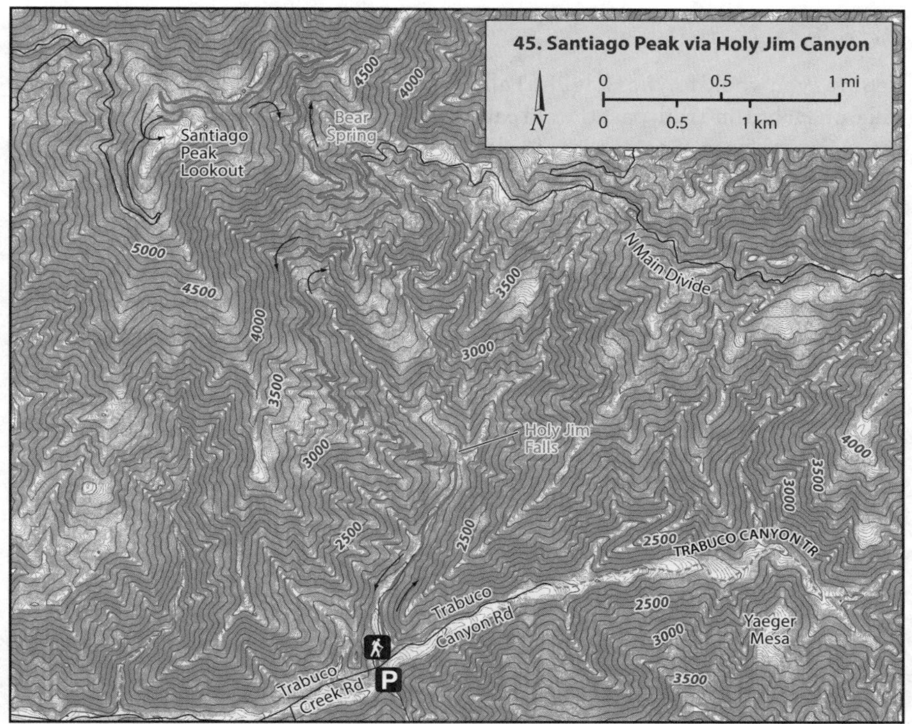


## GETTING THERE

From South County: Exit the San Diego Freeway (I-5) at El Toro Road and head east for 8.6 miles. (The name of the road changes to Santiago Canyon Road.) Turn right at Cook's Corner, location of the noted motorcycle bar, onto Live Oak Canyon Road, which turns into Trabuco Canyon Road. Drive a total of 5.2 miles, past the entrance to O'Neill Regional Park and over the bridge, then make an immediate left onto Trabuco Creek Road, where you see a large dirt clearing to the left. The rocky, rutted road, which travels through scenic areas along the creek, has a lot of teeth-rattling washboarding and after rains collects difficult-to-ford pools of water. Timing your hike to be at least a week after the most recent heavy rain will give the pools a chance to dry a bit.

After 4.4 miles on the rutted road, you'll see a wide, flattened area for parking with chemical toilets and a visitor's kiosk. This is the entryway to Holy Jim; the road continues straight ahead to the Trabuco Canyon Trail (see the chapter on the Trabuco Canyon-West Horsethief Loop). Walk up the dirt road that heads uphill to the left.

From North County: Take the Chapman Avenue exit from the Costa Mesa Freeway (CA 55), heading east for 15.4 miles and making a left onto Live Oak Canyon Road at Cook's Corner, location of the noted motorcycle bar. Proceed as above.

## THE TRAIL

Begin as you would for the Holy Jim Falls hike, on Holy Jim Trail, past the old cabins on forest leases. (See Chapter 46 also for the history of "Cussin'" Jim Smith, who used to run a beekeeping operation in the lower canyon, and points along the way.) At 1.2 miles, where a spur trail goes off to the right toward Holy Jim Falls, you'll stay left on Holy Jim Trail and begin the switchback ascent up to Main Divide. Here you'll leave the cool shade of the trees that brought you this far and enter a more exposed stretch for the next 3.8 miles.

This single-track trail is well maintained, thanks to the volunteer efforts of the Warrior's Society, a civic-minded biking group. And because this is a favorite trail among bikers, keep an eye out for them going both ways.

This is the steepest going of your trip, along a trail that is often thickly lined with manzanita and fragrant blue-flowered ceanothus blooming in springtime. You'll ascend up some 15 switchbacks; in areas, the chaparral will thin out to give you a view back into Holy Jim Canyon. The trail then levels out slightly—though you're still climbing.

In the lower areas, in early spring, you're likely to find wild peony, with its distinctive burgundy-colored flowers, which smell like licorice. Higher up, you'll see the elegantly contorted limbs

ABOVE IT ALL ON SANTIAGO PEAK

of hoary-leaved ceanothus, or snowball bush. And higher yet, look for an area where the plants change to water-loving bay laurels; except in the driest months, you can find two springs here, one of them seeping with profuse amounts of water.

There are points at which you'll see informal trails that seem to point you straight toward the mountain, but you're on safer footing along the main trail. You'll recognize that you're reaching the top of the trail when you enter a heavily forested area where big-cone Douglas fir trees, found only at the higher elevations of the forest, mingle with oak and sycamore. Bigleaf maple—look for the large, hand-shaped leaves—has the same spinning, seed-containing wings as the Vermont variety and can also produce the makings for maple syrup. The splendid canyon live oaks that grow here—with silvery bark, multiple trunks, and large, rounded acorns—are the less-common cousins of the coast live oak you find in most of the county's oak woodlands.

At 5 miles, you'll come out at Main Divide Road and turn left, almost immediately coming upon Bear Spring (with the concrete tank) on your right, so named because it was favored by grizzly bears back when they still inhabited this area. (They also liked the acorns of the canyon live oaks.) As with all water that doesn't come out of a faucet in the wilderness, this should not be considered safe for drinking.

The rest of the hike is a 3-mile walk up Main Divide, a wide dirt road, with both exposed and loose rock in many places. Watch out for the occasional motorcycle or four-wheel-drive vehicle. You'll climb through thickly forested areas of big-cone Douglas fir as well as spots that are nearly bare of vegetation; in spring, you'll find the bright yellow of bush poppy along the trail as well. At 1.5 miles along Main Divide, you'll come to a small section with a moonscape appearance, called the scar.

At 7.9 miles from the start of the hike, you reach the summit that you may have admired from the lowlands of Saddleback Valley. The ground has been scraped down to raw earth planted with a metallic forest of communications towers, some of them humming. There's no one spot where you can stand to take in a 360-degree view—the antennas see to that—but by walking around the summit, you can see more distant places than you can probably identify. On the clearest days, the sights stretch from the Mexican border up to Santa Monica. If you brought good binoculars, you may be able to make out Mount Wilson with its observatory in the La Cañada Flintridge area to your north, or the high-rise office towers of downtown Los Angeles. San Clemente and Santa Catalina islands might be visible out in the ocean. Inland, you'll see the three peaks known as the "Three Saints"—Mount San Antonio (better known as Mount Baldy), Mount San Gorgonio, and Mount San Jacinto, all three usually covered with snow in winter. Closer to your perch, blue-gray mountains unfold in front of you on every side.

In colder months, you might encounter a dusting of snow up here yourself, and even on a relatively balmy spring day below, the wind was whipping bits of ice off the metal towers. In ways, the experience is even more awe-inspiring on an overcast day, when you can literally touch the clouds as they sail by. Here it can feel as though everything between heaven and earth is contained within a very narrow wedge, indeed.

46

# Holy Jim Falls

**LOCATION**: Cleveland National Forest

**TOTAL DISTANCE**: 3 miles

**TYPE**: Out and back

**ELEVATION GAIN**: 600 feet

**DIFFICULTY**: Moderately easy

**SEASON**: December to May

**FEES ETC.**: Free parking. Good for kids. Leashed dogs allowed.

**MAPS**: USGS Santiago Peak

**TRAILHEAD COORDINATES**: N 33°40.612′ W 117°31.039′

**CONTACT**: Trabuco Ranger's Station, Cleveland National Forest (951 736-1811; www.fs.fed.us/r5/cleveland)

The trail to Holy Jim Falls is laden with both history and natural beauty. The relative shortness of the hike, the sights along the way, and the fun of crossing creeks make it a particularly fun hike for children, as long as they can endure a gentle but steady climb.

You've got to appreciate the mischievous government worker of years long ago who gave this canyon its sobriquet. The falls, and the picturesque canyon in which it flows, are named for pioneer and beekeeper James T. Smith in the late 1800s. Smith was so renowned for the long streams of foul language that would emerge from his mouth, he was nicknamed Cussin' Jim (as well as Greasy Jim, Lyin' Jim, and . . . well, you get the idea). When federal cartographers were surveying the area for a new national forest, the nickname seemed unseemly for an official map; yet one surveyor with a sense of tongue-in-cheek humor clearly didn't want to lose the flavor of the canyon and its idiosyncratic former resident, and came up with the perfect name: Holy Jim. That beats Smith Canyon.

## GETTING THERE

From South County: Exit the San Diego Freeway (I-5) at El Toro Road and head east for 8.6 miles. (The name of the road changes to Santiago Canyon Road.) Turn right at Cook's Corner, location of the noted motorcycle bar, onto Live Oak Canyon Road, which turns into Trabuco Canyon Road. Travel a total of 5.2 miles, past the entrance to O'Neill Regional Park and over the bridge, then make an immediate left onto Trabuco Creek Road, where you see a large dirt clearing to the left. Drive 4.4 miles on this rocky, deeply rutted road

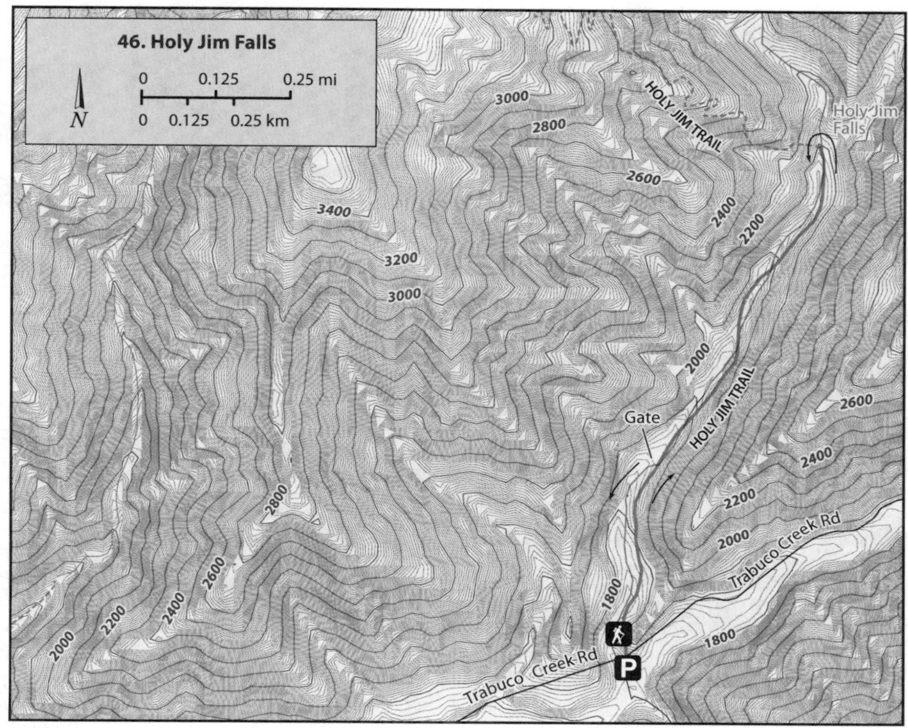


that is more easily traversed by truck or four-wheel-drive than by sedan. But the drive along the creek as the canyon narrows is as beautiful as it is nerve-fraying.

You'll see a wide, flattened area for parking with chemical toilets and a visitor's kiosk. This is the entryway to Holy Jim; the road continues straight ahead to the Trabuco Canyon Trail (see the chapter on the Trabuco Canyon-West Horsethief Loop). Walk up the dirt road that heads uphill to the left.

From North County: Take the Chapman Avenue exit from the Costa Mesa Freeway (CA 55), heading east for 15.4 miles and making a left onto Live Oak Canyon Road at Cook's Corner and its noted motorcycle bar. Proceed as above.

## THE TRAIL

You'll pass rustic older houses, some nearly a century old, on leases within in the Cleveland National Forest, and on the left, century plants, so named because it takes them a long time (but more like 25 years than a century!) to bloom, which they do only once in their lives, and then they die. A form of agave, the plants are natives of Central America that have naturalized to some extent after being cultivated in parts of Orange County. The century plant spends most of its life as just the basal rosette you see at the bottom; then, when it is getting ready to flower and die off, the stem will grow as fast as 2 inches per day. One of the century plants was blooming, with an impressively large cluster of yellow

Courtesy of Cleveland National Forest

"HOLY" JIM SMITH, AT RIGHT, WITH TWO VISITORS, CIRCA 1900

flowers at the end of a 15-foot spike, the last time I was there.

After a half-mile, you'll come to the gate that marks the official trailhead. Start looking to the right for a partial, low stone wall with various rocks scattered about. This is what remains of Smith's late-1800s house. The Forest Service has placed a marker at the spot.

The canyon is deeply shaded and thick with trees as you follow the creek on a gradual incline. Another marker as you ascend will guide you to trees that were downed by a catastrophic 1908 fire that burned 4,000 acres in this area, including Smith's cabin and the fig trees he had planted. The hunters who carelessly left their campfire smoldering were fined.

The flower you're most likely to see is low-growing, blue periwinkle introduced by early settlers in this area; pretty though it is, the Forest Service has been working on eradicating the non-native. Look for the smaller, almost vine-like trees with the big, deeply lobed leaves; these are fig trees, the descendants of Smith's original plants. I've never seen them fruit, but they give off a heavy, sweet scent. At one point along the trail, the fig trees have sprawled toward and over the trail, forming a 30-foot-long tunnel that hikers crouch under as they walk through.

There are seven creek crossings before the turnoff to the falls, most of them easily crossed by hopping rocks or traversing logs that have been laid across the creek. These are great spots to search for California newts, with their standout orange color and bulging eyes.

Along the way, you'll see a stone check dam in the creek, built during the 1950s to create pools for fish—and you might see people fishing for trout as well. The open center of the dam can be closed to block water and form the pool. This marked area is called Picnic Rock. Across the trail at this point is a particularly imposing oak tree estimated to be 500 years old. A short distance after Picnic Rock is an old mulberry tree that probably dates back to Smith's residency here; in June, it's laden with fruit.

At 1.2 miles from the start, after the sixth creek crossing, Holy Jim Trail will fork left, making its grand switchback ascent to the Main Divide. You'll turn right toward the falls; the turnoff is well marked. This area is somewhat thick with poison oak. There will be three creek crossings in immediate succession during the 0.3-mile spur before you reach the chapel-like grotto with its fern-covered walls, where the 18-foot waterfall cascades into a pool.

The return is a fast, easy stroll downhill.

WALKING THROUGH A TUNNEL OF FIG BRANCHES IN HOLY JIM CANYON

# Falls Canyon

**LOCATION**: Cleveland National Forest

**TYPE**: Out and back

**TOTAL DISTANCE**: 0.9 to 2.9 miles round-trip

**TOTAL ELEVATION GAIN**: 100 feet

**DIFFICULTY**: Moderately easy

**SEASON**: December to April

**FEES ETC.**: Free parking. Good for children.

**MAPS**: USGS Santiago Peak

**TRAILHEAD COORDINATES**: N 33° 40.423′ W 117°32.086′

**CONTACT**: Trabuco Ranger Station (951-736-1811, www.fs.fed.us/r5/cleveland)

The biggest trick to hiking Falls Canyon is finding it—and maybe getting past the poison oak you'll encounter for the first 400 feet or so to get to the canyon entrance. It's more than worthwhile for this easy and peaceful little walk to one of the prettiest waterfalls in the county, and one that few people know exists. Just make sure you have a car with a good spare tire and enough clearance to travel miles on the poorly maintained dirt-and-rock access road.

## GETTING THERE

From South County: Exit the San Diego Freeway (I-5) at El Toro Road and head east for 8.6 miles. (The name of the road changes to Santiago Canyon Road.) Turn right at Cook's Corner, where you'll find the noted motorcycle bar, onto Live Oak Canyon Road, which turns into Trabuco Canyon Road. Travel a total of 5.2 miles, past the entrance to O'Neill Regional Park and over the bridge, then make an immediate left onto Trabuco Creek Road, where you see a large dirt clearing to the left.

Drive 3.4 miles on this rocky, deeply rutted dirt road to a point where the road widens slightly on the right, enough room for a couple of cars to park. If others have gotten there first—this is a favorite spot of fishermen—continue 1 mile to the larger parking area for Holy Jim Falls and walk back. It's a level and scenic stroll along flowing Trabuco Creek that turns the outing into a more substantial and varied hiking experience.

From North County: Take the Chapman Avenue exit from the Costa Mesa Freeway (CA 55), heading east for 15.4 miles and making a left onto Live Oak Canyon Road at Cook's Corner, loca-

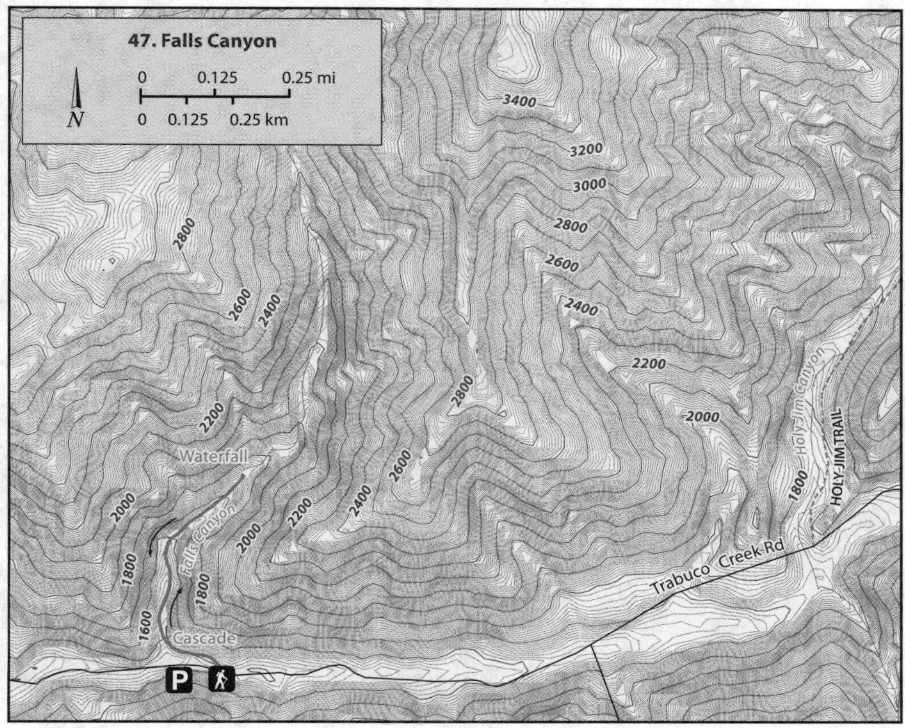


tion of the noted motorcycle bar. Proceed as above.

## THE TRAIL

Most hikers who bother subjecting their cars to jolting, tire-challenging Trabuco Creek Road are headed toward one of the two well-known, marked trails farther along—Holy Jim Canyon and Trabuco Canyon trails. Rare is the visitor who has heard about the short, unmarked creek-side trail through peaceful, steep-walled Falls Canyon to a perennial waterfall more than twice as high as Holy Jim Falls. On a recent visit, even the volunteer officers patrolling the road were unfamiliar with the name. Armed only with vague and slightly inaccurate instructions that turned out to be outdated as well (a berm that served as a landmark had been removed), it took four attempts to locate the opening to the canyon. These directions should put you on the right path the first time.

Once discovered, this might become a favorite hike, in part because though the canyon is relatively convenient and the walk short, almost no one goes there. Within a minute, all traces of civilization disappear. The only sounds are the burbling of the creek and an occasional bird. But it would be smart to bring a companion to Falls Canyon. The trail is primitive and eroded in some spots, and few people come here. Most cell phones get no reception.

The waterfall and creek flow practically year-round but are at their best in the late winter and early spring; how-

THE FALLS OF FALLS CANYON

A SMALL CASCADE IN THE BRUSH MARKS THE ENTRANCE TO FALLS CANYON

ever, if you try this too soon after significant rains, Trabuco Creek Road will be filled with deep pools difficult to cross by car, and the creek itself will be hard to ford. Take basic precautions against poison oak—long pants and a long-sleeved shirt that are washed soon after the hike. Because of the time it takes to drive back via the dirt road, you might even bring a change of clothes and some poison oak wash.

Once you have parked, cross the dirt road and walk back in the direction you came for about 200 feet. Look for a well-worn fisherman's trail cutting diagonally from the road to Trabuco Creek. There are numerous little paths that take you to the creek, but this path will help you avoid poison oak and bring you closest to the mouth of Falls Canyon. In spring, the trailside will be decorated with periwinkle, a blue-flowered cultivar that was introduced into Trabuco Canyon by 19th-century settlers and has made itself a pretty part of the environment, if an unwelcome one. In late summer and early fall, edible wild grape will be fruiting throughout this area.

The path will take you to one of various easy creek crossings, but exercise caution if recent rains have swollen the creek. On the other side, head downstream again, and within another 200 feet you'll find the tributary from Falls Canyon. This can be a little tricky. In all but the wettest conditions, the water does not flow aboveground all the way to Trabuco Creek. To your right, the spot is marked by a small cascade about 50 feet from the main creek. Rocks in the streambed that joins the larger creek also mark the point for turning into the canyon.

Turn right, following the trail into the opening of Falls Canyon. From here, you will follow a narrow but well-worn dirt path along the creek. You're in an area of oak, maple, sycamore, and black cottonwood trees, and occasional bay laurel. California blackberry spreads abundantly, and because birds are a rarity on the dark floor of the canyon, the vines can grow thick with unpicked fruit.

There are several creek crossings, all of them easy, and a few small rises. There are also places where it is impossible to determine whether the trail continues across the creek or on your side. As it happens, you're generally fine either way; the paths will meet up again, usually within 50 feet. In the few cases where one side doesn't work out, it's short work to make your way back to where you were. Most of the hiking upstream will be done on the right side of the creek.

In autumn, the huge bigleaf maples that shelter you turn a glowing orange. Chances are that you'll be able to find California newts in the creek and tree frogs on the nearby rocks.

At 0.3 mile into the canyon, a boulder about 10 feet high must be climbed to continue, but there are plenty of footholds. To the left of this boulder are giant chain ferns, the biggest species of the county's native ferns. Generally, the path to the falls involves a nearly unnoticeable ascent that is slowed only by the creek crossings and eroded patches on soft dirt that require careful treading to avoid slipping.

After hiking for 0.4 miles into the canyon, you'll see a couple of cascades, one right after the other. Shortly beyond this, pass under an archway draped with more wild grape vines. The falls is only about 100 feet beyond, in a small clearing, dropping 40 feet into a pool.

# Modjeska Grade Road and Santiago Truck Trail

**LOCATION**: Cleveland National Forest

**TOTAL DISTANCE**: 7.8 miles

**TYPE**: Out and back

**TOTAL ELEVATION GAIN**: 1,300 feet

**DIFFICULTY**: Moderately strenuous

**SEASON**: December to May

**FEES ETC.**: Free parking. Leashed dogs allowed.

**MAPS**: USGS El Toro (quad to be renamed Lake Forest), Santiago Peak

**TRAILHEAD COORDINATES**: N 33°42.159′ W 117° 38.184′

**CONTACT**: Trabuco Ranger Station (951-736-1811, www.fs.fed.us/r5/cleveland)

With views of Saddleback Valley to one side and the edge of the Santa Ana Mountains on the other, this trail also offers plenty of unusual features close up, enough to keep you absorbed along its length, especially if marine fossils are an interest of yours. In spring, your path is strewn with wildflowers; after major rains, you're rewarded with a dramatic if distant waterfall, one of the loveliest in the mountains. During a good rainy season, a March hike might give you the best of both worlds. Bring a hat and plenty of water; there's little shade along the route.

## GETTING THERE

From South County: Take the El Toro Road exit from the San Diego Freeway (I-405), heading east for 8.6 miles to Modjeska Grade Road (almost 2 miles before Modjeska Canyon Road). Turn right and proceed uphill for a half-mile. The marked trailhead is on your right. Park on the opposite side of the street, obeying signs that prohibit parking or stopping along sections of the road. Ticketing patrols are frequent out here.

From North County: Take the Chapman Avenue exit east from the Costa Mesa Freeway (CA 55), driving 15.3 miles to Modjeska Grade Road (1.7 miles after Modjeska Canyon Road). Turn left and proceed as above.

## THE TRAIL

You begin on a long but gradual climb along the dirt road popular with bikers. The views in this first section stretch across highly developed Saddleback Valley. You'll easily pick out the coastal San Joaquin Hills on the other side of

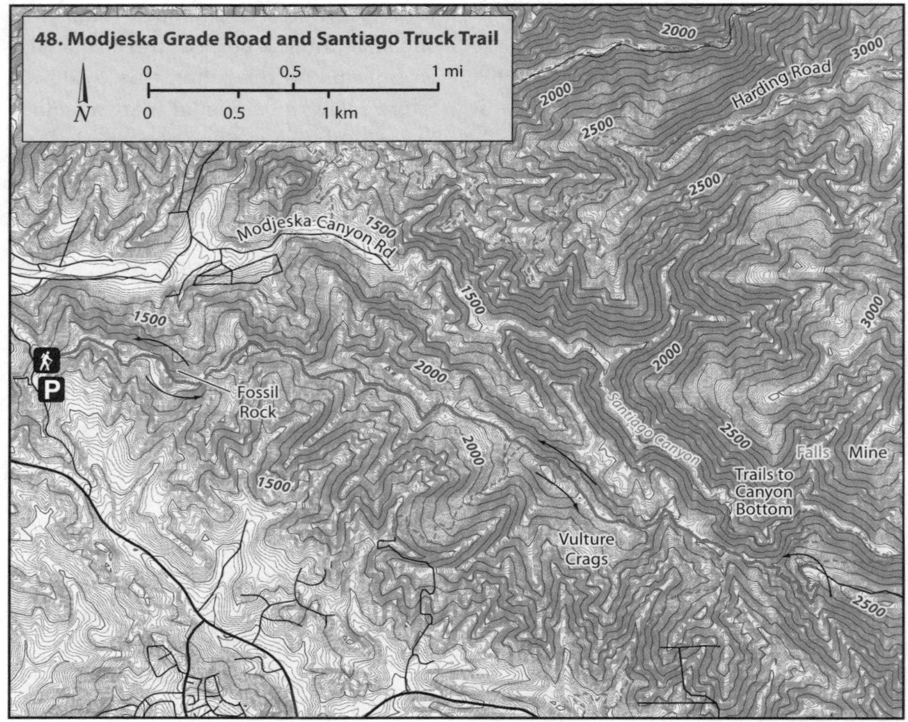


the valley, Newport Center just north of them, and beyond both, the ocean.

Close-up, the first thing you'll notice is that this area is still recovering from the 2007 Santiago Fire. Many of the laurel sumac plants are sprouting healthy greenery at the bottom of blackened skeletons. Other plants, like rare chaparral beargrass, were exposed by the fire for the first time. Though the trail has been reopened after the fire, signs farther along warn visitors to stay on the trail during this post-burn period to give the plants a chance to recover. There are also unfortunate, informal signs that some bikers are ignoring the warnings.

An unusual find along most local trails, exotic-looking chaparral beargrass resembles the more-common yucca called our Lord's candle, but with finer, less lance-like leaves and multiple trunks that are often hidden by the masses of leaves.

At a half-mile, you get your first glimpse northeast into Modjeska Canyon and to the canyons and peaks beyond. Just as that view is cut off again, at 0.6 mile, look on the ground to your left at a triangular rock, approximately 2 feet on each side, with a white layer on top. This layer is laden with remarkably preserved marine fossils, with a few of the shells looking almost as though they might have come straight from the beach. A large rock above this shows a similar white layer wedged through the middle. There are more of these fossil-filled rocks to the right of the trail, slightly downhill.

From this point on, it's worth examining rocks along the path—often in the middle of it—for more signs of these fossils or their tracings. Respect the laws that prohibit collecting.

Flowers will become more numerous as you walk along. Bright-yellow bush poppy, pale-lavender bush mallow, and the giant white blossoms of matilija poppy with the prominent yellow center are all fire followers, sprouting after a burn. But there's also red monkeyflower, vivid paintbrush, morning glory, and deep-purple lupine along the way. Lupine takes its name from the Latin for "wolf-like" because it was believed the plants wolfed up nutrients from the soil, since they seemed to grow well in poor soil. The opposite is true: a member of the pea family, lupine creates nitrogen in the soil. The fire also revealed a large display of Fremont's death camas, a low-growing plant with small, greenish-white petals.

As you continue, climbing 600 feet, you'll see more of the mountains and less of the developed Saddleback Valley, though it remains within view for a majority of the hike.

MARINE FOSSILS EMBEDDED IN ROCK

At 2.6 miles, you can look for more fossils in north-facing rock cut that's covered with lichens and moss. At 2.9 miles, the path takes you past Vulture Crags, though you can't see the formation quite yet. You're descending at this point to a saddle at 2,000 elevation. At 3.2 miles, turn around to take in the impressively craggy sandstone outcroppings, a favorite roosting spot of the California condor when it lived in the Santa Ana Mountains. As happened through much of the state, the majestic carrion-eaters were shot or purposely poisoned. By 1900, they had become rare in Orange County, and the last ones were seen in these mountains in the early 1900s.

You'll begin climbing again. At 3.7 miles, you'll round a hairpin turn to the left, and soon come upon a couple of adits, one much deeper than the other, pecked into the rock, vivid with patches of color from purple to orange, to your right. At 3.9 miles, the trail then veers sharply to the right. Just at this bend, you'll see a small clearing in the promontory straight ahead. Walk to the end for an intriguing view into Santiago Canyon.

From a distance, in a generous rainy season, you can see and hear a splendid waterfall as it cascades noisily down a side canyon immediately opposite where you stand, then falls into a large pool. To the right of that, toward the base of another side canyon, you'll see the large rectangular opening to a mine; there are many other mines near the canyon floor, and various mining artifacts and tailings were left in this area of the canyon. There were two trails in this

Joel Robinson / Naturalist For You

CHAPARRAL BEARGRASS MAKING A POST-FIRE RECOVERY

area, a 0.4-mile one here, and a 0.8-mile path back at the previous hairpin turn, that led down to the waterfall and mining area, but after the fire, these trails have been all but erased. In addition, debris fall has made them extremely perilous. Any attempts at further exploration should wait until the area has had a chance to recover from the fire and the trails are re-established.

This is a good turnaround point for a moderate day hike, but if you're interested in a longer adventure, you could continue for 3.2 miles past this point to Old Camp, a secluded and lovely meadow surrounded by mature oak and bigleaf maple trees. Old Camp also offers safe access to the canyon bottom, though you can expect heavy bushwhacking here.

ADIT

# Harding Road

**LOCATION**: Cleveland National Forest

**TOTAL DISTANCE**: 10 miles

**TYPE**: Out and back

**SEASON**: November to June

**TOTAL ELEVATION GAIN**: 2,300 feet

**DIFFICULTY**: Moderately strenuous

**FEES ETC.**: Parking is in flux. At this time, free parking is still available at Tucker Wildlife Sanctuary, but call in advance. Donation requested to visit the sanctuary.

**MAPS**: USGS Santiago Peak

**TRAILHEAD COORDINATES**: N 33°42.639′ W 117°37.115′

**CONTACT**: Cleveland National Forest (951-736-1811, www.fs.fed.us/r5/cleveland); Tucker Wildlife Sanctuary (714-649-2760, http://nsm.fullerton.edu/tucker)

There's nothing complicated about Harding Road, a fire road that inexorably climbs and curves amid the canyons of Cleveland National Forest, but once you've gone the first half-mile, the vistas never stop. In spring, the flowers seldom stop either, especially after the 2007 Santiago Fire created conditions for the plants called fire-followers. Expect to see plenty of purple lupine, matilija poppy, manzanita, and scarlet paintbrush amid the sage scrub, along with fire-blackened trees.

The reward after the long uphill climb—aside from getting to turn downhill—is a little spring in a dark recess off the trail before your return. If you began very early and brought a surplus of energy, you could climb all the way to Modjeska Peak, the lower peak of Old Saddleback, which would more than double your distance.

Off-trail travel through this area is prohibited while it recovers from the 2007 Santiago Fire.

## GETTING THERE

From South County: Take the El Toro Road exit from the San Diego Freeway (I-5) east for 10.4 miles (the name of the street changes to Santiago Canyon Road) and turn right on Modjeska Canyon Road. Drive 2 miles to Tucker Wildlife Sanctuary on your right. You might find parking on the gravel shoulder, or the larger parking lot just past this area might be open. The sanctuary office and nature center are on your left; check in on the parking situation. The trailhead is behind the office. The parking situation here is in flux. In the future, Tucker might charge for parking; there is very limited parking back along the shoulder of Modjeska Canyon Road.

From North County: Take Chapman

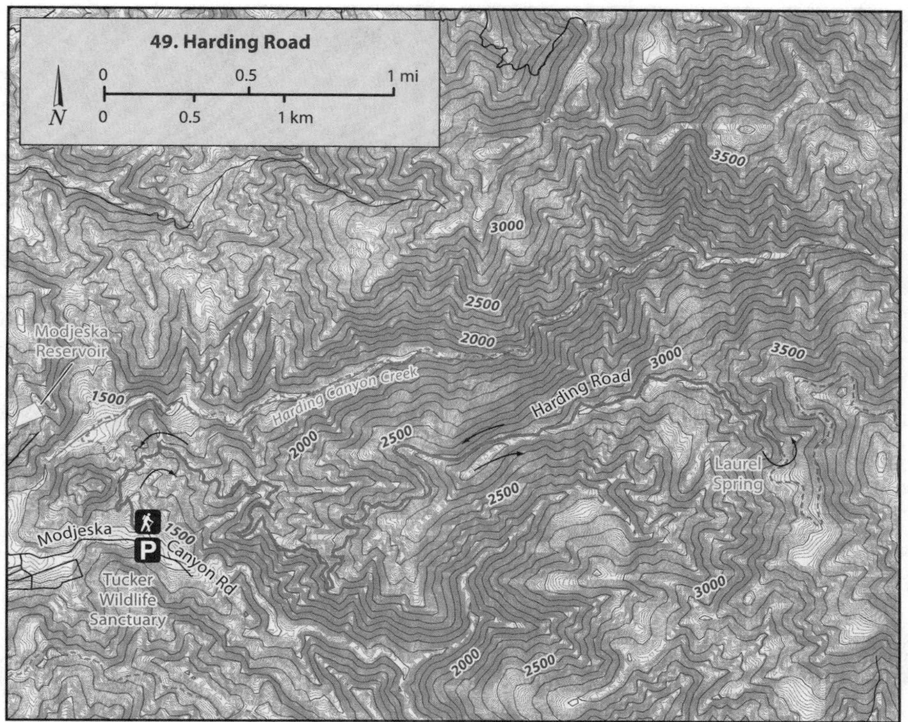


Avenue east off the Costa Mesa Freeway (CA 55) for 13.6 miles (the name of the road changes to Santiago Canyon Road) to Modjeska Canyon Road and turn left. Proceed as above.

The canyon is named for the celebrated 19th-century Polish actress Helena Modjeska, who moved to the United States and built her home, called Arden, in the canyon. Tours of the historic house are available through the Orange County Parks department. Call 949-923-2230.

## THE TRAIL

Up a 50-foot drive is the gate to the road. Climb past Flores Peak, where bandit Juan Flores tried to elude his captors by sliding down a steep cliff with his horse. (See Chapter 23 on the Hanging Tree.) At 0.4 mile, you'll see a trail heading downhill to your left that leads to Harding Canyon. That's a separate, and very different, hike in this book. For this hike stay straight. There will be no more side trails as you climb.

Bring plenty of water—the spring's water isn't potable—and start this hike early. Very early. It can grow uncomfortably toasty on this exposed hike in the back canyons. There's nothing more annoying at 10 a.m. on a hot day than to be sweating your way uphill, only to see a smugly merry band pass you well on their way down because they started before sunrise. Believe me, I know this. Besides, starting in the dark gives you a chance to see a spectacularly starry night sky in an area with very little light pollution.

At 0.7 mile, at a small overlook point,

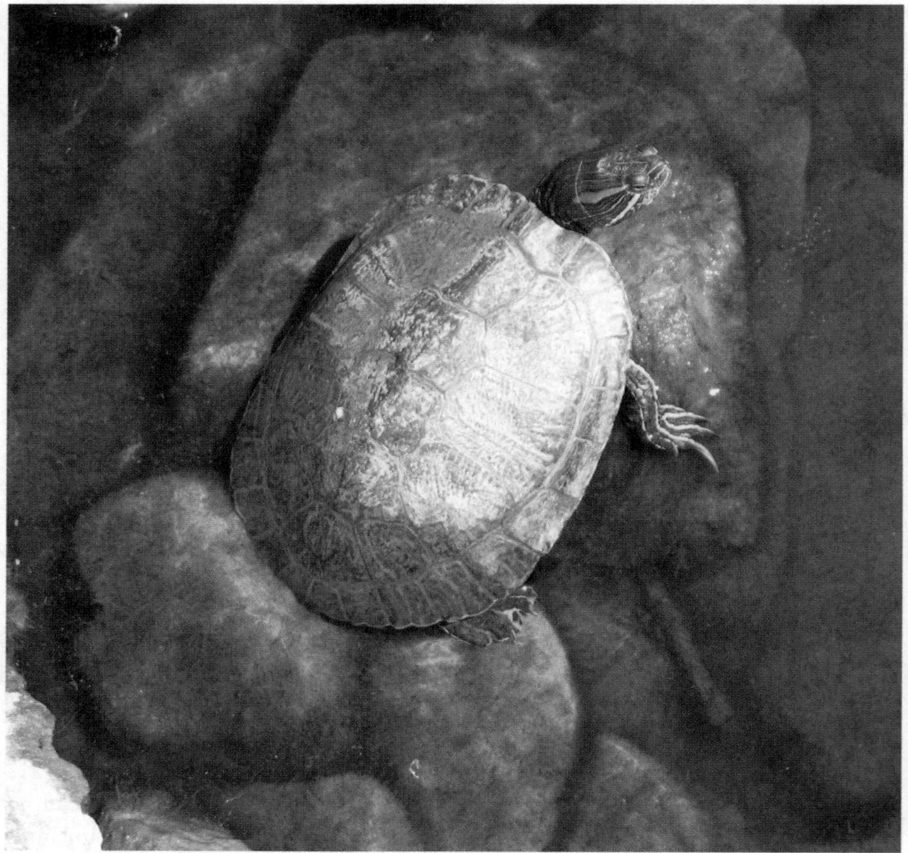

TURTLE AT TUCKER WILDLIFE SANCTUARY

you'll gain vistas into Harding Canyon, which has been considerably scarred by fire and subsequent landslide, and is still one of the most beautiful canyons in the Santa Ana Mountains.

At the 1-mile point, there will be an area in which you're descending around some ravines. Enjoy the break. The next nearly 4 miles will be all uphill.

You'll see plenty of invasive mustard on the way up, but crews of volunteers have worked assiduously after the fire to give the fire-damaged area a chance to recover in the most natural way possible, uprooting opportunistic non-natives like tree of heaven. Many of the blackened native plants also are crowning with new growth. Matilija poppies and bush poppies, two showy fire-following flowers, decorate the path at times.

The view changes as you work your way up, offering vistas into Santiago Canyon to your right as well as Harding Canyon.

As you ascend, you'll see more of the higher-elevation plants such as manzanita, with its reddish bark and flowers shaped like lilies-of-the-valley, and blue-flowered ceanothus, or wild lilac.

AN ACORN WOODPECKER PERCHES ON A BURNED TREE

THE VIEW INTO MODJESKA CANYON FROM HARDING ROAD

Courtesy of the Orange County Archives

ACTRESS HELENA MODJESKA, FOR WHOM MODJESKA CANYON IS NAMED

At the 5-mile point, a quarter-mile past a large cairn, turn right on a small trail that leads into a dark, moist area of mountain mahogany and other mountain chaparral. The trail quickly curves right, just under Harding Road, and leads to Laurel Spring, a small year-round spring. You'd swear the temperature was 15 degrees lower here.

If you've had enough climbing, return down Harding Road. You might want to stop off at the wildlife sanctuary, which along its short, winding trail has a desert tortoise, turtle pond, and a habitat designed to attract birds. You will almost invariably find hummingbirds and scrub jays. Quail are a common sight. If you look up at the wooden power poles outside the sanctuary, there's a good chance you'll see—and hear—busy acorn woodpeckers with their red-capped heads.

# Harding Canyon

**LOCATION**: Cleveland National Forest

**TOTAL DISTANCE**: 5.4 to 10.4 miles round-trip

**TYPE**: Out and back

**TOTAL ELEVATION GAIN**: 900 feet

**DIFFICULTY**: Moderately strenuous because of difficult terrain

**SEASON**: December to June

**FEES ETC.**: Parking situation is in flux. Limited street parking available.

**MAPS**: USGS Santiago Peak

**TRAILHEAD**: N 33°42.639′ W 117°37.115′

**CONTACT**: Trabuco Ranger Station (951-736-1811, www.fs.fed.us/r5/cleve land)

I've been saving the best—in my eyes—for last. With its deep pools, abundant wildlife, and alternating areas of dappled sunlight and close-in rock walls, Harding Canyon—despite recent fire and landslide damage—is a place of breathtaking loveliness with a truly remote and wild feeling.

## GETTING THERE

From South County: Take the El Toro Road exit from the San Diego Freeway (I-5) east for 10.4 miles (the name of the street changes to Santiago Canyon Road) and turn right on Modjeska Canyon Road. Drive 2 miles to Tucker Wildlife Sanctuary on your right. You might find parking on the gravel shoulder, or the larger parking lot just past this area might be open. The sanctuary office and nature center are on your left; check in on the parking situation, which is in flux at this point. In the future, Tucker might charge for parking; there is very limited parking back along the shoulder of Modjeska Canyon Road. The trailhead is behind the sanctuary office.

From North County: Take Chapman Avenue east off the Costa Mesa Freeway (CA 55) for 13.6 miles (the name of the road changes to Santiago Canyon Road) to Modjeska Canyon Road and turn left. Proceed as above.

## THE TRAIL

Begin as you would for the Harding Road hike, up the wide truck trail, but after 0.4 mile and a 150-foot climb, turn left and descend into the canyon. You reach the bottom in 0.2 mile at a large wash. Turn right, going upstream, through an area of showy flowers and along (or into) the gently running creek.

Harding Canyon is the first place I

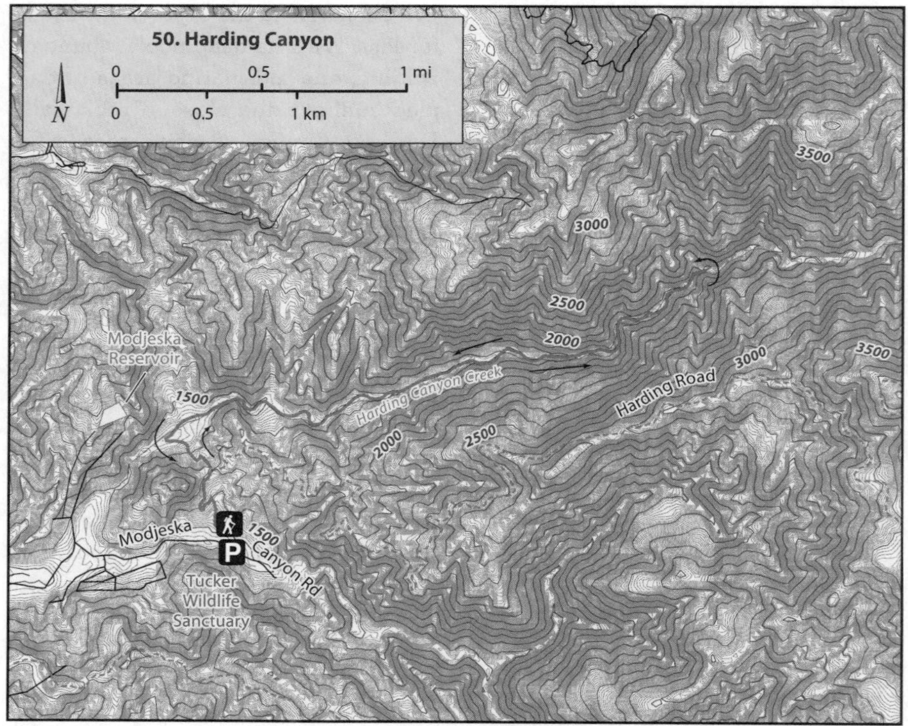


ever hiked in Orange County. I stumbled across it by accident more than 20 years ago (unwittingly trespassing across some private property, which has since been purchased as part of the Cleveland National Forest) and thought it an almost impossibly beautiful place, intimate, bewitching, and completely distant—at least visually—from the rest of Orange County.

The canyon and I have aged since then, not always gracefully. The 2007 Santiago Fire burned the canyon as well as up along the road above. Its steep slopes stripped of vegetation, sections of the canyon walls slid in heavy rains the following winter, burying the seven deep, beautiful pools of crystal-clear water for which the canyon was especially well known among hikers and apparently burying its resident population of rainbow trout. It's possible that these trout could have been steelhead had they been able to migrate to the ocean, but even if they had been inclined to, they were trapped upstream by Harding Dam. Biologists have not yet found a sign of this trout population. Many of the trees up in this area also sustained severe burning. Yet I haven't changed my mind about Harding Canyon. It's still the most magical place in the county.

In the first part of the trek upstream, at least well into springtime, the canyon shows obvious—and sometimes beautiful—signs of the wildfire. The canyon floor is littered with vivid flowers that tend to germinate after fires. One of the most striking is gold ear drops, a bright yellow flower growing on clusters of tall stalks. The blossom resembles a banana with the peel hanging down on two sides. Clumps of matilija poppy, huge white blossoms with prominent yellow centers, grow alongside bright-yellow bush poppies and deep-purple Canterbury bells, a type of phacelia. Many of the trees that were burned are showing new growth; other trees appear untouched by fire.

In late spring, you might find that bright-green stems bearing small yellow flowers are sticking mightily to your shoes and the bottoms of your pants. Once wetted in the creek, they seem almost to embed themselves in fabric. This is aptly named stick leaf. Once you get home, a combination of pulling, scraping, and laundering will remove them.

This first section, though shaded by trees, is still bright on a clear day, the sun glinting off the creek water. There used to be informal trails on either side of the creek for the first half-mile after you enter the narrower part of the canyon, and some segments of these remain. But for the most part, you'll pick your way through the brush, rock hop, wade, and generally do whatever it takes to work your way upstream.

It's slow progress, but who wants to move fast through Harding Canyon? The sound of the creek's water rippling over rocks and down small cascades is downright hypnotizing. Tiny California tree frogs call out to each other and show, if you look carefully, how perfectly camouflaged they are on the speckled rocks. Bright-orange, big-eyed California newts zip around in the water

CAN YOU FIND THE MOTTLED GRAY TREE FROG ON THE MOTTLED GRAY ROCK?

Joel Robinson / Naturalist For You

HARDING FALLS

along with an occasional garter snake. So quick in the water, the newts are surprisingly slow and waddling on land.

Keep an eye out for poison oak during the first three-fourths of a mile or so, though the fire seems to have put a temporary check on it. Eventually, the canyon grows so rocky that even poison oak has a tough time growing. Be careful to stick to the canyon bottom rather than trying to scale the slopes, which are treacherously steep and unstable in places.

As in most of the canyons in the North Main Divide area of the Santa Ana Mountains, Harding Canyon was the site of a mining craze in the late 1800s, in this case, for lead and silver.

At 1.8 miles from the start, the cascades in the creek grow taller and you're forced to do more scrambling over boulders along the sides. At 2 miles, you come across a beautiful, shaded glen as the canyon walls pull in close around you. If you're using a GPS device, you might notice that you lose satellite contact at 2.2 miles, so tightly surrounded are you by rock.

You'll clamber over an outcropping at a place where a cascade tumbles down from 7 feet above. The canyon then makes an abrupt turn to the left. At this point, you'll feel as though you have left the world behind and entered a new one of steep rock walls and cascades and pools perfect for a dip. Side drainages add their water to the flow from the hills above and huge bay laurel trees reach 30 to 40 feet high. You'll know them from the bay leaves—check out the familiar scent from your pantry.

At 2.6 miles, the canyon reaches a more exposed zone, where damage from fire and mudslides is more apparent. You're reaching the area where the seven pools used to brim with sparkling water; now they are filled in with dirt. This is the turnaround point, though for a longer hike you could continue for an additional 2.5 miles ahead—the passage was actually made easier by the landslide—to reach glorious, two-tiered Harding Falls.

BUSH POPPY AND PURPLE CANTERBURY BELLS

## APPENDIX 1

# A Guide to Guided Hikes

One of the best introductions to hiking—or ways to learn more about already-familiar trails—is a guided hike. The following organizations lead hikes on park, forest, and reserve lands in Orange County. Most of these organizations provide a wide variety of hikes, from yoga in the backcountry to birding walks to strenuous cardio hikes. There's no way to be all-inclusive; it's worth contacting individual parks as well.

**Amigos de Bolsa Chica** (714-840-1575, www.amigosdebolsachica.org/tours.htm). Holds monthly tours of Bolsa Chica wetlands from 9 to 10:30 a.m. on the first Saturday of each month and organizes larger group tours for a small fee.

**Back Bay Science Center** (949-640-0286, www.backbaysciencecenter.org). Regular monthly tours of Newport Back Bay animals and habitat.

**Irvine Ranch Conservancy** (714-508-4757, www.irlandmarks.org). The largest and most professional of the organizations, the conservancy manages open-space reserves of the Irvine Ranch and offers a boggling array of hikes, bikes, and other events on a variety of lands, both private reserves and public holdings.

**Laguna Canyon Foundation** (949-497-8324, www.lagunacanyon.org) offers 25 or so events each month in Laguna Coast Wilderness Park and Aliso and Wood Canyons Wilderness Parks. There are hikes specifically targeted to the elderly, young children, or themed to birding, geology, or edible and useful plants, or providing tai chi or yoga lessons in the parks. Most events ask a $2-per-person donation.

**The Reserve at Rancho Mission Viejo** (949-489-9778, www.theconservancy.org). This private preserve on Rancho Mission Viejo was set aside as mitigation for development. It offers light but interesting programming including astronomy nights, bat walks, and mushroom hunts. There is usually a fee of about $10 per person.

**Sea and Sage Audubon Society** (949-261-7963; www.seaandsageaudubon.org). Everyone expects birding hikes from the Audubon Society, and it schedules them in abundance, in spots all over the county. What you might be more surprised by are the wonderful summer bat hikes at San Joaquin Wildlife Sanctuary.

**Sierra Club, Angeles Chapter** (213-387-4287, www.angeles.sierraclub.org). Hikes and service days throughout the region, including many in Orange County.

**Starr Ranch Sanctuary** (949-858-0309, www.starrranch.org) offers camps for children, two open "Family Days" per week, and fascinating field-ecology programs and hikes, arranged by the group. Some programs include the ability to hike in this beautiful, seldom-visited preserve. Varying donations requested.

## APPENDIX 2

# A Guide to Field Guides

Learning about nature begins with a hiking guide like this. Once you're out there, you'll start wondering what those extraordinary flowers are, or birds or insects. Fortunately, Orange County recently got its own wildflower book, an extraordinarily complete and beautifully illustrated guide.

***Wildflowers of Orange County and the Santa Ana Mountains*** by Robert L. Allen and Fred M. Roberts, Jr. Published by Laguna Wilderness Press, Laguna Beach, CA. The definitive guide to the county's flora.

***Flowering Plants, the Santa Monica Mountains*** by Nancy Dale. Published by the California Native Plant Society, Sacramento, CA. A useful handbook that will cover most of the plants you'll commonly see.

***Edible and Useful Plants of California*** by Charlotte Bringle Clarke. Published by University of California Press. Written by a life sciences teacher who gives the uses of many wild plants, both native and exotic, and even provides recipes.

***Healing with Medicinal Plants of the West*** by Cecilia Garcia and James D. Adams Jr. Published by Abedus Press, La Crescenta, CA. Much of the information about medicinal uses of wild plants involves lore. This unusual book, written by a Chumash healer and a pharmacologist, provides information about both the traditional healing uses of plants and what's known scientifically about whether or not they work.

***Birds of Los Angeles*** by Chris C. Fisher and Herbert Clarke. Published by Lone Pine Publishing, Auburn, WA. This is a lightweight handbook with drawings. It's particularly helpful for people just beginning to be interested in the birds around them. Not comprehensive, but the limited number of entries will cover most of the birds you see and make it easier to find the bird for which you're looking.

***Birds of the Los Angeles Region*** by Kimball L. Garrett, Jon L. Dunn, and Bob Morse. Published by R.W. Morse Co., Olympia, WA. This small, chunky book uses photographs rather than drawings, which many people find more helpful.

***Sibley Field Guide to Birds of Western North America*** by David Allen Sibley. Published by Knopf Doubleday Publishing Group. The Sibley bird guides are the classic comprehensive books for birders.

***Insects of the Los Angeles Basin*** by Charles L. Hogue. Published by the Natural History Museum of Los Angeles County. Illustrated with both photos and helpful sketches.

## APPENDIX 3

# Annual Parking Passes

If you plan on doing a significant amount of hiking over the year, annual passes will save you money and time. There are three kinds of passes for Orange County hiking.

**Forest Adventure Pass.** It's complicated. Parking in Cleveland National Forest used to require a Forest Adventure Pass ($5 for the day, $30 for an annual) that covered four national forests in southern California. But after a series of court rulings, the forests were no longer allowed to charge a fee just for parking, though it left open the charging of fees for use of developed amenities. The problem is, it's unclear exactly what those amenities are, though they include such things as bathrooms and picnicking facilities, or what combination of them must be used to constitute fee-worthy use. The forests continue to work on the policies. For now, if you're just parking to hike and happen to use a bathroom, you should be fine without a pass. If you do want one, they're sold at some small stores near the forest such as the Ortega Oaks Candy Store on Ortega Highway.

**County Pass.** As of this writing, county parks were charging $3 per day for parking, with many raising it to $5 on weekends. A $55 annual pass provides access to all Orange County regional and wilderness parks. An $80 pass provides access to the parks and county beaches. People 60 and older pay $35 for the parks-only pass and $50 for the combined pass. The passes are sold at most county parks, but call 1-866-OC PARKS to confirm locations and availability.

**California Vehicle Day Use Pass.** Daily parking fees at most state parks increased substantially with California's budget problems. They are now $15 at San Onofre State Beach and Crystal Cove State Park, and $8 at Chino Hills State Park. The annual pass good at all state parks is $195, not worthwhile unless you live near one of the county's two state parks and visit them multiple times per month. The less expensive Golden Poppy Pass, $125, is even less useful because it's not accepted at Crystal Cove. The limited-use Golden Bear Pass, $20 a year, allows senior citizens unlimited use of the parks, but only during off-season. That's actually a good thing in Orange County, because the best hiking at Crystal Cove is during the non-summer months. (www.parks.ca.gov/?page_id=1049)

**The free route.** Have a favorite park that you'd like to visit regularly? Many county and state parks provide free annual passes to those who volunteer three or four hours a month.

## APPENDIX 4

# Resources for Children

Best hikes for children: Many of the hikes in this book are marked as good for children, but the ones listed below maximize the sights that intrigue them and minimize distance and difficulty:

Arroyo Trabuco
El Cariso Nature Trail
Horseshoe Loop Trail
Lower San Gabriel River to Turtle Overlook
Maple Springs Road
Roadrunner-Bluebird Loop
Pecten Reef Loop
Vernal Pool Loop (can be shortened to a 1.6-mile out and back to the large vernal pool)

**Exhibitions and nature centers:** The county is full of nature centers, many at parks. Here are the best:

**Bowers Museum** (714-567-3600, www.bowers.org). In its courtyard, the Bowers exhibits the Bell Rock and Maze Stone, ancient artifacts from Bell Canyon (see chapter on Starr Ranch Sanctuary). The permanent collection of the Santa Ana museum includes an impressive room of local Native American artifacts such as cogstones from Bolsa Chica (see chapter on Bolsa Chica Ecological Reserve).

**Environmental Nature Center** (949-645-8489, www.encenter.org). It's amazing how much this Newport Beach nature center packs into 3.5 acres. Its garden has been landscaped to contain various native habitats. Exhibitions include a butterfly house. There are nature programs for children and families, from stargazing to learning such wilderness survival skills as building a shelter.

**Laguna Hills Community Center** (949-707-2680, www.gotfossils.com/community_center.html). It has the best hours, some of the best exhibitions, and it's free. When Laguna Hills built its community center, it included excellent displays of local fossils, many gathered during the construction of the center. There are large fossil scallop shells and shark teeth as well as mastodon and Ice Age camel bones.

**Naturalist For You** (www.naturalist-for-you.org/calendar.htm). Not a place, but an organization that offers various family-friendly activities, usually in the Santa Ana Mountains, such as processing acorns to eat, fire-making, mountain music jams, and easy exploration hikes. Donations of about $10 are requested.

**Ocean Institute** (949-496-2274, www.ocean-institute.org/). Open weekends from 10 to 3, this Dana Point research facility has small exhibitions of interesting sea creatures and a tide pool exhibitions in which children are allowed to touch the animals; the institute also offers ongoing programming during these public days during which children can join such activities as dissecting squid. Admission is $6.50 for adults and $4.50 for children 3 and older. Various marine-related camps and programs for children are offered at the institute and on its research vessel.

**Peter and Mary Muth Interpretive Center** (949-923-2290, www.ocparks.com/unbic). The interactive exhibitions on the habitat and animals of Upper Newport Bay are riveting for both children and adults; there are also some small but nice archaeological displays.

**Ralph B. Clark Regional Park Interpretive Center** (714-973-3170, www.ocparks.com/clarkpark). This park is located on a site teeming with Ice Age fossils. The interpretive center is like a mini-paleontology museum, with fossil exhibitions of a local Ice Age bison, mastodon, and ground sloth. Call beforehand to make sure the center is open.

**Starr Ranch Sanctuary** (949-858-0309, www.starrranch.org). A private reserve not open to the public most days of the year, the Starr Ranch Sanctuary offers unusual, more-in-depth educational programs for groups of children during the school year, and weeklong ecology camps during the summer.

# Index

## D

## M



## N

O

## P



## R



## S